FAMILY AND FAITH IN ASIA:
The Missional Impact of Social Networks

Other Titles in the SEANET Series

Vol. 1   Sharing Jesus in the Buddhist World

Vol. 2   Sharing Jesus Holistically in the Buddhist World

Vol. 3   Sharing Jesus Effectively in the Buddhist World

Vol. 4   Communicating Christ in the Buddhist World

Vol. 5   Communicating Christ Through Story and Song: Orality in Buddhist Contexts

Vol. 6   Communicating Christ in Asian Cities

Family and Faith in Asia:
The Missional Impact of Social Networks

Edited by Paul H. De Neui

WILLIAM CAREY
LIBRARY

Family and Faith in Asia: The Missional Impact of Social Networks
Copyright ©2010 by Paul H. De Neui

All rights reserved. No part of this book may be reproduced, stored in a retrieval system, or transmitted in any form or by any means—electronic, mechanical, photocopy, recording, or otherwise—without prior written permission of the copyright owner, except brief quotations used in connection with reviews in magazines or newspapers.

Unless otherwise noted, all scripture is taken from the HOLY BIBLE, NEW INTERNATIONAL VERSION®. Copyright © 1973, 1978, 1984 International Bible Society. Used by permission of Zondervan. All rights reserved. The " NIV" and "New International Version" trademarks are registered in the United States Patent and Trademark Office by International Bible Society. Use of either trademark requires the permission of International Bible Society.

Published by William Carey Library, an imprint of William Carey Publishing
10 W. Dry Creek Circle
Littleton, CO 80120 | www.missionbooks.org

Naomi McSwain, editorial manager
Johanna Deming, assistant editor
Rose Lee-Norman, assistant editor
Jonathan Pon, graphic design

William Carey Library is a ministry of Frontier Ventures
Pasadena, CA 91104 | www.frontierventures.org

23 22 21 20 19 Printed for Worldwide Distribution

Library of Congress Cataloging-in-Publication Data

Family and faith in Asia : the missional impact of social networks / edited by Paul H. De Neui.

    p. cm. -- (SEANET ; v. 7)
Includes bibliographical references and index.
ISBN 978-0-87808-022-9 (alk. paper)
 1. Missions to Buddhists. 2. Christianity and other religions--Buddhism. 3. Buddhism--Relations--Christianity. 4. Asia--Religion. 5. Family--Religious life. 6. Social networks--Asia. I. De Neui, Paul H.

DEDICATION

This volume is dedicated to the extended family network of SEANET
To those who have gone before us and marked the path in
which we are following,
To our spouses and children who sacrifice for ministry
and do not seek recognition,
To the future generations that will gather with us around the great feast.
With David we say, "Who am I, Sovereign Lord, and what is my
family that you have brought me this far?
How great you are, Sovereign Lord! There is no one like you."

In Memoriam

Henry Joseph De Neui
(1929–2009)

Alfred Garnett Smith
(1919–2009)

CONTENTS

Introduction   i

Contributors   iii

I. FAMILY NETWORK

1. Evangelizing Whole Families:
   The Value of Family in the 21st Century   1
   Alex G. Smith
   Trends in the new millennium indicate the increasing importance and changing role of families in evangelism in the Buddhist world.

2. Catalyzing "Insider Movements" in Buddhist Contexts   31
   David Lim
   Family units must serve as the basic model for house church and insider movements in the Buddhist context.

3. Family Networks: The Context for Communication   47
   Alex G. Smith
   Family networks in the Buddhist world provide one of the best platforms for Christian evangelism and church planting.

II. FILIAL PIETY

4. Duty, Obligation and Prostitution: How Family Matters in Entry into and Exit from Prostitution in Thailand   77
   Christa Foster Crawford
   Within Theravada Buddhist society familial obligations are gendered in nature.

5. The Ritual of Reconciliation of Thai Culture   101
   Ubolwan Mejudhon
   This discipleship tool can assist in healing relational wounds caused by Christian conversion within Thai families.

6. A Day in the Life of a Sinhala Buddhist Family and
   its Relevance for the Evangelical Christian   131
   G.P.V. Somaratna
   Understanding Buddhist families' reverence for the
   religious can facilitate meaningful Christian witness.

III. VENERATION

7. The Struggle of Asian Ancestor Veneration   161
   Alex G. Smith
   Christianity must provide functional substitutes that reflect
   important cultural values held towards ancestors.

8. Ancestor Veneration and Family Conversion Revisited   183
   David S. Lim
   Refusal to adapt to the cultural values in the Buddhist world
   will continue to hinder response to the Christian gospel.

IV. MARRIAGE AND FAMILY LIFE

9. A New Family Model for Japanese People   217
   Mitsuo Fukuda
   Japanese dissatisfaction with the pursuit of wealth
   indicates a need to reprioritize relationships and the family.

10. Christianity and Buddhist Marriage In Sri Lanka   229
    G. P.V. Somaratna
    Sri Lankan Christians must recover their godly
    cultural heritage in wedding ceremonies in the face
    of rising post-colonial, anti-Christian sentiment.

11. Biblical Ideals and Buddhist Images   257
    M.S. Vasanthakumar
    Obedience to the biblical perspective can restore
    Christian blessings upon Sri Lankan marriages.

References   281

Index   313

INTRODUCTION

"Therefore, go and make disciples of panta ta ethne"
Matthew 28:19

If Christian mission in Asia and most of the non-western world is ever to advance, it must seriously consider the importance of family networks. Far too long the strategy of a "one by one" approach has stifled the spread of the gospel, reinforced a highly individualized unbiblical theology and destroyed social relationships that might lead to conversation, conversion and social transformation. With this concern in mind, SEANET is proud to present another volume in its series addressing critical missiological issues relevant to the practice of mission in Asian and many other non-western contexts. Our title Family and Faith in Asia: The Missional Impact of Extended Networks attempts to issue a wake-up call to serious reflection upon a highly ignored social reality in one of the largest unreached regions of the world.

The following chapters are an edited collection of several of the papers presented at the SEANET XI missiological forum in Chiang Mai, Thailand in January 2009 on several issues related to family and mission in the Buddhist world. Each presenter was a practitioner willing to take the time to reflect upon her or his own ministry and share missiological reflections verbally and in print with others. These chapters represent the perspectives of mission and ministry in China, India, Japan, Philippines, Sri Lanka and Thailand.

In reviewing the papers it became apparent that the issues presented could be categorized into four major categories: Family Networks, Filial Piety, Ancestral Veneration, and Marriage and Family Life. The eleven chapters in this volume are presented under these four headings in hopes that, along with the index, this will be a resource that will be useful for anyone wishing to study practical approaches to issues related to family and faith in Asia, particularly in Buddhist contexts for mission.

SEANET serves as a networking forum wherein groups and individuals can meet to reflect and strategize together on topics particular to their collective mission. SEANET does not promote one particular strategy or approach but seeks to learn from models of hope of what God is doing around the world. Over one hundred and sixty attendees from seventeen countries contributed in a wide variety of roles to this conference for which we are grateful. Special gratitude is given to each of these chapter's contributors as well as their respondents whose invaluable comments improved the articles immensely.

No volume could be produced without the effort of many individuals. Special recognition goes to Zachary Lovig who worked tirelessly in collating, correcting and improving the main text of this volume. SEANET is indebted to William Carey Library for their help in bringing this volume into print. I am personally appreciative of the careful support of editorial manager Naomi McSwain, her faithful assistant editor Johanna Deming and the creative work of graphic designer Jonathan Pon.

Paul H. De Neui
July 2009

CONTRIBUTORS

Christa F. Crawford is from the United States and spent most of her life in Southern California. A graduate of Harvard Law School and Claremont McKenna College, she currently lives in Thailand with her husband Mark and Thai son Ahm. In 2003, with her husband she began The Garden of Hope, a ministry that reaches out holistically to victims of trafficking, people in prostitution and children-at-risk in Thailand and other parts of the Mekong region. Christa speaks and teaches internationally on issues of trafficking and prostitution. She has published several articles on the subject, as well as written a book on combating human trafficking for the United Nations. Christa also serves as a missionary with Mission to Unreached Peoples, an adjunct professor with Fuller Theological Seminary and Food for the Hungry's GoED Program. Christa is an entrepreneur, starting businesses to provide the vulnerable and exploited with sustainable livelihoods. She is currently working on an M.A. in Holistic Child Development from the Malaysia Baptist Theological Seminary.

Mitsuo Fukuda is from Japan. He is the founder and director of a mission strategy think tank, Rethinking Authentic Christianity (RAC) Network. His main ministry is to design effective training programs for church planters to catalyze church multiplication movements that are grassroot and contextualized to Asian contexts. After graduating from Kwansei Gakuin University with a Bachelors degree in theology and an M.Th. in Japan, he studied at Fuller Theological Seminary as a Fulbright Graduate Student earning an M.Th. and D.Miss. there. Areas of research for him include: Japanese Identity; paradigm shift; Postwar Japanese Family Model; Intimacy in marriage relationships; 'the New Economy'; 'Kakusa-Shakai' or the stratification of modern Japanese society and its effects on work, marriage, and values; empowered, transformational discipleship which results in mission and church multiplication through house churches. Mitsuo has been married to his wife for twenty-eight years and has two grown sons.

David S. Lim is from the Philippines. He serves as the President of the Asian School for Development and Cross-cultural Studies (ASDECS), and previously served as the Academic Dean at the Asian Theological Seminary (Philippines) and the Oxford Centre for Mission Studies (U.K.). He also serves as President of China Ministries International-Philippines, and as a key facilitator of the Philippine Missions Mobilization Movement that seeks to mobilize and train 200,000 Filipino missionaries to reach the unreached peoples of the world. His Ph.D. in the New Testament was earned from Fuller Theological Seminary. He has an adult son (and a granddaughter) and a teenage daughter.

Ubolwan Mejudhon is from Thailand. She has her D.Miss degree from Asbury Theological Seminary. She is the co-pastor of the Muang Thai Church and co-director of the Cross-Cultural Training Center, both in Bangkok.

Alex G. Smith is from Australia. He earned his D.Miss. and M.A. degrees at Fuller Theological Seminary; His M.Div. is from Western Evangelical Seminary. Veteran Missionary to Thailand, co-founder and coordinator/chairperson of SEANET (South, East, Southeast, and North Asia Network); He was Adjunct Faculty at Multnomah University for 18 years; presently he serves as Minister-at-Large for OMF International. Author, Trainer, Lecturer; His church planting experience in Asia convinced him of the need to reach whole families, not just individuals. He resides with his American wife, Faith. They have three sons and four grandchildren in the USA.

G. P. V. Somaratna is from Sri Lanka. He has a Ph.D. in South Asian History from the University of London. He serves as senior research professor at Colombo Theological Seminary, in Colombo, Sri Lanka. Somaratna has worked in the metro-political cities of Sri Lanka for the last forty-five years.

Michael S. Vasanthakumar is from Sri Lanka. He has a B.Th., a M.A., a M.Phil., and D.Min. degrees. He has been involved in Christian ministry for the past twenty-four years including teaching and training Christian ministers and lay people at Lanka Bible College, Sri Lanka and editing for Tamil Christian magazine for the Back to the Bible Broadcast Ministries in Sri Lanka. In 2005 he formed the Tamil Bible Research Centre in London in order write and publish biblical commentaries and study materials in the Tamil language. In addition to this he is involved in teaching and pastoral ministry among the Sri Lankans in London. He has written more than forty books and study materials in the Tamil language and contributed numerous scholarly articles to Tamil magazines and English journals.

1

Evangelizing Whole Families: The Value of Family in the 21st Century

Alex G. Smith

Celebrated American actress, Reese Witherspoon, said it best, "Family is all we have in life" (Rader 2008:5). Wife of an Australian publishing tycoon, Ros Packer, who lost her husband in 2006, poignantly declares, "My family is the most important thing in my life. Being separated from them for eternity is too terrible to think about. If you love your family, I simply can't see how you can feel otherwise." She adds, "Yes, I'm a spiritual person and it's all to do with family" (Writer 2008:47). Her gregarious heart reaches out in enormous help to hosts of hurting families through her extensive charity work. They are like an extension of her family. This eclectic and rich Arts patron and philanthropist, who helped National Gallery to purchase the largest Buddha image in Australia, also has a couple in her own home. She said she finds Buddhas "soothing and calming" (Writer 2008:52).

Family helps consolidate individuals into a sociological if not biological kin and value group. It generally gives one identity in society. It also provides the means for nurture, protection and provision for the members' survival. A true story from Thailand illustrates the power of family and its influence on lives. Wat Thammakaya, a large Buddhist monastery, has a strong presence at nearby Thammasat University on the outskirts of Bangkok, the capital. One of the lectures was attended by thousands of rowdy students. To quell the growing noise level already elevated to a high crescendo, the Thai professor calmly requested the assembled students to cooperate and be quiet. He spoke slowly, with extended pauses in between each of his phrases, asking the scholars to close their eyes, breath slowly, put down their pens, think of their responsibility to the government, and to their parents, and remember the sacrifices their parents made so they could study. Slowly the students began to respond and come back until all finally quieted down. Significantly, the professor's reference and emphasis on the parents helped to defuse the rumbling din in this situation. Family, along with ancestors, not only signifies one's identity, and provides sustenance and shelter, but is also a key point of reference for respect and loyalty.

Recognizing the worldwide importance of the family, the United Nations declared 1994 to be the "International Year of the Family." The U.N. 1959 Universal Declaration of Human Rights stated that "The family is the natural and therefore fundamental group unit of society and is entitled to protection by society and the State." In his 1970 book, *Future Shock*, Alvin Toffler said, "The family cycle has been one of the sanity-preserving constants in human existence."

Buddha and Buddhist Scriptures on the Family

Generally, Buddhist scriptures contain little instruction on specific matters related to family. The Siddharta Gautama, known after his enlightenment as Buddha, was married at sixteen to his cousin Yasodhara. At twenty-nine they had their only son, who was named Rahula, meaning "a chain, fetter." What was the reason for selecting such a name, whose interpretation seems to indicate a burden and be anti-family? Soon after, Gautama, who had been protected in a life of luxury and affluence, had occasion to secretly leave the confines of the palace. On this escapade, he saw four sights that disturbed him greatly, including a sick person, another aged one, a corpse and an ascetic guru. Gautama returned home, renounced his privilege, position and status, and immediately left the palace that night, abandoning his wife and infant son. In Buddhism this is known as "The Great Renunciation." He went to join the ascetics to search for an answer to the problems of life and suffering. From the time of his Enlightenment at Bodh Gaya about six years later, he advocated celibacy for himself and his monks, the Sangha brotherhood. In time some of his extended family became Buddhists, but Buddha himself never returned to the norm of accepted family life.

Teaching on the family in the Buddhist scriptures is quite limited in terms of personal responsibilities of the spouses, social duties regarding the children or ethical issues affecting society. However, much instruction and many precepts were developed to guide and assist individuals in their quest to escape the cycle of life with its suffering in order to attain nirvana. The main emphasis of Buddhist practice revolves around listening to and following the dharma (Buddha's teaching), which strongly emphasizes karma, the bane of all beings. Each one's current existence is the product of karma. Because Buddha taught that humans have no essence of soul or spirit, this "karma remains untouched by death and continues to live" (Carus 1997:IV). Therefore as no soul exists, karma is primarily the only thing that is recycled into the next rebirth. In turn this produces more suffering through craving and attachment to empty illusion, the immaterial, and the transitory cycle of life. One must escape suffering by eliminating desires and craving, developing contentment, having compassion for all sentient beings, and by respecting life. Each person must overcome suffering through self-effort by doing good deeds or merit (*dana*) and by keeping the basic Buddhist precepts (*sila*). Self-reliance and self-dependence alone help the individual attain nirvana, which is the state of release from the cycle of birth, death and rebirth.

To illustrate the general emphasis noted above, the Buddha's relation to his family requires further mention. After seven years of not seeing Siddharta, his son, King Suddhodhana sent a message to Buddha saying, "I am growing old and wish to see my son before I die. Others have had the benefit of his doctrine, but not his father nor his relatives" (Carus1997:59). The Buddha consented and came to Kapilavatthu to see his father. He acknowledged the love that the king had for his son, mixed with grief in losing him to religious devotion. The next day the Buddha came with his bowl to beg food, house to house. This embarrassed the king, but he still received Buddha's preaching of the dharma along with the relatives and friends gathered in the palace. However, Yasodhara, Siddharta's wife and mother of his son, Rahula, refused to come. The Buddha then went to her apartment with his two disciples, where they found her in inferior clothing with her hair cut, possibly a sign of mourning. On the Buddha's entry she held him by his feet and wept bitterly, having not seen her husband for seven years. On the seventh day of Buddha's arrival, Yasodhara dressed seven year old Rahula in his princely robes. She told him that Buddha was his father and sent him to ask for his inheritance. Rahula replied that the only father he knew all those years was King Suddhodhana (his grandfather). When Rahula came to Buddha he greeted him saying, "My father" and asked for his inheritance. The Buddha responded by offering his the Four Noble Truths and the Eightfold Path, "a treasure that will not perish." He then asked if Rahula wanted to enter brotherhood of the Sangha. He agreed to do so and Buddha ordained his own son. Having already lost his son and other close male relatives to the Sangha, King Suddhodhana spoke to Buddha about his ordaining his grandson also. From that time on Buddha promised not to "ordain any minor without the consent of his parents or guardians" (Carus 1997:59-63).

Some 547 of Buddha's previous births were detailed in the Jataka tales, a section of the Tripitaka (Three Baskets) of the Pali Buddhist scriptures. Many of these stories were set in contexts of families or related communities. However, the punch lines of these stories always focused around the dharma and the precepts noted earlier. The objective of each lesson centered on the specific individual, including his release from suffering or karma and clearly not directly around instruction to better the harmony or growth of the family. In like manner many of the sutras were illustrated through family narratives, but the key point and conclusion of the teaching always related to freeing oneself from karma, through practicing dharma and in the end, attaining nirvana. Making merit was enjoined as part of self-salvation. Thus the individual was called to escape the emptiness of life and to detach from desires, which also included attachment to relationships, including family.

Though not in the *sila* or a specific tenet of Buddhism per se, the major exception concerning the family concerned a strong respect for parents, honoring forebears, and particularly venerating ancestors. Like the time King Bimbisara invited the Buddha for a special meal, in honor of his ancestors. The Buddha affirmed that transferring merit to ancestors was deemed a good thing to do. Buddha gave rules and guidelines on how that should be accomplished (Smith 2006:167). One well known legend tells how Buddha ascended into one of the heavens to preach the dharma to his mother (though some say it was one of the hells). In both Theravada and Tibetan Schools Buddha's alleged return to earth (*Assayuja*) is celebrated annually, usually in October, coinciding with the end of the Buddhist Lent (*Vassa*). This festival is excluded in the Mahayana School of north Asia where they focus their festivals on Kuan Yin's birth, enlightenment and death, rather than on those of the Buddha. According to Chinese scholars, by the second century B.C.E. Chinese filial piety became formalized into ancestor worship through the Buddhist practice of burning incense in front of altars and the ancestral tablets. Offering incense clearly indicates worship in Chinese culture (Smith 2006:167-168).

In some ways the Buddha substituted the Sangha for family. The Sangha became the new community, virtually replacing the family in position and importance. Monks were to be celibate. Their families visited them in the temple, but always venerated and gave obeisance to them primarily as monks, rather than as father, son, uncle or grandfather. Monks and novices lived in the monasteries, ate their food twice a day there (no meals after 11am), and were assigned chores and duties therein. Female nuns and novices sometimes were quartered in the monasteries too and were expected to be celibate. They were respected, but considered to be of a subordinate status and degree below males. Patriarchy reigned and women were relegated to a lower value—not good for normal family orientation. Basically Buddhism teaches that "women are burdened with bad karma, thus born inferior to men, so they must endure for the sake of others" (Ekachai 2008:1) Consequently women could not achieve nirvana until they are reborn as men. This is still a fundamental teaching to this day, though not often emphasized in Western contexts. The

Buddhist feminist's struggle for the same level of acceptance and equal ordination is still an ongoing battle.

FAMILY DISINTEGRATION AND TRAUMA TODAY

During the past half century an increasing breakdown of families has become a worldwide problem for all religious traditions. This erosion of family values, both in fragmented relationships and in looser morals, has accelerated at a heart-rending pace, especially since the end of the Second World War. While evil practices and excesses have existed in all eras of times past, the current increases in worldwide crime, violence, murder, rape, robbery, corruption, mass destruction and such like, seem to be of such a magnitude as to reach enormous proportions. Is all this merely the result of karma, as Buddhism would suggest? Is the world only getting worse? Evil seems to prosper, and the environment for families continues to become more harsh, unfriendly and uncertain. Is there no increase of those entering into the state of nirvana? Why does its effect seem so negligible on the planet? Why does Asian theater not become more peaceful?

In the West it is little better. In the cover story of USA TODAY, December 2007, Jill Lawrence described the shifts of family emphases in a changing America. The 2004 election in the United States had family values at the heart, particularly regarding maintaining marriage between one man and one woman, as a backlash against pressures to formalize same-sex marriages. Periods of political reactions against the earlier feminist movement and the sexual revolution also followed them. By the build up to the 2008 election, family values were, however, much lower on the political agenda. Mitt Romney was almost alone as a strong advocate of family values (2007:1). Reflecting the changes in societal values, many of the other candidates did not emphasize "family" in campaign rhetoric, but favored issues like war, terrorism and the economy instead. Lawrence noted that a number of those running for this high office were divorced, some into their second or third marriages. Recent pollsters discovered that modern Americans had little concern for the personal lives of future presidents, as long as they exhibited wisdom, showed ability and provided swift action in "getting things done." In the last decade, Americans "have seen major cultural changes become woven into society. Divorce, blended families and women in the work force are common." Even family values are "open to interpretation" today. Some define them, according to Lawrence, in terms of embryonic stem-cell research, legal abortion, women working outside the home, health care, opposition to Equal Rights Amendment, and issues with religious connotations (2007:2A).

Yet in a November, 2007 USA TODAY Gallup Poll, three quarters of the respondents indicated "family values are extremely or very important to them." One third said they defined family values as "strong families." More than half of the voters said it would matter a great deal or a moderate amount to them if a candidate had an extramarital affair." Yet a strange ambivalence hovers around family issues. According to the U.S. Census, the traditional "family—a married couple with kids—made up fewer than twenty-two percent of US households in 2006, down from forty percent in 1970. Approximately one-fifth of Americans have been divorced ." (Some say fifty percent of marriages today end in divorce, and the ratio for Christians is no better than in the general population.) "Nearly two in five US births in 2006 were out of wedlock, more than twice as high as in 1980." A considerable discrepancy seems to exist between ideal standards in family values and honest realities. This is a mark of the times in our twenty-first century. The deeply disturbing thing about it is that so many people seem to have compromised their traditional moral standards so as to no longer consider evil, with all its variegated tentacles, to be that insidious or damaging to society.

The extent of this declension and its serious effects on the children of families are quite disturbing and deeply concerning. In an article, "Toddlers in Distress," published in Australia, the rise in mental illness in our modern day was blamed on the breakdown of the family. Dr James Scott at the Royal Children's Hospital in Brisbane confirmed the findings of recent research. Shockingly, children as young as three years old are being treated for mental health conditions in some hospitals there. Research reveals that now younger people are more likely to have a mental disorder than older people. One in four teenagers in Queensland experience mental problems, including panic attacks, obsessive-compulsive disorders, depression and substance abuse. According to the Australian Bureau of Statistics, one in five Australians will suffer from a mental health issue at some stage of their lives. Dr. Scott said that a big part of the burgeoning problem was due to changes in the family environment. He emphasized that a secure relationship with at least one parent was "enormously important." He added that "the biology of people hasn't changed, but everything else in society has. Family break-ups, single parenting, blended families are a big part of it." He added, "Kids need to be part of a family and feel safe" (Hinde 2008:7).

Accompanying this scary trend is the burgeoning problem of domestic violence. This abuse is not limited to race or color, rich or poor, female or male, the religious or atheist, west or east, or to upper or lower echelons of society. It has become a universal tragedy of gigantic magnitude across all segments of global humanity. Erin Marcus says that those in the medical profession "who support routine questioning, say domestic violence is as or more common in women, than many diseases, which doctors regularly check, including breast and colon cancer" (2008:03). Unfortunately fear, ignorance, bias and neglect add to the dilemma. One national survey in USA found only seven percent of women had been asked about domestic abuse by their health professionals. The US Bureau of Justice Statistics indicate that "from 2001 to 2005 there was an annual average of nearly 511,000 violent assaults against women—and 105,000 against men - by a spouse or intimate partner, about half resulting in physical injury" (Marcus 2008:03). Abused humans are at "increased risk of chronic pain, depression, anxiety and alcohol and substance abuse." In the West, it is estimated that domestic violence accounts for seventy percent of police calls. The presence of churches everywhere does not seem to assuage the chaotic pain of this terrible trend.

Asia, like other areas of the world, is not immune, despite the prevalence of Buddhism with its purported peace-loving, compassionate approach. According to a 2005 survey the "Ministry of Planning estimates that 22.5 percent of women in Cambodia are victims of domestic violence." Children are often the objects of frequent abuse in the families also. Cambodian and other Asian men, like those in many areas of the world, regard women as sex slaves, including their wives, believing they have a right to sex whenever they want it, whether the wife agrees or not. "In most households the man is the only one earning money, so many women remain in violent marriages because leaving would make their future uncertain" (Chamroeun 2008:5). It is encouraging that in these days more Asian women are being empowered to break the cycle of habitual abuse, but still little is being done to educate the men concerning this despicable practice.

As a child in north Thailand, Ouyporn Khuankaew, now a Buddhist peace activist and feminist, experienced along with her mother, her father's violent treatment. She struggled to understand how her father, a devout Buddhist who frequently made merit at the temple, could treat her in this abusive way; or why others cognizant of his abuse did not do anything about it. She recognized that "patriarchy distorts Buddhist teachings to keep women down." She saw patriarchy was also the root of abuse of young rural girls naively recruited into prostitution. Ouyporn says, "Breathing patriarchy, (Buddhist) monks teach that women are burdened with bad karma, thus born inferior to men, so they must endure for the sake of others" (Ekachai 2008:01). Yet in seeking to free herself of her anger towards her father, she found solace in Buddhist spirituality. Her practice of meditation for compassion and mindfulness, and her recognition of impermanence and of non-self helped her to feel the sufferings of other beings. She now prays for her father "for his chance to be born again in the lands of Buddhism so he can practice dharma to free himself from suffering." Some experts believe more children, including in Western countries, die from abuse injuries than from all common childhood diseases.

China, the most populous nation on earth, has a potentially escalating problem with their angry youth (*fen qing*), particularly ages fourteen to eighteen. "These young people are just angry, not necessarily at anything in particular. One moment they are angry at Japan, the next at the USA; angry at any criticism directed at China; angry at anything that questions their patriotism" (Pruitt 2008:2).

This powder-keg of emotions under the stress of life and strain of societal uncertainties is likely to explode in vicious violence at any moment.

In both the East and West the rate of suicides and attempted destruction of one's own life has dramatically skyrocketed during the last few decades. Shockingly, this covers an indiscriminate age spread from children to the aged. This self destructive trend has many causes, including inability to deal with stresses, the lack of coping skills in the face of complicated issues, and intense massive societal pressures. Liz Lipski tells of her brother who, in Australia one hot day in January 1992, "jumped off the eighth floor of a city parking building." In 2005 the Australian Bureau of Statistics recorded that "there were 2,101 deaths from suicide." (That is more than one in twenty thousand of population). Nearly eighty percent of them were males. Neither fame nor fortune precludes such tragic deaths as All Saints actor Mark Priestley joined that number in 2008 (2008:13).

The serene expressionless faces of the Japanese and other devout Asian Buddhists may come from the long influence of Buddhism, which tends to help produce a calm and quiet look. However, repressed emotions, overly calm control outwardly, or latent deep-seated revenge from an unforgiving heart may be psychological volcanoes just waiting to erupt and explode at a future time, like Oregon's Mount St. Helens did in May 1980. The author remembers a discussion with a Chinese-Thai businessman in Bangkok. He had two wives, chosen from different social strata so they would be unlikely to meet. He told how his Chinese wife, when she was upset at him, would promptly yell at him and tell him off, ripping him to shreds with her biting tongue. On the other hand his Thai wife would be patiently calm and serenely cool until one day, out of the blue, she would attack him from the kitchen with a butcher knife. No longer able to be ignored, her pent-up frustrations and repressed anger eventually exploded.

On another occasion the writer's attempted mediation between a rural pastor and a female church member indicated that Asian Christians, like Western ones, have a hard time forgiving, even within the church family. In spite of counseling with God's Word, the obvious conviction of the Spirit and copious tears, the middle aged Thai woman refused to grant forgiveness over her loss of face. Like fleeing the tiger only to encounter a crocodile, all efforts to resolve the matter encountered a wave of repressed wrath that would not be assuaged.

Despite the gloomy realities described in the above section, hope in the resilience of the human spirit suggests that better things may still be ahead for families in the future.

TRENDS RENEWING EMPHASIS ON FAMILY IN THE TWENTY-FIRST CENTURY

Down through history until the Industrial Revolution of the 1800s, the major pattern of families was the extended family, more than the nuclear family. The clan, tribe and extended networks of family webs were generally self-sufficient, supporting the members through hunting, gathering, gardening and animal husbandry. Everything they needed for food, clothing and housing, they produced together. Through trading they also gained additional income and so extended families were fairly economically independent. They married, raised their own children, cared for the aged generations and buried their own dead. Mostly they lived in their own villages from birth to death. Their domicile was in local communities the whole of their lives. Inheritance of lands was passed on to children generation after generation. Normally, the occupations of parents were passed on to the sons and daughters also. Skills learned over generations were thus preserved.

By the mid-1800s the Industrial Age had arisen. Manufacturing cities became the major population and work centers, drawing the masses from the rural and tribal areas. As families left their villages and kin, these nuclear units became free of the controls and restraints of the village and ancestors. They also became exposed to and often involved in social evils that they would never have considered participating in back in their traditional familial settings. As Communism dawned, Karl Marx saw the family as an antiquated structure and predicted it, along with capitalism, would vanish. He was wrong. His experiment in encouraging casual dating and easy divorce, as well as the later "free love" movement went awry. In fact, after the Revolution of 1917 Joseph Stalin stopped those kinds of practices and declared the family to be "the basic cell in society."

Everything, including economics, styles of living, and means of employment, changed in this new world of industrialization. Farming families especially, were drastically affected. In 1900 ninety percent of Americans lived off the land by farming. They also lived on their own land. In 2000 less than ten percent in the USA were farmers. Over time this mobility during the Industrial Age caused a break up of many extended families, as nuclear families became the dominant economic earning units in the cities of industry. Up until the early twentieth century, grandparents lived in, with or next to the members of their extended families. In the latter half of the twentieth century that pattern increasingly changed to isolated, independent units of living, often hundreds of miles apart. By then most extended families did not live together or even nearby.

However, in recent decades that is now changing. The pendulum is swinging back slowly. In November 2008, Britt Hume reported on television's Fox News that four thousand households in America now have three or more generations living together. In "Grandparents under the same roof," Hume noted that the decade between 1990 and 2000 experienced thirty-eight percent increase of this phenomenon of three or more generations living together. This trend of multi-generational domicile indicates a new feeling and sense of people needing family. The stress of modern economics and high housing costs put much pressure on families. Families of the younger generation frequently recognize the need to share expenses with someone else, including parents. Aging parents face the increasing cost of assisted living or of nursing homes and are likewise opting for life with their offspring and grandchildren. This is a general trend opposite an earlier era's attitude of independent living and not needing family help.

Greg Toppo and Anthony DeBarros in *USA TODAY*, relayed data from the U.S. Census Bureau, indicating that "the number of parents, siblings and other relatives who live with adult heads of households grew forty-two percent from 2000 to 2007." Parents increased sixty-seven percent to 3.6 million and other relatives by forty percent to 6.8 million. The increase of grandchildren in households was above ten percent, reaching almost six million (2008:1). While intergenerational households are more common among the growing immigrant populations, especially from Asia and Latin America, this phenomenon is a major trend among Caucasians and others also, in both groups of under and over sixty-five years of age.

This intergenerational living has advantages of fostering a sense of family closeness, continuity, cohesiveness, caring, sharing and mutual respect. Cross generational bonding is tighter. On the downside this close-quarter living also provides potential avenues for disagreement, stress, conflict and codependence.

Similarly, because of the rising cost of rents, single folk are opting to share rooms with other single roommates, sometime unmarried ones of the opposite sex. From 2000 to 2007 the households with non-relative live-ins increased eight percent to more than six million (Toppo 2008:1).

Significantly in "The Family: At Home in a Heartless World," Rowland Croucher affirms the extended family model. He writes that "no (nuclear) family can provide for all the needs of its members. I believe it's time to re-tribalize. The extended rather than the nuclear family is the best model (and always has been). As we live in 'community' incarnational love is experienced again and again; we are loved in spite of our faults and failings and even our sinfulness" (1994:3).The extended family has a long history of stability and "the backing of Christian teaching," says John Court (1975:2).

In the East, China is undergoing some major sociological changes in family also. One interesting fact of Mao's earlier influence on society in China was his demand that their young be responsible to look after their aged parents. "China's Constitution says children must support their parents." But "many now neglect them" (Liu 2008:18). The unpopular one-child policy, instituted in 1979, attacked basic family values. Its excesses of forced sterilizations and consequent female infanticide in that male oriented society, distorted the gender composition, resulting in an imbalance of population. It is now comprised of a considerably greater majority of largely spoiled, self-centered males. Significantly, the one-child practice also dramatically limited the number of offspring available to care for aging parents. Melinda Liu notes that "China's one-child policy is broken" irreversibly, in "a manner that threatens" China's future.

"This has become a big issue, among decision makers." In "Playing With the Old Blood Rules," Liu explains that China's traditional filial piety is no longer a sacred family value. "The most pressing problem is a break-down of filial piety, the sense of loyalty and shame that drove generations past to protect their elders no matter the cost" (2008:17).

Today China faces another kind of challenge that is changing basic traditional family values. Older Chinese are adapting modern pragmatism that leans on females more than males for their future. Ignoring their former prejudice for sons, elderly parents are adopting adult daughters to look after them in their old age, because "daughters are more likely to grow into loyal caregivers." This significant change was reinforced in one 2007 survey where "a thin majority of parents" preferred to have girls over boys. As for the aged Chinese, life expectancy has increased from fifty in 1949 to seventy-two today. In 2005 government statistics indicated that forty-two percent of Chinese families consisted of "an old couple living alone." In today's cities it is "more than fifty-six percent." Another reality acerbated this need, "Less than 1.2 percent of China's retirees have access to nursing homes, compared to eight percent in developed countries." China's authorities are working on a nationwide system of home care for the aged. Other private schemes like "kids for hire" are forms of insurance against old-age neglect (Liu 2008:17-20).

These changes that accommodate the pressing needs of families in the twenty-first century suggest that positive renewal models for families are increasingly being implemented.

HISTORICAL CHANGE OF APPROACH FOLLOWING THE REFORMATION

Another kind of change, discussed next, seems to have become detrimental to the extension of the church and its pioneer outreach in virgin missions following the 1700s. Prior to the Reformation, much pioneer church growth occurred, mostly from in-gatherings of whole families, clans, tribes and peoples. Historians like Kenneth Latourette (1953:100) and Stephen Neill (1973:31-77) as well as missiologists such as Bishop Waskom Pickett (1933:37f) and Donald McGavran

(1970:173f; 296f) affirmed that from the earliest centuries of the church, family, group and people movements were foundational to the extension of the church. Stephen Neill's chapter, "Conquest of the Roman World, A.D. 100-500," indicated that the key to the extension of the church was the movement of the gospel from people to people and country to country until the whole of the Roman Empire was reached. Writing about Asia Minor to Emperor Trajan about 112 AD, Younger Pliny "was dismayed by the rapid spread of the Christian faith in the rather remote and mainly rural province of Bithynia in north-west Asia Minor." Pliny made note of "many in every period of life, on every level of society, of both sexes… in towns and villages and scattered throughout the countryside." The "evidence of Pliny is unimpeachable; we seem to encounter here one of the first mass movements in Christian history" (1964:31). Here was an obvious major family movement. Near the end of the fourth century in the time of John Chrysostom, the population of Antioch was not less than a half a million and "half the inhabitants at that time were Christian" (1964:32). Neill reported that "The church of North Africa was a church of bishops. Every town, almost every village, had its bishop," in contrast to the rest of Christendom, where "bishops were located only in the cities," and were few in number (1964:38).

Armenia became another Christian kingdom, reached through witness from Cappadocia. Tradition says that when Gregory the evangelist and wonder worker became Bishop of Cappadocia "there were only seventeen Christians in the city, but when he died thirty years later there were only seventeen pagans" (Neill 1964:53-54). Armenia became the first known case in which the conversion of the king was the first step in the conversion of the whole country. King Tiridates accepted Christianity as the religion of his state. The families of aristocracy and common people followed en masse. A second factor was the association of the church with the language and thought of the people, for Gregory preached in Armenian. The third element came as the New Testament was translated into that language in 410 (1964:54).

Another case occurred through Patrick who returned to Ireland in 432 staying until his death in 461. At the time of his return "Ireland was almost wholly, if not entirely, a heathen country." By "the time of his death, Ireland was largely a Christian country" (1964: 56). In 493 Clovis, King of the Franks married a Christian princess of Burgundy. She did her best to convert him. Later, in a crisis, "Clovis swore that, if victory was his, he would become the servant of the God of the Christians. He kept his vow; on Christmas day 496, he was baptized with three thousand of his warriors." (1964:58). In 596 Pope Gregory the Great sent Augustine to Canterbury, England. King Ethelbert of Kent had married Bertha, a Christian princess from Gaul. Augustine's preaching converted the king and by the end of the year Augustine baptized 10,000 Saxons (1964:67-68). Among the Franks and other Europeans, Boniface had a particular practice or habit, "When a group, often under the influence of a chieftain or ruler, had decided to become Christian, it was customary to baptize" them "without any long delay" (1964:77). Thus for more than a thousand years the church expanded across nations through massive family movements.

The Reformation of the 1500s faced a different situation than the early pioneer settings which were mostly among unevangelized people groups. Primarily, the reformers were dealing with largely nominal, already churched communities. Throughout the Dark Ages moral corruption and unbiblical practices had saturated the church, resulting in spiritual weakness and large-scale nominalism. Under these conditions the primary focus of the Reformation was *within* the churched communities across Europe. In these Christianized populations the call for renewal of personal faith and individual salvation was rightly warranted. In that context a change of emphasis to the individual was correct. The Reformation thereby brought renewal and revitalization to the existing church. Faced with the consequent Roman Catholic Counter Reformation, much energy of the Reformers, at least until 1648, was spent in "fighting for their lives" (Neill 1964:220).

As Ralph Winter pointed out, the Reformers did not organize new mission structures comparable to the former missionary training monasteries. In fact, they discarded the monastic system (1999:226f). It was likely that Christian meditation, frequently nurtured in the monasteries, also ceased to be practiced around that period. This was one weakness of the new movement. Thus the Reformation did not spawn major missions across cultures to new unevangelized populations for more than another two hundred years (Pierson 1999:263). There was little thought of missions (Neill 1964:220-226). During the seventeenth century a few exceptions arose in Europe, notably the Moravian mission movement, which started in 1732. Consequently when William Carey and others launched the Protestant's Modern Mission Era in the late 1700's, the Reformers' pattern of converting "individual by individual" was carried over as a dominant evangelistic and mission strategy. Unfortunately this renewed pioneer outreach to frontier unreached peoples did not generally return to the earlier biblical model and historical pattern of evangelizing whole families, tribes and ethne. At the restarting of the major mission enterprise, a definite change in methodology seems to have occurred.

In his 1970 article R. Pierce Beaver succinctly noted this changed emphasis of mission strategy following the Reformation. The aim of 17th seventeenth Protestant missions of the Dutch, British and Americans was that peoples like the East Indians and Native Americans "would be converted, *individually* receive salvation, and be gathered into churches." In reaching the Native Americans at Martha's Vineyard, Thomas Mayhew followed "a slow, individual, personal approach." Beaver summarized nineteenth missionary strategy of the Protestants as being "aimed at individual conversions, church planting, and social transformation" through actions of "evangelism, education and medicine" (1999:244, 249).

When did the family approach change to an individual one? At the point when Reformation mission to unevangelized nations was restarted almost three hundred years later. The Reformers' theology and practice in reaching out to new unreached peoples did not return to the earlier biblical family approach. Instead a theological shift to individual evangelism, individual salvation, and calling to individual personal holiness were emphasized. The move from biblical theology to systematic theology helped advocate this ignoring of family evangelistic approaches too. Calvin's Institutes, as well as synthesized or summarized creeds, or shortened theological tenets, like the *Westminster Catechism*, tended to focus on the individual growth and not on evangelizing and discipling whole families and their entire extended families.

Nevertheless, God's Spirit often overruled in His harvest and spontaneously gathered some whole family networks, tribes and people groups into the church, especially in the non-Western world. One wonders how much greater the ingathering might have been and how much speedier evangelization accomplished had family and group evangelistic approaches been the intentional method of modern missions, particularly among Hindus, Buddhists and Muslims.

Modern illustrations of family and people movements include the Mizo, Naga, Karens, Toba Bataks, Karo Bataks and many others who transferred their allegiance to Christ as family after family came into the church fold, until a large majority had become Christians. An interesting case in the last half-century is the Dalits (Daliths), the untouchables without caste in India. This was not a people movement into the church, but the conversion of millions from Hinduism to Buddhism. The pattern was largely family by family, often in whole extended families. Over eight million or more Dalits were garnered into the Buddhist fold. Some Indian reporters quote the numbers as high as thirty million, which is about one third of all Dalits in India. This dramatic example emphasizes the principle of family focus in dynamic religious change. It also calls for a re-examination of family approaches to community development, local Christian service and outreach as well as in evangelism. Working with whole families is not only biblical and sociologically sound, but also desperately needed in the societal chaos of modern times.

Introducing Changes on Modern Socio-Cultural Issues

All over the world, the family generally provides emotional support, expects loyalty with elders and often exercising control over younger and sometimes older members. This solidarity affects the receptivity of family dynamics to outside or unusual influences. Family bonds and filial unity generally resist or oppose changes coming from without, through fear of the effects on existing kin ties, traditional loyalty and financial stability. Where a strong sense of family is missing through the lack of setting proper boundaries, establishing common mores, or teaching moral obligations, fragmentation and break-ups often occur. Where these are in place, family solidarity stands strong and secure.

For example, ancestral worship is a major family issue in China, Japan, Korea and Vietnam, and found in many other Asian settings. The family is central to Chinese worldview because the group gives meaning to the individual. Three strong elements that affect the Chinese cultural map and integrated mindset are: 1) Buddhism relating to one's ultimate end of life, 2) Taoism along with naturalistic, animistic spirit forces and 3) Confucianism which defines relationships (*kwang shi*) between levels of humans, including continued connection with the ancestors. Filial piety provides structure for loyalty, continuity and responsibility. The deceased ancestors are deemed such an important part of the living family, they must be honored. Family members are required to show respect, express filial piety and conduct the appropriate rites. Emotional ties to family structure are so strong that responsibility and loyalty to family supersede all personal preferences in this matter. Any attempted change or disruption in this realm is resisted.

A recent example on China's mainland poignantly re-enforces this powerful drive. During the Chinese New Year season of 2008 the snow and rains produced floods, particularly in South China. The resulting chaos shut down the operations of trains, airlines and busses for a week or more. This immobilization caused Chinese emotions to boil over, mainly because of planned family visits over this festive event. Many Chinese were in "panic mode" trying to get to their extended families for the New Year and its filial rites of showing respect to parents and ancestors. Deeply frustrated by long delays, many started riots, attacked transport workers, and blamed the Central Government for the situation. Fulfilling proper rites for ancestors is a strong emotional issue in many Buddhist cultures.

In many dire and abusive situations in families, change is urgently needed. However, change often comes slowly. In the past, though outlawed in 1829, the practice of *sati* or *suttee* (burning of the living wife on the husband's funeral pyre) persisted. It was a familiar family expectation, particularly in India. Occasionally, this is still carried out in modern times, including in the high castes, as late as 2002. In similar fashion today, through an adaptation of this, widows are publicly degraded, shamefully have their heads shaved, and frequently are robbed of their property rights, among other atrocities they endure (Meroff 2004:182-183). In India and Bangladesh 25,000 brides per annum are deliberately set on fire. In Delhi a woman is burned to death every twelve hours. Most of these crimes go unpunished (Meroff 2004:132). How can lasting change be implemented within such entrenched mentalities and ingrained societal practices?

In face-saving societies not only do individuals partake of shame, but their families and their communities experience it also. To illustrate the point, in 2007 the South Asian cricketers were deftly defeated by the Australian Team, who badly beat them in just two innings of the Test-Match. The shame and loss-of-face could be clearly seen on the countenances of the Asian players shown on television. Following the collapse of the team, with deep mortification they left Australia as soon as possible to return home. They were deeply embarrassed, as equally were their families and their communities back in their homeland. It is difficult to deal with, and almost impossible to change, the deep sense of shame in face-saving communities.

The following story pointedly illustrates the power of shame in the East. An Indian daughter began to develop a relationship with a man whom the family did not choose nor endorse. Suppose she is shown on television in a public compromising situation with him or is found to be pregnant. The family members are not only likely to be violently angry and embarrassed, but also deeply ashamed, causing them to arrange for family members to murder the girl as an "honor killing." In the latter months of 2008 in America, two separate South Asian fathers disposed of daughters in honor killings. One was killed merely because she asked for a divorce from a pre-arranged marriage. Shame was too much for the family's head to endure. Asian family ties hold such high values, that the demands on members and the consequences for infractions are substantial. Introducing change here is difficult.

Child prostitution is a worldwide problem. It plagues many countries in South and Southeast Asia. At least a million children are exploited for sex in Asia, half of them in India, with large numbers in Thailand, Taiwan and the Philippines. Then another one hundred million work and live on the streets (Meroff 2004:137-138). A different source claims there are "160 million street children in the world, 143 million orphans, 400,000 child slaves in Haiti, thirteen million AIDS orphans in Africa, and over one million children (many of them only five, six, or seven years of age) living on the streets of the Philippines" (Nichols 2008:1). These statistics magnify societal problems across the globe, needing serious attention and definite changes. Most of these enormous concerns arise out of families in distress, disorder, disarray or dysfunction. How can change be affected?

The church has a responsibility to care for widows, the poor, the orphans and the down trodden. Christians are to be examples of what family truly means as well as models of the true compassion and redeeming grace of Christ? They are one of the change agents available to help through their relationships, community service, counseling and spiritual outreach. However, some authorities and community leaders may oppose these efforts because of their vested interests in the abuses. The churches' attempts to bring about change may also encounter reaction from the local community, who may question their motives. The best approach to change the situation is through advocating and catalyzing it in local families of need. The indigenous insider can appropriate change and spread the model of change much more readily than the outside advocates.

This is true of religious change also. For example, *Business Week*, in the January 14, 2008, reported on "China's Spiritual Awakening." This was not a movement into the church, although that too is occurring in this most populous country on earth. This was an awakening of Buddhism. Reporter Lenovo identified "Why a growing number of successful urban professionals are flocking to Buddhism." Interest in and commitment to Buddha is booming. A growing number of Chinese celebrities and urban professionals are becoming "tired with their old toys of luxury and turning to more spiritual sense of fulfillment." Behind this phenomenon is a sense of deficiency and lack of deep, heart-felt satisfaction in the midst of obvious affluence and hard-earned progress. The emptiness of modern advancement often leaves China's yuppies and DINK (double income no kids) families with inner aching voids. Religious aspiration seems to provide some satisfaction.

Opposition to change or spiritual conversion is not always primarily religious, but frequently the result of social solidarity. Family consolidated unity is often the major barrier to significant change. The family opposes outside influences because it feels threatened, needs to protect the family, to maintain and keep its appropriate place in society, and to reinforce loyalty to each other.

The more the whole family can be approached, recognized and influenced, the more likely innovation can be catalyzed, accepted and changes effectively implemented. The flow of change is reflected in Van Gennep's model of Rites of Passage starting with the old state, moving through reorientation (usually by rite or ritual), and passing into a new state. The process of separation from the old condition moves through a transition into the incorporation of a new form. Likewise, for innovation of new ideas to be adopted in families with success, it usually follows a similar process. This entails several successive stages: Initiation, Permeation, Group Commitment and Consolidation (or Incorporation). Starting with the old values, time is required for the penetration of any new concept to take hold. Educational input once initiated takes time for diffusion and saturation within families. Once the group adopts and accepts that change, the final stage is set for its integration into the new value, attitude and action. This explains the general process of introducing change and of religious conversion of a family, a group or a people.

Observe an important practical application of this. The crucial fulcrum in moving this process forward is the initial one, that of building solid and deep relationships with the family. Applying the above principles, some practical approaches and tactics to develop effective relationships with families might include:

1) *Initiation* - take time to build relationships with the whole family. During repeated interaction with them tell them about your family, your parents, grandparents, extended families. Show them photos of your family, your parents and siblings. Explain how your family works and interacts, shows respect to each other, and makes decisions together.

2) *Permeation* - in similar fashion, ask them to explain to you about their family, children, grandchildren and extended families. Carefully jot down the special linguistic terms they use for each class of relative. Specifically observe the pronouns they use for themselves and the key terms for their various relatives. Record what they call each level of family relationship and how they address each one from their position in the family.

3) *Commitment* - when, in due course, the family or group is ready to act together, encourage the whole group to decide together mutually as a united family to commit to the desired action and where appropriate, to commit the family to Christ.

4) *Incorporation* - identify the words and terms they use for their new life changes and new practices. Start using the various indigenous terms for different family relationships in each category of relatives. Ask families who these extended family relatives are, and encourage them to begin sharing the changes they have experienced with each family on their broader family tree.

MYTHS AND OBJECTIONS ON THE FAMILY GROUP APPROACH

Myths and ignorance concerning individual evangelism or conversion abound. Some sound quite plausible, but deeper scrutiny often explodes the myths. The *first* objection is "salvation is only an individual thing, not a family thing." Individuals can and do convert but, among resistant populations, usually will lack the solidarity of the group's backing, often essential for survival and added growth.

Family and Faith in Asia

Individual converts can soon become social misfits, or fringe people in society. Where a movement of families or multi-individual, mutually interdependent decisions of small or large unified groups occur, stability is more likely than that of several scattered individuals. Strong individuals sometimes can be innovators and catalysts to reach their own family networks, if motivated to do so.

A *second* retort says "Students are so receptive we should go for them now and not worry about their families." Asian youth in universities have some freedom to choose. But what about after they graduate? Who chooses their wives, work and jobs? Mostly the parents and elders come back into force after graduation. Even student churches do not remain student oriented forever.

Thirdly, "Youth work and children's ministry are superior because they build for the future generation. The old generation is 'dyed in the wool,' of the old way, and can't change." Again in Asia the family structure and its control indicate that most children have no power of decision or control of action until adulthood. So while we should not neglect the youth we are wiser to reach them along with their families.

Fourth, some advocate "Children and youth are more important because they are easier to reach and mold. Save a child and you save a life. Save a broken adult or family and you have no end of troubles to solve." Generally, conversion and growth in family groups provide the best stability, normality and strength for youth. They should be cherished and reached, but this is best done in the context of the whole family. Taking deliberate steps to reach out to the families of interested scholars and children is a vital strategy. The worst sin of evangelism is to reach a child, but neglect his or her family, which is their nurturing ground and controlling entity.

Fifth, some say "It is better to have a few individuals who are genuine Christians than whole families that need so much work that you never are sure that they will become strong." There is no guarantee that "our" isolated individual believers are holier, stronger or more stable than those in family groups.

Sixth, "Separating individual believers from their unsaved families is biblical, better and builds them stronger in face of opposition."

They are to "come out from among them and be separate." This misinterprets the Word. History proves these views are wrong, on all counts. Co-dependent "rice" Christians usually turn out not to be the strongest disciples.

A *seventh* objection is, "Only individuals can have a relationship with Christ, not so for the diverse family." This is true for "personal" salvation generally, but here we are talking about the best strategy for producing long term stability against often fierce opposition, particularly among resistant peoples. The family comprised of a majority of new believers becomes its own nurturing force, closing ranks on the outside powers of opposition. Families throughout Scripture have been kept by the grace covering of God.

Eighth, "Group and family movements are shallow, weak and unstable." This can be true if post-decision nurture and teaching are absent. Family movements require suitable post-conversion evaluation with sustained teaching, training, discipleship and consolidation. But in the end the strength and solidarity of the Christian family stands tall. The strong Christian family can be a powerful model and tool for extending the gospel throughout the extended family and local community. History proves this.

Ninth, is a sad commentary, "Winning one by one individually is always the way we did it back home in our churches, so let's do it in missions too." The thinking advocate of indigenous methods will question this as a theologically good mission strategy. It has the seeds of proud ethnocentrism and ignorance of social and family structure across cultures.

Tenth, "Massive numbers of families coming into the church dilute it and produce nominalism." Not necessarily so, depending on the prompt nurture and training given. Individual converts can be weak, nominal and just as easily dilute the church. Often they may not have the strength to stand alone against the opposition of the family or village.

An *eleventh* view suggests that "Doing God's work with a few individuals is better than distributing our energies among the multitudes or multiple families." This mentality can produce the small insular ghetto church and favors a fortress mentality, instead of the vision for reaching out to the whole community or people group in self sacrificing service.

Twelfth, some feel "If we do not accept the individual when opportunity to believe arises, they usually miss the salvation boat." While not advocating the rejecting of individuals, the group approach is one of faith in God and hope for the family by exercising love to the whole interrelated group. Often the "one by one against the tide approach" only shuts the family off from the gospel. Ideally by delaying individual decisions or baptisms, the family has the opportunity for the diffusion of the good news so that all the members can consider it and mutually decide together.

Lastly, "Individual salvation through "one on one" is the proven, successful method of some major evangelistic agencies. This form of evangelism is taught in churches, seminaries and Bible colleges." Unfortunately, it is also passed on to new and old native converts of foreign missions as "the best or only way to do real evangelism." Maybe changing this approach to "one on a whole family" might be an even better method with stronger and more extensive effect. It would be more culturally appropriate too.

Concluding Practical Applications and Suggestions

A worldwide disintegration of family is beginning to be reversed, of necessity, through a return to extended family living. The biblical emphasis is strongly on families, but following the Reformation, a major change moved that focus away to one on individuals, often at the expense of the whole family. Modern societies face growing dilemmas of enormous moral declension and ethical challenges. These complexities demand that the church return to stress the family in its involvement with local communities, rather than remaining apart in insular isolation. The more the church is involved locally with the families of its surrounding society, the more effective and valued it will become. This conclusion primarily offers advice to Christians; it suggests some vital principles to apply to reaching families; and finally it recommends a key simple model to win families.

First of all, the church must accept responsibility in regards to family groups. Christians might well repent for failures to serve families in their immediate communities. Often the church's ambassadors have unwittingly contributed to family breakdowns and domestic divisiveness, not only through neglect, but also by their policies and practices in service and evangelism. Their tactics have frequently isolated individual converts from their families, instead of integrating loving ministry to their whole families through the church. Broken society needs mending not meddling, healing not harassment. Often the unity and support of the family provides the best nurture and encouragement for the individual members of the family. To this end the church can focus on the family more than on the individual. Furthermore, Christians who have neglected or possibly rejected their non-believing relatives need to rebuild bridges to their own family networks. One South Asian pastoral leader shared that he had not seen, contacted or visited his in-laws for decades. From their particular religious perspective, they had reacted to a Christian marrying their daughter. In turn the pastor ignored the in-laws from that time on. Many Christians in Asia and elsewhere need to mend family fences and rebuild communication with their unsaved relatives. This will not be an easy task, but humbly needs to be done.

Church workers and missionaries should study and understand the sociological and cultural dynamics of families, the familial structures and their decision making patterns. Making decision in Asian families is often not an individual thing, but a family affair. The author remembers one thirty year old Thai man who was thinking of taking a teaching position at the local school. When asked if he had decided yet, he replied that he had to ask his parents first, even though he was an adult, married man with his own children. Later he responded that he did not take the job because, though his father was agreeable, his mother was not. Decision making is often an extended family matter. So the church needs to take the whole family into account when anticipating increased and lasting conversion.

Notice that Christ's Great Commission commands us "to make disciples" (plural) not disciple (singular). Neither did Jesus instruct us to do that individually, "one by one." The emphasis is more likely "ethne by ethne," or family group by family group, tribe by tribe and people by people (Matt. 28:18-20). The Apostles obviously understood Jesus' command as from the beginning they won and incorporated whole families into the church. Few isolated individual converts are highlighted in the New Testament. The Apostles then extended the family movements out to reach Romans, Greeks, Gentiles, Goths and so forth. "Family by family" was the primary approach and mostly the usual mode of response for more than a millennium and a half.

Second, here are some vital principles and practical tactics for reaching whole families:

- Change the way we pray, from patterns of just individuals to lifting up whole families, their extended families and their family webs and networks before God.
- Focus outreach ministry and service objectives on specific families as the clear goal or reason for evangelism. This intentional strategy may produce quite surprising results.
- Experiment with creative ways to reach whole families. Test models, methods and strategies to do this. Research the effects of the process and its results. Recycle the best lessons learned.
- Foster building friendly relationships with whole families over time. Effort taken to invest in gaining connections with families does take energy, but is well spent.
- Develop family friendly tools and approaches to families rather than just to individuals. Mass media has tended to major on resources focused on individuals, little on families.
- Teach and encourage new interested seekers to begin sharing the good news with their families and their relatives, even before they themselves become committed believers.
- Allow time for the dissemination of the good news to penetrate and permeate whole family networks, before calling families to commit prematurely. Diffusion helps here.

- Consider delaying the baptism of individual members until the whole family is ready to follow, or at least to endorse the individual's baptism. More of the family may join in.
- Practice patience, persistence, and perseverance in order to see whole families reached, penetrated, won and discipled. Pushing for speedy decisions, pressure to show results back home, and commando approaches are to be resisted rigorously. As Rome was not built in a day, nor are genuine converts or family conversions produced instantly.
- Immediately incorporate family accessions into house churches from the start. Most of the cutting edge extension of the church and its multiplication in Asia are found in tiny fellowships—usually less than fifteen or twenty members, sometimes only five to eight.
- Evaluate results in terms of families won, not just individual converts. Statistics should reflect both categories. The most vital one is the number of new families brought into the Kingdom.

Third, take note of a model that has been used for forty years in parts of Asia. The Five Finger Family Evangelism approach was initiated in 1970 in Central Thailand. It spread throughout the land and crossed into other regions and peoples of Asia. The philosophy and method of this simple strategy to reach family networks was published in Thai and later in English as *Multiplying Churches Through Prayer Cell Evangelism: A Manual for Church Planting Movements* written by the author.

The five fingers of family evangelism emphasize the whole family context in reaching networks of natural relationships of relatives and close friends. The visual hand of five fingers is taught to all members, who memorize the five elements, and begin to practice them as soon as possible. Though these five core strategies stand alone through their connectedness to the whole process, they are also integrated into a cycle of reproduction which propels new church plants into being. New converts from their families and friends become part of the continuing reproduction and multiplication. Here are the five basic precepts:

1) Pray specifically for your relatives and close friends by name.
2) Witness to them, sharing God's Word and your testimony of God's grace.
3) Go back to visit regularly those families who show interest, until they believe.
4) Teach them to know all you know about God, to help them grow spiritually.
5) Instruct them to repeat and practice the whole process of the five fingers.

Not only can heads of households start family movements, but sometimes they are started just from one relative's Christian witness to the family also. From there the movement is purposely spread throughout the extended family networks, across natural bridges of relatives and friends. It takes discipline to keep the group in mind. Normally, time for diffusion of the gospel and its permeation to all members of the family network is required. Clear understanding and acceptance of the gospel may take even up to two and sometime more years. The consistent change of life and the faithful witness of relatives, as well as their indigenous sensitivity to Buddhist cultural issues, have a marked effect on the acceleration of the process for the conversion of the whole family, extended network, tribe or village. By not withdrawing from normal relationships, interaction and customary events of the family and the local community, Christians' witness can portray genuine faith and commendable ethical living to the society at large.

As family movements occur, it is essential to nurture the movements so that each member of the family affirms personal faith and relationship with Christ. Nurture adds spiritual depth to the members of believing families. Usually family house church fellowships are easily initiated. Unpaid local family leaders can be trained to function in them and to mobilize relatives for more extension into other family networks.

2

Catalyzing "Insider Movements" in Buddhist Contexts

David S. Lim

What is happening in the Buddhist world? A little has been heard about church planting movements (CPMs) among Muslims (Garrison 2005; Travis 2000, 2006) and Hindus (Richard 1999; Hoefer 2001; Raj 2004; Pierson 2004:34-59). But in spite of the Church Growth phenomena (esp. the mega-church kind) and multiple talks about CPMs, there seems to be no significant impact on the Buddhist world, except for some regions in Cambodia (Carlton 2000), China (1993; Deng 2005; Pierson 2004:60-86; Tang 2005; and Wesley 2004), Thailand (Among the Isaan, cf. Wetchgama 2006) and Vietnam As our Lord's Great Commission includes discipling these major blocs of people groups,[1] which model of evangelism and mission will be effective in reaching Buddhist-majority nations and peoples today, that will bear fruit and even much fruit among them? Our evangelistic and missionary efforts have not been wanting in zeal, holiness, dedication, prayer and even sacrifice. The problem seems to be with the church model and mission strategy that have been used. Are we willing to make a major paradigm shift for the sake of putting closure to the Great Commission, even if it may mean breaking with some of our sacred traditions in doing church and mission?

---

1. Spaulding 2006 raises the issue of why we are not prioritizing the least reached populations who happen to be the dominant peoples in Buddhist lands, albeit they may have a viable small church (often uncontextualized) among them.

Understanding "Insider Movements"

The phrase "Insider Movements" (IM) has been popularized recently through the September-October 2005 issue of U.S. Center for World Mission's *Mission Frontiers*. It was also the theme of the 2005 annual conference of the International Society for Frontier Missiology last September 12-15 in Denver, Colorado: "Insider Movements: Doing Church Where There is No Church."

IM is synonymous with "gospel movements," "people movements," "Christ-ward movements" and "disciple-making movements" as long as these phrases refer to a nuanced understanding that CPM should be combined with "radical contextualization (RC)" (cf. Lim 2003). Some even contrast IM from CPM:

> The term "Church Planting" implies inventing a new structure. No matter how contextualized the "church" may be, it is still a new structure that is foreign to the people group. Church-planting work of various levels of contextualization is necessary in some contexts. However, our primary desire is for the spontaneous spread of culturally relevant Gospel movements through *pre-existing networks*. We believe that the extended family unit is the primary and foremost biblical model of *ecclesia* ("Seeking..." 2005).

They say further:

> Our aim is to be *catalytic agents* in the spawning of new movements. We do not have a prescribed methodology. We focus on facilitating the inductive learning of the scriptures that will enable indigenous believers to define their own convictions in their daily living. Using the scriptures as the primary and foremost authority, we trust in the self-correcting power of God's Word that is lived out through obedience and the work of the Holy Spirit to lead the indigenous believers (ibid.).

In the contextualization continuum of C-1 to C-6 introduced by John Travis (1998),[2] many advocates of contextualization have accepted up to the C-3 and C-4 levels.[3] But IM pushes for C-5 or even C-6. Gladly, several evangelical missiologists have welcomed this, perhaps with Donald McGavran as their forerunner.[4] The theoretical and theological framework of this approach to church and missions has been summarized well by John Travis. Working in a Muslim context, he enumerates ten, which can also be applied to Buddhist contexts:[5]

- *Premise 1:* For Muslims, culture, politics and religion are nearly inseparable, making changing religions a total break with society.
- *Premise 2:* Salvation is by grace alone through relationship/allegiance to Jesus Christ. Changing religions is not a prerequisite for, nor a guarantee of, salvation.
- *Premise 3:* Jesus' primary concern was the establishment of the Kingdom of God, not the founding of a new religion.
- *Premise 4:* The very term "Christian" is often misleading—not all called Christian are in Christ and not all in Christ are called Christian.
- *Premise 5:* Often gaps exist between what people actually believe and what their religion or group officially teaches.
- *Premise 6:* Some Islamic beliefs and practices are in

---

2. C-1 is "least contextualized," while C-6 is "most contextualized" with "secret believers."
3. Cf. Patterson 1988; Parshall 1998; and Garrison 2004.
4. McGavran 2005, Kraft 1979; 2005; Berentsen 1985; Winter 2005; Travis 2005 and Lim 2003. Perhaps also Smith 1993.
5. In the case of China, the early missionary implementers were W.A.P. Martin, Timothy Richard and Karl Ludwig Reichelt (Covell 1993:136-137; Lai 2000:146-147), and church leaders were Wang Zhixin, Francis C.M. Wei and Xu Song-shi (Lai 2000:146-158).

- keeping with the Word of God; some are not.
- *Premise 7:* Salvation involves a process. Often the exact point of transfer from the Kingdom of darkness to the Kingdom of light is not known.
- *Premise 8:* A follower of Christ needs to be set free by Jesus from spiritual bondages in order to thrive in his/her life with Him.
- *Premise 9:* Due to the lack of church structure and organization, C5 movements must have an exceptionally high reliance on the Spirit and the Word as their primary source of instruction.
- *Premise 10:* A contextual theology can only properly be developed through a dynamic interaction of actual ministry experience, the specific leading of the Spirit and the study of the Word of God. (Travis 2005:13).

In all these, the assumption is that vast numbers of peoples can be converted *en masse* as we allow new converts to remain vital members of their families and communities. "Fighting the religion-changing battle is the wrong battle" (ibid.). The strategy is that of infiltration,[6] to transform the people with the gospel from within their social structures, preferably without setting an alternative religious structure among them.

CALL TO PARADIGM SHIFT OF "CHURCH"

Unless church leaders and missionaries who have been ministering in Buddhist-majority contexts shift paradigms of church and ministry, they will remain ineffective, even if they seem to be winning a number of converts at a time. In the milieu of rapid population increase and growing mission activities of Buddhists, especially among the poor, we need to adopt a more effective approach, otherwise millions of Buddhists will continue to die and go to eternal destruction by the millions each year.

---

6. Travis 2006; cf. *International Journal of Frontier Missions* 17.1 (2000) and 21.1-4 (2004), and their website *http://www.ijfm.org.*

Global Christianity (including Evangelicalism) has unwittingly fallen into a trap, which is historically known as "the Babylonian captivity of the church," that constitutes the Christendom paradigm of church and also often called "western shape" which most third world churches have adopted. Thinking that this will result in better church growth, Christian leaders have been promoting "the local church is the base for ministry and/or world evangelization." By "local church" is meant a congregation that seeks to have a full-time pastor (and a pastoral staff as it grows bigger) and her own sanctuary (ideally bought and owned rather than rented), in order to attract and maintain an ever-increasing attendance in her weekly Sunday worship services.

Though this looks appealing (and not many have seriously questioned this tradition), it has been a self-defeating (and historically, quite self-destructive) trap. The maintenance mode of local churches has almost always killed (often sooner than later) the mission mode of the whole church. A lot of Christian resources become absorbed into the maintenance of church activities (e.g., evangelistic rallies, Sunday Schools, youth camps, mission conferences, building projects, etc. etc.) for nominal believers who offer to God (often hypocritically) what are conveniently "extras" from the "abundant blessings" that He provides in their middle class comfort zones. Usually only a pittance are actually spent to help reach out to non-church member. In secular terms, this is not cost-effective. In spiritual terms, it is poor stewardship. Why?

May I suggest that there are at least three ways by which local church structures become hindrances to church growth: they stunt quality growth, quantity growth and long-term growth.

They Hinder Quality Growth

In spite the zeal and fervency affirmed in the songs, prayers and sermons of worship services, they actually nurture nominalism. Disciples are made in small groups, not big meetings. Yet most, if not all, local churches would emphasize congregational assemblies rather than cell groups. The best proof is to ask where do they look to count their weekly church attendance? Such emphasis is perhaps

35

inevitable, because of the hierarchical and clerical model of church in the minds of most Christians ever since the Edict of Milan (in AD 313 when Constantine enforced Christianity in the Roman Empire) when the bishops introduced the diocesan and parish structures to the church.

Thereby almost inevitably, most church activities (including the central "Sunday worship services") have helped keep Christians spiritually immature. They are kept perennially as spiritual babies who are dependent on pastors, church buildings and church programs to feel spiritual or even just to "be in God's presence." Almost all lay-people, even after forty or fifty years in faith, would still need to be visited or counseled or prayed for/blessed by pastors; are still self-centered and needing to be served rather than being equipped to minister to others (cf. Eph. 4:11-16). A majority hesitate to lead in public prayers or to do personal evangelism. Instead of spiritual empowerment, they experience spiritual disempowerment. In short, local churches normally produce nominal (or baby) Christians, not committed disciples.

They Hinder Quantity Growth

Moreover, local churches stunt the amount and the rate of numerical increase of the church. We have mentioned above how they waste a lot of resources in maintenance, mostly on more costly ways to keep the members happy, if not "spoiled." In fact, to attract more people to Christ, they create more "come structures" (church programs that almost always has to border on entertainment; how else are they going to be seeker-friendly, given the competition "out there" in the world?), rather than more "go structures" (more secular-looking programs not held in church buildings).[7]

And instead of "total church mobilization" to evangelize their community and the ends of the earth, local churches elicit low commitment from their members (besides weekly church attendance

---

7. As seen below, the best "go structure" is to "make disciples" through informal "friendship evangelism" and bringing converts and interested parties to "come and see" the (informal) body-life of one's cell group/house church (a la Acts 2:42-47).

and giving their offerings), hence the need to constantly cajole people to be more active in church. Meanwhile, they enhance the role of full-timers (pastors and missionaries) to be the key players in doing evangelism and missions. Reaching out to the lost becomes the job of specialists, and not of the whole body. No wonder the rate of growth of local churches decreases as they often slowly increase in size. How tragic!

Should we not be longing for a more spontaneous expansion of the church involving the *whole* church to reach the whole world? Hardly any local church has been able to sustain rapid quantity church growth for ten years—with the only exception that they were able to institutionalize a strong cell multiplication program whereby every member is encouraged (or required) to be a member of a small group. Yet, how many have been able to maintain and sustain such structure beyond twenty years?

They Hinder Long-Term Growth

And worst, local churches are structured in such a way that qualitative and quantitative future growth, if any, will be stunted. The emphasis on big assemblies, magnificent buildings and super-gifted "full-timers" seems to fit into the less democratic, or more authoritarian, societies in Asia (or perhaps in most Christian and Buddhist subcultures). But in the long term, this breeds the "superstar complex" in the church leaders and "hero (bordering on demi-god, as in Korea) worship" among the members. Tragically, in the long term this results in the appointment or election of "lay leaders" (often called trustees, elders or deacons) who are chosen on the basis of their popularity—often due to their giftedness in public speaking (or singing) and/or in political savvy, including the use of wealth for self-promotion (perhaps often unintentionally). The almost inevitable rise of such populist leaders, especially as the church grows richer and becomes middle- or upper-class (known as "redemptive lift"), usually results in the degeneration of the quality of church leadership—often sooner than later. Normally, the second generation of local church leaders (both clergy and lay) would be good bureaucrats (knowledgeable in maintenance management) rather than good entrepreneurs (who can provide visionary and creative leadership).

But more tragic, their concept of spirituality also often degenerates into "spiritual showmanship" (usually on stage, something which our Lord Jesus clearly denounced in Matt. 6:1-18), thereby placing non-functioning people (who are not doing actual disciple-making) in positions of authority, while the functioning ones (who are doing actual disciple-making) are busy taking care of the flock, often in their silent ways (even shying away from accepting administrative roles that entail a series of committee meetings). Thus, local churches produce spiritually immature, and even hypocritical, leaders who hardly contribute to quality or quantitative church growth at all.

So, are we destined to have local churches that gradually become less and less effective in evangelism, discipleship and missions? Not necessarily, but it comes at great cost to our present local church structures. Are we willing to shift to a more decentralized (less hierarchical and less clerical) paradigm of church? That is, to transform our local churches into house-church networks, where small group meetings increase, while big assemblies decrease? The challenge is to work for the multiplication of more small churches (each self-governing, self-supporting, self-propagating and self-theologizing) rather than for the addition of more mega-churches. The key is to remember disciples are made in small groups, not in big meetings.

The secret to maintain a long-standing revived state of the church is to keep strong small group structures, just as it stretched for more than a hundred years at least twice in history: in the Moravian community in Herrnhut (with its cells called "choirs"), and during the Wesleyan Awakening (with its cells called "classes"). However, in both these cases, gradually small group meetings decreased, while big worship services increased. This is due, in my view, mainly to human weakness, as usual. Attendance in big meetings where one can remain anonymous require less commitment than participation in small groups where one can hardly hide any secrets. We tend towards cheap grace rather than costly discipleship. Hence, under normal instances, mega-churches will grow at the expense and loss of small churches.

Thus, the ultimate challenge is, Are local churches willing to die, so that house churches can be born and flourish? Then and only then will there be the possibility of all converts growing into mature Christians who can be disciple-makers and be sent elsewhere as tentmakers to make more disciples. And church leaders will only be those who are true servants with proven pastoral gifts. Thereby, the whole church will be empowered to reach the whole world in the fastest way possible through this IM or rapid disciple-making strategy done by hardly visible house-church networks.

Biblical Basis for IM

Actually, Jesus' mission paradigm was IM. His CPM was C-5—Jews multiplying disciples among Jews without creating another organized religious system parallel or counter to the synagogue (of early Judaism). He did not intend to found a new religion, but his movement later on became an institution (Bosch 1991:50-51). He even had C-6 converts in Nicodemus and Joseph of Arimathea, and perhaps through them, Gamaliel.

The early Christians followed the same pattern, too. They reached out to their compatriots as Jews to Jews within the Temple and synagogue structures of Jewish society, and just met "from house to house," evangelizing and discipling a few households at a time. Within a few years of such IM, they had literally turned the Roman Empire upside down (Acts 17:6 KJV). They did not create a clergy class, nor construct (or even rent) a special building nor hold regular religious services, except to break bread weekly in their homes (Davis 1993).[8] It was the teaching and practice of the apostle Paul (perhaps the best model of a cross-cultural missionary) not to plant a growing "local church," but an indigenous disciple-making movement in house churches that are formed by converts who did not have to be dislocated from their homes and communities (cf. 1 Cor. 9:19-23).

---

8. For biblical precedents for RC, esp. in relation to religious rituals and customs, cf. Davis 1993:128-143 and Lim 2003.

This New Testament practice is not different from that of Old Testament (OT) Israel, which shows God's design and structure for a reached, discipled or transformed people:

1) There were no local shrines or temples in each village or town.
2) There were no weekly Sabbath worship services (synagogues came later in 200 B.C. for teaching Diaspora Jews) (Lim).
3) There were no weekly nor monthly collection of tithes and offerings.[9]
4) there were no "full-time" clergy (the levitical priests were provided not just with cities, but also with pasturelands. (Josh. 21).[10]

The OT Jews were required to celebrate communally as a people in the national Temple (note: God's design was a portable and transportable Tabernacle) only three times a year: Passover, Pentecost and Tabernacles (Deut. 16:16). The actual teaching and obedience of the "way of God's righteousness" was in the homes (Deut. 6:1-11).

Biblical Christianity is therefore structured as a network of simple churches (usually called "house churches"). It is not churchless Christianity nor religionless Christianity (cf. *IBMR* Editorial 2005; Tennent 2005), but simple Christianity. Its mission is to reproduce simple groups of Christ-worshippers without elaborate religiosity. Thus, the mission statement of the Philippine house church movement is, "to multiply God's church throughout the world, one household at a time." This seeks to fulfill God's covenants with Abraham that through him every family on earth will be blessed (Gen. 12:3, cf. Gal. 3:14, 29), and with Israel that she will be a kingdom of priests (Ex. 19:6, cf. 1 Pet. 2:9-10).

---

9. 1 Cor. 16:1-4 shows weekly offerings in the early church were mainly for immediate survival needs, esp. of widows and orphans (cf. Acts. 6:1; Jas. 1:27).
10. Were they exempt from being stewards of God's resources, to be shepherds and cowboys to provide livestock products for their neighbors and nation (cf. 2 Thess. 3:6-10)? And where else did the priests learn to be expert butchers of animal sacrifices in the Temple three times a year?

PRACTICAL STEPS FOR CHURCHES

How then can church leaders in Buddhist lands shift into the IM paradigm? Most of them look foreign to their own peoples.[11] They just need to follow the simple yet effective strategy which Jesus and his first disciples used. It is based on a simple doctrine ("priesthood of all believers") and a simple practice ("making disciples") in a simple structure ("house-church networks"). Churches can be transformed from centralized Christendom (traditional local churches) to decentralized house-church structures. Although, by God's grace, it is possible to skip some steps, it seems best to work out a three to five year plan to take one's church through the transformation process so as to avoid unnecessary conflicts and splits (cf. Southerland 1999). It may be best to transition first into a "mega-church" (church with cells) to a "cell church" (church of cells) and finally to "house church" (church is cells) (Zdero 2004:110-118).

First of all, the church leadership must make a policy that membership in their church entails the commitment to be a faithful participant in a small group (maximum of fifteen members in cities, and twenty in villages). If they are alone or just a few, they can start by forming a cell and multiply from there. Start like Jesus, who began with twelve disciples. Alongside this decision, training sessions for cell leaders should be scheduled. After the initial orientation and training on the basics of leading cells, the cell leaders (and their assistants) should meet at least monthly for fellowship and mutual learning. Each cell leader should know who is his or her coordinator, who is facilitating their cell leaders' meetings and who is monitoring their ministry. To ensure cell growth, all cell members must be trained to do "friendship evangelism." If they have no more non-Christian relatives and friends, they should learn how to make friends with their neighbors, their fellow workers, and their schoolmates to win them for Christ.

Then the church is ready to become a cell church (church of cells model). They should work towards turning all church activities

---

11. On how foreign Christianity looks in Sri Lanka, cf. Somaratna 2006; and in Buddhist societies, cf. Smith 1993:126.

into cells: prayer meetings into "prayer cells," youth fellowship into "youth cells," Sunday School classes into "children's cells," choirs into "singing groups," etc. They can start training and delegating the administration of the sacraments/ordinances to the cell leaders; after all, they are truly the "pastors" of their cells.

And finally, they are ready to become a "house church network," where each cell *is* a church indeed—self-governing (with its own leaders), self-supporting (with its own budget), self-propagating (with its own missions program) and self-theologizing (with its own doctrinal statement).[12] Each cell can collect and spend their own funds (so-called "tithes and offerings"), giving at least ten percent for the support of their "favorite" leader/minister/missionary; they should aim to allocate at least fifty percent for ministry beyond their in-group. The Sunday service becomes cell meetings, perhaps alongside (ministerial or practical) training workshops or open forums as needed by the network. And better, slowly lessen "celebrations" from weekly to monthly to quarterly (or even just three times a year, as was instituted in the Torah for O.T. Israel). The church building can be transformed into a multi-purpose ministry center to serve the needs in the community. If they don't have a building, there is really no need to have one. Whenever they need a large space for big gatherings, they can resourcefully find free or rented facilities for their purposes.

By this time, the church has become a "community church," with direct attachment, ministry and witness in her (even if it were Buddhist) neighborhood and locality. The cells will be sending their members to serve in the community and to form partnerships with other Christians in their community, perhaps starting with a monthly prayer meeting and forming a "local leaders" (or ministerial

---

12. In *post-denominational* Christianity, churches do not need to be Roman Catholic, Eastern Orthodox, Anglican, Lutheran, Presbyterian or Reformed, Methodist, Pentecostal, Full Gospel or whatever! They can name their own names! What label(s) and theology(ies) did Paul want the factions in Corinth to have (1 Cor. 1-4)?

fellowship.¹³ They will be teaching and submitting to one another, learning to work as fellow servant-leaders with those who share common convictions on the essential doctrines, and allowing (and delighting) in the diversity of views on non-essential ones. Welcome to post-denominational Christianity!

Then they should have formed the habit of counting church membership, not according to how many attend Sunday worship services, but according to those who participate regularly in the cell meetings. What a good way to really count true "disciples of Christ" and to clear our church rolls (and David Barrett's annual statistics on global Christianity) of nominal Christians.   And what's the curriculum for each house church? Simply, life as it comes! The agenda is set by the members as they share their concerns and prayer requests, actual needs and interests are discerned, and thereby opened for discussion, aiming at their mutual edification (cf. 1 Cor. 14:26-33). As they follow the NT teaching to serve one another with their spiritual gifts (Rom. 12:3-8), exhort one another (Heb. 10:24), teach one another, even confess sins to one another (Js. 5:16), share insights into what the Bible teaches, they will find concrete applications to obey God's word in their own context/life-situation. If they feel that they have not resolved the doctrinal or practical issues adequately, they can assign someone (usually the cell leader) to research and/or ask his mentor or co-coordinators, and report in their next meeting; or they can invite an expert to share.

How then will each full-timer be supported? Well, there's really no need for full-timers until there are about 500 members meeting in thirty to forty house churches. Anyway, technically one house church can support a "full-time" minister (pastor-coordinator of about six co-coordinators, each serving five or six house churches) or a missionary (preferably in pairs, sent to plant house church networks elsewhere) through their regular tithes and offerings. Jesus and the Twelve had their own "common purse" and were supported by just one small group of women (Lk. 8:1-3). Once Christians learn to relate to one another in love, and pastors serve their little flock, their disciples will

---

13. The importance of this show of unity can not be over-emphasized, cf. Jn. 13:3435; 17:21-23.

naturally provide for their family's needs and their ministry expenses. (Remember also that their collections are no longer used for church paraphernalia and building maintenance).

IM AT THE FRONTIERS

But perhaps it is even better to start from scratch; to pioneer an IM in virgin territory among a truly unreached people group where no known Christian or church exists. The key to this incarnational or infiltrative approach is to be as low profile as possible. Until the converted become a majority, they must not be de-culturized from their social and religious communities. And even if they become the majority, they must avoid establishing elaborate structures for religious purposes.

In fact, all social affairs in Buddhist societies can be sanctified and transformed, for all things belong mainly to God; and those that have become sinful and evil can be redeemed through prayer and the Word (cf. 1 Tim. 4:3-5). Almost all religious activities can also be redeemed and transformed into Christ-centered and Christ-ward worship.[14] What makes them biblically "Christian" is the heart or motive, almost always regardless of the forms. What counts is that these activities and rituals are led by those who have been and are being nurtured or discipled in the low profile cells or house churches, which almost always are informal and therefore do not require formal and elaborate rituals. Missionaries and new converts may create new organizations and programs, but these should be community-based (not church-based) structures that cater to the real needs and aspirations of the people.

Keeping the faith simple, to just change allegiance from Buddha to Jesus, is essential to IMs. The essence of the Christian faith lies not in a philosophy or an ethic but in a Person. Thus, any religious or cultural artifact, belief or value must be evaluated in light of God's revelation of the historical Jesus revealed in the four (not one) gospels. Aiming just at eliciting simple faith in Christ makes evangelism quite

---

14. On the witness of God's revelation among the religions, cf. Kraft 1979:239-253; Richardson 1981; Seamands 1981:173-199; and Travis 2005:13-14.

easy, thus ensuring rapid multiplication of converts.[15] It makes possible the easy passing on by word of mouth of the Jesus story within a community, as is recognized in all CPMs (Garrison 2004:209-210). Each person and household can be discipled as insiders in their own contexts (cf. Petersen & Swamy 2003).

Historically, we can also read the conversion of Armenia, the European peoples and other Christian-majority lands like Latin America, the Philippines, northeast India (Mizos, Nagas, Karens) as different forms of IMs. The missionaries were able to win the top leaders of their societies, so that these indigenous leaders influenced, if not coerced, their constituencies as a people to join them in the faith. The days of those top-down approaches to mass conversions is almost gone. The challenge through IM today is to catalyze bottom up mass conversions following the pattern of Jesus and the early church, as China's Back to Jerusalem and the Philippines' missionary movements are trying to do, mainly through friendship evangelism with "an army of ants, worms and termites (and not elephants)" (cf. Hattaway 2003:90-94).

Yet, to achieve community or mass conversions, missionaries must aim at winning the leaders, especially the top two or three. This may be done through the community development approach. One must get immersed, integrated or, better yet, incarnated in the community while befriending and serving the people, hence gaining the attention and friendship of the local leaders, including the religious leader(s); yes, even Buddhist abbots, monks and nuns.

Hence the ideal missionaries should be "tentmakers," Christian professionals or businessmen, or skilled workers who have secular skills to serve and earn a livelihood in the community. Their witness to Christ will not be viewed as the expansion of a religious movement.[16] It is interesting to note that the *Mission Frontiers* issue on IM also includes articles on "social entrepreneurs" (Lewis 2005; Wall 2005; cf. Bornstein 2003). Community service by ordinary lay Christians not only helps Christianity gain a good reputation among a people

---

15. Garrison 2004:241-243 considers "Improving the Bible" as the second deadly sin against CPMs.
16. For more details, cf. Lim 2004.

group, it also helps gain the trust and respect of community leaders, thereby opening the opportunity for the conversion of these leaders and eventually the whole community as these influential converts protect, if not encourage the "house to house" multiplication of disciples in their midst (cf. Lim 2004).

Conclusion

Christianity, even among predominantly Buddhist lands and peoples, will then return to what Jesus Christ originally intended His Kingdom to be: a personal relationship with God through simple faith in Him, liberated from sin and the complexities of both primitive/animistic/folk religions and major/great organized religions, which results in works of sacrificial love for Him and His creation/creatures' liberation from sin's effects on the poor bound to their poverty and on the rich bound to their prosperity. No more need for elaborate religiosity with elaborate theologies, liturgies, temples or clergies. His kingdom and mission is to bring forth a spiritual (read: moral) transformation rather than a religious reformation of "nations." And his mission strategy is humble service (way of the cross) rather than triumphalistic crusades (way of the world).

Let us spread simple Christianity. Let us not burden people of other faiths, particularly Buddhism, with "stumbling-blocks" other than the simple gospel of following Jesus. Let there be "more Jesus and less religion." May IMs multiply soon across the Buddhist world, so that "the earth will be filled with the knowledge of the glory of the Lord, as the waters cover the sea" (Hab. 2:14, NIV).

3

Family Networks: The Context for Communication

Alex G. Smith

The December 2005 issue of *National Geographic* featured an article with a startling title, "Buddha Rising out of the Monastery into the Living Room" (88f). Buddhism is fast becoming a popular folk religion across the planet. It has a growing global influence on family structures as it adapts its communication to penetrate the homes of the West in particular. The church in many quarters is being caught off guard.

God desires that his church multiplies in numerical growth, in spiritual depth and fervor, and in geographical expansion - extending His Kingdom to all ethnic peoples, nations, tongues and tribes on planet earth. Scripture declares that God is "not wishing for any to perish but for all to come to repentance" (II Pet. 3:9). This mission to all families on earth is the particular, primary priority of business for the church in the last days before the Lord's return (Matt.24:14). This entails urgently communicating Christ to all peoples (*panta ta ethne*). While the major focus of this writing is Buddhist Asia, the issues discussed here are equally appropriate to Hindu and Muslim peoples as well as tribal groups.

Serious questions arise. What are the best ways to communicate to family-oriented Asia? What might be the most efficient strategies to implement? What patterns of the past give clues that can assist in the acceleration of future Christ-ward movements? This paper will concentrate on family networks and their strategic value for concerted evangelization, especially among the inadequately reached Buddhist peoples, mostly concentrated in Asia. These networks provide the context for basic communication of the Kingdom of God. Historically, the rapid spread of the early church through family networks turned the Roman Empire upside down, transforming it from the bottom up into the Kingdom of Christ (Acts 17:6).

Paul G. Hiebert points out that people are social beings. "In their relationships, people form groups and societies." Usually these do not exist in complete isolation. "Most tribes have trade, social and ritual networks that link them to their neighbors, while complex societies (composed of great numbers of groups) increasingly grow to be parts of a worldwide community of societies" (1983:177). Today, enhanced and immediate communication through the worldwide web, cell phones, instant messaging, the internet, and satellite television bring even tribal areas and isolated rural villages into the global village. It is deceptive to interpret this phenomenon only negatively as a threat to basic communication within traditional family lineages and networks. Positively, family networks, both close and distant in space (if not time), now have immediate access for quicker communication as never before.

DEFINITION OF FAMILY NETWORKS

Generally a family, according to Robert B. Taylor, is the fundamental "social unit established by a man and woman who live together, who co-operate economically, and who produce and rear children. In harmony with this the family has often been viewed as a residential unit" (1973:255). No matter how independent and basic this nuclear family unit is, it also has strong connected links through its extended family networks associated with the partners. In tribal cultures this family network may be broader than in industrialized states, being incorporated into structures of clans, tribes, consolidated communities and sometimes nations.

Donald McGavran frequently used the term webs or web movements. By these terms he meant "movements through ramified family or class relationships." He recognized that faith "flowed along kin lines." By webs he referred to "close family ties" or "tightly knit webs of relationships and many extended families." He saw extended families had "a close blood and marriage web." These "webs of relationships" were "organisms composed of individuals closely and permanently linked together" (1970:174, 320f). In today's parlance McGavran likely would have used "family networks," a current term more commonly in vogue. Socio-anthropology has identified these family networks with kinship ties, kinship groups or kinship systems (Hiebert 1983:195f).

Help from the Social Sciences

Anthropologists, sociologists and psychologists recognize many different ways of viewing basic human interaction, expressed through societal family networks. In the social organization of marriage and the family, Taylor suggests two distinctions of basic importance. First, a social group "defined by actual interaction among the members who perform roles in relation to one another" and second, a social category "defined by something the members have in common, independently of whether or not members interact with one another." The basis of human interaction and communication revolves around various statuses and roles, as well as other components like kinship, sex differences, age differentiation, residence expectations and mutual interests or affiliations, which develop a consciousness of kind or identity (1973:243-248).

A plethora of terms (not defined here) are commonly used to distinguish a broad spectrum of familial kinds such as: exogamy, endogamy, sororate, levirate, monogamy, polygamy (polygyny, polyandry) and rarer group marriages. Cultural rules on marital residence add conditional terms like neolocal, virilocal (matrilocal), uxorilocal (patrilocal), avunculocal, duolocal (Hiebert 1983:198-217; Taylor 1973:249-255). Other descriptive classifiers portraying the parameters of family networks or kinship systems (bilateral or unilateral) include matrilineal, patrilineal, matriarchal, patriarchal, the extended family (patrilocal, matrilocal, ambilocal), the joint family, and the agnatic family. The fundamental nuclear family (father, mother and offspring) is the primary familial unit. It has network connections backwards, linking it with the parents' extended lines, as well as forwards by developing additional networks as new marriages are contracted. Upon the marriage of one child, the nuclear family changes to become an extended family. The composite family, clusters of households (domestic groups) and the expanded family through polygamy are unique aberrations of the extended family (Hiebert 1983:214-233; Taylor 1973:255-259). In recent years, blended families and single parent families have also gained common acceptance. All these variegated shades of societal familial structures come together in one large human family—the human race.

Understanding the complexity of many different types of families becomes increasingly more complicated for intercultural workers researching and evaluating family networks across cultures. Differing ethnicity, caste categories, clan structures and even rigid religious creeds and restrictions compound the confusion. This manifold multiplicity of patterns complicates the clarifying of the maze of significant parameters that affect family networks and communication within specific cultural peoples. No wonder anthropologists have been unable to agree fully on a precise definition of the family (Taylor 1973:255).

BIBLICAL VALIDITY

Is there any Scriptural validity for family networks or for concentrating communication on them? Scripture indicates there certainly is.

Significantly, from the beginning, God emphasized family. The involvement in creation of the Father, the Son and the Holy Spirit identifies God as a unified trinity—these terms connote family. God recognized Adam needed Eve to be complete. Following the Fall, the redemption of families, peoples and individuals was accomplished through this eternal, united, divine "family of the living God." The salvivic process was initiated by the Father, incarnated by the Son, and implemented by the Holy Spirit.

Alan Tippett points out missionaries often have portrayed "a truncated theology of God as Creator," leaving the impression

He created only in the past instead of emphasizing His ongoing involvement in creating still now and into the eschatological future. The Psalms are full of His present creative works, as well as His provision in current and continuing action for all families of the earth (1987:80-81). Buddhist peoples reject an outside supreme personal Creator, yet still bow down to images made with their own hands. The reality of this living Creator who is daily working on their behalf and is concerned for their families should be the clarion cry of the church.

In the final interaction with Laban, Jacob swore by "The God of Abraham and the God of Nahor, the God of their father" (Gen. 31:53). Spiritual connection, accountability and continuity of the family were reinforced repeatedly in Scripture as noted in the call of Moses, "I am the God of your father, the God of Abraham, the God of Isaac and the God of Jacob" (Ex. 3:6).

The early church experienced growth in three primary ways, all currently still relevant. In all three some evidence pointed out the significance of family movements.

The first avenue for growth came from adding members to existing groups of believers and congregations. During the immediate post-resurrection period, 500 followers met in Galilee (I Cor.15:6). About 120 were present while praying in the upper room just prior to the Day of Pentecost. This included Jesus' mother and His brothers, the eleven apostles and likely other families too (Acts 1:13-15). Approximately another 3,000 persons were baptized that historic Pentecost Day (Acts 2:41). This occurred in Jerusalem, but the crowd was from all over the Roman Empire. They represented up to 3,000 families. Jewish heads of families were required to be there for the Feast of Pentecost. By tradition they met at David's Tomb, which is near the traditional site of the upper room. Luke reported that "the Lord added to the church daily" (Acts 2:47). In Acts 5:14 "multitudes of men and women were constantly added" to the church. Disciples continued to increase greatly in Jerusalem and "a great many of the priests were becoming obedient to the faith" (Acts 6:7). This early movement therefore included many married priests of Levi as well as other families of the Diaspora and local

51

Judean Jews. Thus hundreds of families were affected in this initial growth of the church. Obviously, with the male leadership pattern of Jewish groups, many families were gathered into the church, not just the men alone.

The second pattern of expansion was multiplying churches across the empire. In spite of the Acts 1:8 specific commission of the resurrected Christ to his disciples, the church in the period of Acts chapters one through seven remained concentrated in Jerusalem only. Then, after the martyrdom of Stephen, "a great persecution arose against the church in Jerusalem." While the apostles remained in the capital, the believers were "all scattered throughout the regions of Judea and Samaria" (Acts 8:1). After Saul the persecutor was converted, peace came to the fledgling churches, which were started through the witness of those followers who were forced to disperse throughout Judea and beyond. "So the church throughout all Judea and Galilee and Samaria enjoyed peace," and "continued to increase" (Acts 9:31). As the movement accelerated through the proclamation of those scattered by Saul's persecution, churches arose in Phoenicia, Cyprus and Cyrene (northern Africa). Some believers from this Mediterranean area broke the pattern of reaching only Jewish families and preached Christ to the Greeks in Antioch, where "a large number who believed turned to the Lord," likely in family groups (Acts 11:19-21). F.F. Bruce affirms, "The context plainly requires the sense "Greeks" (as opposed to Jews) and not Grecians or Hellenists;" the preferred interpretation "must be used in a wider sense "Greek speakers" which includes Greek-speaking Gentiles as well as Greek-speaking Jews"(1979:237). Antioch later became the primary missionary sending church (Acts 13:1f). From here Paul and his comrades planted churches among both Jews and Gentiles in cities throughout Asia Minor and Greece. Many of these churches were initiated or organized around converted families.

The third way the Good News spread and churches multiplied was through the gathering in of households and family networks. The early Jerusalem movement focused around families. While the believers continued to meet in the temple day after day, they also were "breaking bread from house to house" in communal fellowships -

likely around nuclear families, family networks or groups of believers and friends meeting in homes (Acts 2:46). Significantly, when Saul started "ravaging the church" he systematically entered "house after house" and was "dragging off men and women" (Acts 8:3). Frequently in the early Christian movement, house churches arose around these family networks. Churches functioned in family homes such as the house of Nympha (Col. 4:15). Basically two kinds of house churches existed: first, the church comprised of the household of the family, and second, the church gathered together in the home or house, comprised of family members plus others from the community.

Later Paul testified that his pattern was to teach publicly and "from house to house," or as a marginal reading notes, "in the various private homes" (Acts 20:20). In Philemon verse two Paul addresses Archippus, his fellow worker, and "the church in your house." Philip's ministry in Samaria resulted in multitudes responding and being "baptized men and women alike" (Acts 8:6-12). Again this hints of families accepting the gospel, just as did the "multitudes of men and women" in Jerusalem (Acts 5:14). Clearly the family network of Cornelius is specifically noted in Acts 10. This Roman centurion was a God-fearer along "with his household" (10:1-2). When the apostle Peter and some brethren from Joppa arrived at his home in Caesarea, "Cornelius was waiting for them, and had called together his relatives and close friends" (10:24). When his household and family network received the gift of the Holy Spirit and spoke in tongues, Peter "ordered them to be baptized in the name of Jesus Christ" (10:44-48). In Acts 16 Lydia was among the first converts in Philippi. "She and her household" were baptized, including "presumably her servants and other dependents" (Bruce 1979:331). She became "the person of peace" and the apostles stayed with her household (Matt. 10:11-13; Acts 16:14-15).

Immediately following the imprisonment of Paul and Silas, the Philippian jailor "and all his household" were dramatically converted and baptized (16:31-34). Note Paul's basic theology in verse thirty-one. In answer to the jailor's question on how to be saved, Paul confidently replies "Believe in the Lord Jesus and you will be saved, *you and your household.*" In another case at Corinth, "Crispus, the leader of the synagogue, believed in the Lord with all his household and many of the Corinthians when they heard were believing and being baptized" (Acts 18:8). Also Paul "baptized the household of Stephanus," the first fruits of Achaia (I Cor.1:16; 16:15). The impact of the family of Prisca and Aquila was significant in their service, along with the households of Onesiphorus and of Aristobulus and Narcissus in Rome and elsewhere (II Tim. 4:19; Rom. 16:10).

THEOLOGICAL INSIGHTS

Throughout Scripture the terms house and household occur hundreds of times. In many of these, house refers to the household concept (especially in the Old Testament). At other times it obviously relates to the physical house. This household and family network concept is firmly rooted in the Old Testament. The New Testament also affirms this principle.

It is like a kind of covenant, where the whole family placed faith in God. Noah is a dramatic example. God said, "Enter the ark, you and all your household" (Gen. 7:1). The whole extended family was included. They all obeyed and were consequently saved (7:7, 13; 8:15-18). Another classic example is Joshua, "as for me and my house we will serve the Lord" (Josh. 24:15). Even Gentiles like Rahab were granted salvation along with her parents and their whole extended family network (Josh. 2:12-19, 6:22-25). Faith often flows along family lines and across generations as modeled in Lois, Eunice and Timothy (II Tim. 1:5). One notable teaching on this covenantal aspect indicates that the believing spouse sanctifies the other unbelieving spouse and the children (I Cor. 7:14-16).

For two millennia historical church practice has emphasized this family covenant concept, as many church traditions faithfully performed infant baptism. Like Roman Catholics, Reformers, including Lutherans, Episcopalians, Methodists and Presbyterians, practiced this custom and rite. Most also recognized the need for reinforcement and confirmation of true faith, usually during puberty.

Animal sacrifices started in Genesis when God provided clothes for Adam and Eve. Similar forms of family covenant are frequently reflected in the Bible. For example, In the midst of grief, High Priest Aaron placed his hand on the sacrificial animal as a symbol of substitution, confessing the sins on behalf of himself and his whole family, to "make atonement for himself and for his household" (Lev. 16:6, 11). The lamb's sacrifice was a symbolic covering for the sins of Aaron's family. Poignantly, in the Exodus, the Passover lamb was offered for the whole family. The members of the family all ate of it. Only "a lamb for each household" was required, not a lamb for each individual present. This covenant symbol covered the whole family, "according to their father's household." Some of the lamb's blood was sprinkled on the two doorposts and the lintel of each house where the gathered household ate the Passover (Ex. 12:1, 7, 13). The blood of one paschal lamb was sufficient to cover the whole household and adequate for the family's protection and salvation.

Similarly, on the Day of Pentecost, the Apostle Peter exhorted the assembled "devout men from every nation under heaven" to repent. He affirmed "the promise is for you *and your children*," a reflection also of the Psalmist and prophets (Acts 2:5, 38-39; Ps. 22:27; Isa. 54:13). God's mission through Abraham is also in view, "in you all families of the earth will be blessed" (Gen. 12:3). Interestingly, "God set the solitary in families" or literally "makes a home for the lonely" (Ps. 68:6).

The Levites' compensation granted from the temple offerings was for the sustenance of their whole households (Num. 18:31). Jacob instructed and led his household to repent of idolatry (Gen. 35:2-4). In his old age Jacob responded to the invitation of Joseph and Pharaoh to find succor and preservation in Egypt with his whole household—all his sons and their extensive family networks (Gen. 45:5-11, 18). Later Moses returned to Egypt similarly with his wife and sons (Ex. 4:20).

Abraham and the heads of later Jewish households were responsible to teach their children and their extended families (Gen. 18:18-19; Duet. 4:9-10). The Israelites were to celebrate before the Lord in households (Duet. 12:7; 15:20). During Passover all the family members were to gather as whole families. The heads of families recited, reviewed and re-enacted the redemptive works and actions of God (Wright 1952:13). The family thereby became both the object and the agent of salvation (Ex.12:3-4).

In cases of serious disobedience, such as Aachan, a man and his household received God's judgment (Deut. 11:6; Josh. 7:14, 18; Acts 5:1-10). Therefore God seemed to place a high value on families and extended family networks in the transmission and reception of His word and will.

During Christ's ministry on earth, notable mention was specifically made of households such as the salvation of Zachaeus and his house (Luke 19:5-10) as well as that of the nobleman from Capernaum and "his whole household" (John 4:53). Jesus also advised those he healed to return to their homes and family networks rather than to continue to accompany him in his ministry across the land of Israel. Two outstanding cases were the blind man at Bethsaida (Mark 8:26) and the demon possessed man of Gerasenes (Luke 8:38-39). On another occasion Christ interacted with the woman of Samaria, who had previously had five husbands and was currently living in a common-law relationship. Recognizing Christ as prophet and Messiah, she left her water pot at the well, went into the city, and began to proclaim "to the men" about her encounter with Christ. One wonders if these men were her former husbands or partners. Probably some of them were (John 4:16-18; 28-29). Connectedness to family networks and the communication of God's purposes to and through them was a paramount practice of Christ's earthly ministry. He focused much of His ministry around or related to the families.

The primary prayer Jesus taught His disciples is family oriented, "Our Father who is in heaven." This indicates the trinity is family oriented. Heavenly relationships are family ones. God uses family related terms to help humans comprehend spiritual relationships, which are supernatural, supra-cultural and superior in quality. Though begotten of God, the miraculous virgin birth placed Jesus in a human family. Though Jesus did not marry and had no children, He extended His grace to all families on planet earth. He frequently performed miracles in the households. Many significant events in His ministry occurred during His visits to homes of families. At a higher level than natural family such as mother and brothers, Jesus declared "These are my brother, and sister and mother" (Matt. 12:46-50). Still while on the cross, Jesus honored His mother and arranged continuing care for her, "Behold, your mother!" From then on John "took her into his own household" (John 19:26-27). Christ recognized the church as God's family and household of faith. Later, Paul reinforced the church as "the household of God" in Galatians 6:10, Ephesians 2:19, and I Timothy 3:15. In Christ's training of the twelve, primary discipleship occurred in community, not in isolation. Most significant growth is through interaction in the context of the family. A good proportion of Christ's preaching of his gospel was given in family settings.

HISTORICAL REFLECTION

As the communication of the Good News radiated out from Jerusalem in all directions to earth's peoples, the historical pattern of effective advance across cultures and epochs of time was primarily that of the impressive gathering in of many family networks. At times these were through smaller units of nuclear families or local households. In many cases dynamic multiplication occurred through the concurrent communication along family networks, lineages, clans, tribes and whole people groups.

The church started from movements within the family networks of the Jews, *first* from those of Judean Aramaic background and *second* among those of the Hellenistic Jews. Individuals like Saul of Tarsus and the Ethiopian eunuch were not rejected, but for the most part the majority of growth came about through connected groups rather than isolated individuals. In the early years and in later centuries the communication of Christ continued to advance across new cultural basins through the conversion of families and their networks among the Gentiles including Greeks, Romans, Barbarians (Goths, Visigoths, Vandals), Celts, Vikings (Northmen), and many other people groups. Through his prolific writings, Kenneth Scott Latourette described many of these people movements, which cascaded whole family networks and tribes into the Kingdom. "The Goths were the first of the northern peoples among whom Christianity had a marked effect."

Family and Faith in Asia

Two means of communicating the gospel were Christian captives from Gothic raids and Arian believers who had been expelled from Catholic Rome. "Arian Christianity continued to spread among the Goths until most of them belonged to that branch of the faith" (1953:100). Obviously such a movement rose on the wave of massive family network conversions. The author will continue this discussion later, along with the effects of the Reformation in another chapter concerning evangelizing whole families.

In the modern mission era, the extension of the church, under the Holy Spirit, gained large harvests from close knit family networks such as Hmong, Mien, Lisu and others. The reaping of tribes into the church has been matched with strong movements among whole people groups like Toba Bataks, Karens, Nagas, Torajans and many others. In a considerable number of these kinds of growth movements, the communication through family networks has been so effective and comprehensive that it is not unusual to find upwards of ninety percent of those particular people groups becoming Christian. Unfortunately this has not been generally true of Buddhist peoples. Is this because the advocates of the gospel have not sufficiently implemented intentional strategies for reaching whole family networks?

NETWORKS AS BRIDGES OF TRANSMISSION

In Romans chapter 16, prior to his visit to Rome, Paul identified twenty-six names of people in the Roman capital, who were either his earlier associates or relatives of believers elsewhere in the Empire. These relational contacts, like the God-fearers and Gentile proselytes connected to synagogues in Acts, provided immediate access as natural bridges for the further spread of the gospel. Crossing over into new family networks facilitated continuing communication of the gospel for the extension of the church.

Interestingly, Jesus chose two sets of brothers to be among the Twelve: Peter and Andrew, and James and John, the sons of Zebedee. All four were also fishermen (Matt. 4:18-22). So one third of the disciples had close immediate family connections. Andrew also brought Nathaniel to Jesus. He was from Bethsaida, Peter and Andrew's town and thereby known to them (John 1 41-45). Christ's own younger siblings had part in the kingdom (Acts 1:14). Jesus frequently visited homes and participated in family events such as healing Peter's mother of the fever (Mark 1:29f), attending the wedding at Cana (John 2:1f), and dealing with grief of Mary and Martha over their brother Lazarus in Bethany (John 11 & 12).

There are several reasons that make family networks feasible as vital keys for communication. Family networks already provide established relationships. These natural relations make it automatically easier to reach relatives, since few barriers exist to bar those openly accepted within their own family network. Usually the problems, difficulties and joys of relatives are known beforehand to network members. They understand and empathize with their kin. This normally precludes rejection and exclusion as network members are insiders, not outsiders. So the door is open for unlimited access and for open communication between members of the family network.

In much of Asia the family with its extended network is a wonderful natural bridge for communication. While family networks are among the primary means for expanding the Kingdom, frequently Christian workers inadvertently overlook this in proclaiming the evangel. Instead, they mostly emphasize the individual, independent approach, which is a dominant trait of many Western societies. Individual identity in the West tends to define a person. In nonwestern societies the connectedness of belonging to the group has a greater influence on consolidating one's identity. The Japanese are an example of this. In Chinese culture the family gives meaning to the individual. Family is central to Chinese worldview. Mixtures of Buddhism (and the ultimate), Confucianism (and ancestors), and Taoism (harmony with nature) surround and strengthen the centrality of family.

Certain dynamics within these networks increase their potential for speedy and effective communication. Relatives are often in the same or nearby villages or suburbs, providing convenient access for interaction. Even where the major network is located in outside towns or distant provinces, transient workers in the big cities maintain regular contact with the family network back in rural areas. For example, large Asian cities like Bangkok, Thailand provide economic opportunity for men from northeast Isaan to work and earn income as taxi drivers in the capital. Back in the northeast they would struggle to eek out an existence. Nevertheless, the obligations of family networks require them to send funds back to parents and relatives in the rural regions. This kind of economic flow is common around the world; Asians working in America or Filipinos working in Saudi Arabia are two examples. Asian family responsibilities maintain cultural and social expectations within family networks. Blood ties provide connections for economic help and continuing communication. In times of economic crisis the family is the first source to be tapped. Those in the family network feel obligated. Furthermore workers in the cities of Asia usually return to their home villages at least twice a year to help with plowing, planting and reaping the rice fields. A missionary working with this labor force of northeast Thai in Bangkok has capitalized on this natural bridge for communication by simultaneously planting churches among this group, both in the capital and in the distant rural areas. Tapping the family networks is a wise approach for communicating the message. Among affluent people and sometime rural ones, multiple marriages or the keeping of minor wives, though not as common today as in the past, does provide possibilities for reaching new family networks of the multiple spouses. Normal marriage always creates new links to the in-law family networks. These need to be considered as bridges for extending the church's communication. Therefore awareness of the family structures is helpful, whether patriarchal or matriarchal and so forth. The more precise a family network structure is defined and understood, the better it can be strategically utilized to reach the full potential of purposeful communication across family lines.

EXAMPLES OF COMMUNICATING ALONG FAMILY NETWORKS

Many close knit Asian family networks provide either a bulwark for resistance or a doorway for responsiveness. During the late

1800s Daniel McGilvary, a pioneer Presbyterian missionary to north Thailand, observed the tendency for Lao (Khun Muang) family members to become Christians along network lines (Smith 1982:74f). A significant movement among these families resulted in tens of thousands entering the church during a half century. One practical value was the solidarity that Christian families provided against strong village opposition and social rejection. When the majority of the family network converted, their unity and commitment to each other and to God helped them withstand the broader social pressures, which they would not likely have been able to do as individuals in a face-saving society. During that era groups of families approached the missionaries to come to their villages to teach and help. Usually missionaries required those families first to build a place for instruction and worship as a genuine evidence of their sincerity. Often the families responded and soon many extended families became followers.

In the 1970s a Marburger missionary in Barn Tham, a village in the Province of Phayao in northern Thailand helped spark a family network movement, which brought about 1,000 or more into the local church. During the same time Fred Magbanwa in the Philippines reported the conversion of a Filipino military Colonel who, within three years, won 62 of his family members to Christ (Smith 2003:19). During the 1980s an Australian Seventh Day Adventist worker helped stimulate a movement of churches among related family networks in a couple of provinces of Isaan Thailand. The movement gathered in approximately 600 converts, mostly from family networks. Some years later I remember talking with a brother named Thor Therng in northern Chiang Rai Province. He reported that fifteen of his extended family had become believers through attending the church with him in Mae Khai Nang Bua. When Asians become Christians as families, their relatives often feel more comfortable to come into churches with them also. Outside relatives are more likely to participate in Christian activities when they have significant family members present.

During twenty years of working in the hot plains of central Thailand, I observed and researched patterns of family networks entering the church. An elderly Lao uncle in Ipung Noi taught me the lasting effect of family ties and networks. He remembered that his grandfather, who had lived in a far northern province of Thailand, was a Christian. He recollected that his grandfather was buried as a believer. Decades later Uncle Tong and his family had contact with the gospel through our rural evangelism and accepted Christ. The memory of his family connection helped him decide. As he could read the old Lao script better than the Thai one, our team got him a copy of the Bible in that ancient script from Chiang Mai. His family believed and a church was started in his village.

Forty years ago, in one city of central Thailand, missionaries witnessed to an elderly Buddhist grandmother. She was converted, but her family resisted the gospel because of local social pressure. Nevertheless, this grandmother kept faithfully sharing her testimony with her children and her grandchildren, seemingly to no avail. As she grew older she craftily asked them to read her the biblical stories, saying her eyes were too bad to do so. She also taught the youth to sing gospel songs. Some twenty years after her death, one of the daughters, now grown, married and with her own offspring, went through a shattering divorce in the capital city. This crisis caused her to reflect on her life. She decided to return to her village birthplace. There she remembered her grandmother's life as a follower of Christ and what she had taught her. Admitting the failure of her own marriage and disintegrated family, she called all her siblings and their offspring together. She rehearsed her plight before her family network. Then she reminded them of their grandmother's faith and called them to commit to following her example. Twenty-two of them began to meet weekly to recite the Bible stories, sing the childhood songs, worship and read the Scriptures. They started a house church comprised of many in the family network.

Another powerful example in Thailand was the holistic ministry among leprosy patients, which included meeting the physical, spiritual and social needs of their families. This produced movements of whole families and their networks coming into the church. Though marginal in society these families found renewed hope and dignity together in the church (Smith 1977:125-144).

As I did pioneer work in the Barnrai district, I noted that often faith followed along family networks. In one sizable village the witness of the first convert affected his extended family dramatically. Within a year most of his family network had turned to Christ. Within a couple of decades the church in that village comprised five generations spanning several extended family networks, produced through the marriages of the members. This was so significant that we changed our strategy from a focus on the individual to concentration on the family and extended family. In 1972 the implementing of this new family-focus reoriented the team's prayers and outreach methodology. This resulted in the conversion of twenty new couples and other relatives. Several new house churches were initiated around these families. A year later another small family network movement began, when twenty-six new believers were baptized. My careful analysis discovered that twenty of them were related.

My conclusion was that family networks provide one of the best platforms for evangelism and church planting. Intentional focus on communicating through family networks transforms praying, strategizing and practical evangelism in order to produce stable and lasting congregations. In contrast a senior church planter in Asia summarized an evaluation of his ministry of some twenty years. He observed that on returning from furlough after each term of service, those churches which had been built around individual converts had ceased to function, while only those established around families survived.

COMMUNICATING THE GOSPEL MESSAGE

One important area of weakness in Christian witness to Buddhists and their families relates to ineffective communication. What are some obstacles to sharing biblical concepts with Buddhists and their families? How can we make the meanings of biblical concepts clear, when Buddhist thinking perceives them differently? How can we discern when that is occurring? How can we clarify the difference of meaning between seemingly similar Buddhist/Christian terms? Another problem is that many believers, both missionaries and native members, proclaim the gospel with a Western style of approach to evangelism. Usually the focus is on the individual only and not on the wider context of his/her social relationships, which are particularly centered in the family network. To be effective a better understanding of the local family networks needs to be defined and reached. More native approaches in spreading the Good News must be used. Basic principles of communication should also be understood and taught to believers.

Let us note some practical principles for communicating with Buddhist families: First, communication is not only what is said. Primarily it is what is heard that counts. While a clear presentation of Christ is important, it is the reception of that message in the mind of the hearer that is crucial. Just because we told someone something does not mean he or she understood our anticipated, projected message. A potent example is what Buddhists might hear when we give them the gospel by quoting John 3:16. All believers have memorized this verse, but what do Buddhists understand this to mean? From their worldview they may hear, "For God (*god does not exist*) so loved (*that's a passion to be extinguished*) the world (*I need to be detached from it*) that He gave His only begotten Son (*no substitute is possible for karma*) that whosoever believes in Him (*self-effort alone delivers one's self, not faith*) should not perish but have everlasting life (*my Buddhist goal is to reach nirvana (death and escape) not continue in life and suffering forever*)." Rarely are Christians even aware of this possible discrepancy in meaning in the minds of thinking Buddhists. Major conflicts occur because of the differences and clashes of worldviews.

Second, communicators cannot transfer meaning. They only encode a message by transferring bits of information. That data is then re-formed or decoded in the mind of the hearer. The real meaning is what the receptors understand (D. Smith 1984:32f). Sometimes we wonder why a person or his family does not follow our instructions. Often, it is because the message that they decoded through their personal, cultural grid differs from the one we thought we had clearly given. So the intended message we send may be understood differently, depending on how the hearers perceived the message.

Third, the messenger needs some feedback mechanism so he can evaluate what the hearer has actually understood. Suppose, for example, Christian Sally shares the gospel with the family of Buddhist Billy. She says, "We are all sinners and need Jesus." Billy responds in his mind, "I did not kill anything today, so I am not a sinner. Nor do I need someone to help me get rid of that sin, which I did not commit anyway." Sally must use some means to find out what Billy is really understanding and thinking.

Fourth, a good communicator must understand his/her audience. People receive our message in a social context not in a vacuum. That context comprises cultural complexity, family relationships, historical significance and usually religious tradition. So the messenger must know how to present the message within the linguistic, social and religious framework of the hearers. A clear comprehension of family networks in the audience's specific culture is also crucial. Establishing personal rapport and credibility with the audience is vital. Above all, as Schramm emphasizes, "communication is based on relationship" (1954:13). Often relationships in Buddhist Asia are intricately related to family networks. The successful messenger has an empathetic heart. He knows how to speak to the felt needs of the audience and how to bridge over into the wider family network.

Fifth, an effective communicator must know his message accurately. Our message is "good news to all people" (Luke 2:10). It is not propaganda, nor is it ideas clouded by the messenger's own cultural bias. Christians need to discern precisely what the biblical gospel is and what is cultural Christianity. Usually, their own culturally colored glasses distort the biblical gospel, at least to some degree. I like to give my students an assignment. I ask them to think carefully and write in fifty words or fewer, what the essence of the gospel is. Maybe you could do that in your own language later today. We must know God's message clearly. The gospel is expressed concisely in 1 John 4:14, "The Father sent the Son to be the Savior of the World." Christ, fully equal with Creator God, came down to earth and took on the form of a human servant. He lived a sinless life and voluntarily died on the cross to redeem humankind from its sins. He rose from the grave, victorious over Satan and death. He ascended into Heaven and will return for His people in the final days of all humanity. He extends His grace and grants forgiveness to those who repent and accept Him by faith as their substitute. This is good news to all families, peoples, tribes, and nations. This is the gospel.

This message of grace is not only for isolated individuals, but primarily for all groups of peoples. Family networks are the basic platforms for communicating this message. Hesselgrave notes that humans are social beings and communication, by its root meaning of "commonness," operates in community not in isolation (1978:31).

Sixth, the use of indigenous forms of communication is superior to using imported outside ones. Here are some suggestions for using local ways to share the message with families:

1) Use oral stories, analogies, illustrations, myths or parables commonly known and suitable to the culture of the family network (Jesus did this frequently). Tell particular stories of family conversions, resolution of conflicts within family networks, and similar family themes rather than only ones about individuals.

2) Use visual pictures, posters, and symbols that the audience easily comprehends to complement the story of the gospel. One such tool has been in print for around 300 years. Though initially published in French, it has since been translated into various languages including, since 1879, Chinese. Its title is "*The Heart of Pak*" (or "*The Human Heart*"). It uses different animals to describe human emotions. Many editions also tell the way of effective salvation found in Christ. Families and individuals easily identify with the expression of these feelings. Interestingly, Tibetan Buddhists have assigned particular animals to represent different negative human emotions too. Consider developing and using art and other tools, which portrays the family in common familial life situations, along with practical solutions for their struggles against failures, passions and evil.

3) Use idioms and paint word pictures drawn from nature, history or culture. These make excellent examples for interaction and discussion, especially when they relate to family networks and relationships. The more familiar these are, the more likely communication and understanding will occur within the group.

4) Study in family groups the biblical wisdom books of Proverbs, Ecclesiastes as well as Job—a vital book about suffering. Discover ways to stimulate the minds of Buddhists, who are usually interested in and affected by proverbs and sayings of wisdom. Assign a topic and suggest that the family discusses it over meals or in the evenings in their homes. Note the Bible is full of stories about complications around in-house relationships, conflicts within families, and concerns about extended family. Study these contexts and ask families to discover similarities in their own situations.

5) Use techniques like discussion, question and answer, or conversational exchange about some topic, rather than preaching or debating. Encourage questions and feedback from the family. Suggest they discuss the topic with their extended families. Also encourage involving the whole family in this, so that young and old alike can participate and share their views and feelings. Emphasize the need to listen to each other with courtesy and sensitivity.

6) Make good use of local grassroots media such as native drama, dance, song, and indigenous music. These are powerful tools for communicating, particularly to people who have low rates of literacy. Don't hesitate to encourage believers to experiment with these modes of grassroots communication. Encourage the families to act out the stories of biblical parables and events with a dramatic, local flavor. In January 2006, while in Chiang Mai, I was watching Buddhist priests communicating their message on television. Surprisingly there

were no Buddhist idols or similar props in the studio. Two yellow robed monks in their forties simply sat on two chairs facing each other. Using local Thai language and indigenous forms of music, they sang alternatively. Their teaching was given by antiphonal song. Here was a creative way to reach out to the younger generation. I was struck by one particular Thai phrase they used to authenticate their Buddhist tenets, "This is the message that our fathers and mothers taught us in handing down the Buddha's principles."

Creative Indigenous Communication

Here is a true story of the native development of local media which became an effective tool for reaching whole families and networks of the community. A Buddhist man who became a Christian was formerly a member of a Li-kae (professional drama troupe) in central Thailand. The troupe went from village to village night after night acting out their quite raucous and course plays. The colored, costumed actors presented drama and dance befitting the culture. Music was played on indigenous instruments, along with local styled singing and dialogue. The Li-kae performed nightly from dark to dawn. Villagers from nearby communities came to watch and listen with their whole families. Usually they stayed all night long. The people sat on the barren, dry fields in front of the simple stage with its colorful backdrops and banners. Near the crowd, enterprising vendors sold food and drinks. Spontaneous interaction between the players on stage and the audience seated on the ground kept a keen festive spirit alive. Some succumbed to sleep, others remained alert the whole night through.

A few of us encouraged this former Li-kae member and his family to develop a Christian drama troupe. But he was adamant that he could not do so in good conscience. His reason was that he was ashamed of his former acting lifestyle, which he left when he was converted to Christ. He said, "In those days I spoke crude words, got drunk, used drugs and played around with many women.

That is Li-kae to me. Since my life has been changed, I don't want anything to do with it." For several years attempts to change his mind failed. In the meantime, he moved with his family to a distant area. They witnessed to the families there and within a couple of years started a little church. He became the volunteer pastor of the group of growing families. Then, one day while working his fields, he developed serious internal bleeding and collapsed. The local believers found an old truck and transported him across the rough trails to the Christian hospital about ninety kilometers away. On arrival, he was unconscious and the doctors did not think he would survive. They treated him, gave him many blood transfusions, and prayed.

Back in his village lived a blind Lao woman, whose parents had abandoned her as a little child, because they believed bad *karma* had caused her blindness. Through this man's witness, she had come to Christ, along with the Karen family who took her in and raised her. While he was at death's door in the hospital, she had a dream in his village. "I dreamed that God healed our pastor and that he will return home," she declared. The villagers, Christians and Buddhists alike, said, "You are crazy. We saw him before he was taken to the hospital. He was in such bad shape, there is no possibility he will survive or return here. He's gone forever." Undeterred, she got an elderly Karen Christian to lead her around through the forests to the surrounding villages. She declared her dream and proclaimed her testimony before many families.

Meanwhile, back in the hospital the man slowly started to revive. After a couple of weeks, he had a dream in which God spoke to him about starting a *Christian Li-kae* troupe. "Lord, I can't," he said. "You know what that evil lifestyle was like." Then God told him again that He wanted him to develop a *Christian* Li-kae. "But Lord, I can't use those crude scripts of the old troupe. It just won't do," he responded. Then God told him to use the Scriptures to compose themes and scripts for the new dramas. So the man told the Lord that he would try to do so. When he returned home alive, he surprised everyone, except the believing blind Lao lass. He visited nearby villages and told the families how God had spared his life for a reason. Many families believed and were baptized. The church grew considerably.

New house churches were begun in some nearby villages, mostly through family networks and connections.

Then this man started working with his own family members and some of the local Christians to get a Christian based Li-kae troupe going. They prayed together for this project. With his wife, he prepared dialogues and stories from the Scriptures. The gospel message was interwoven clearly indigenously within the performances. He taught his own children to act, dance and sing the parts in Thai style. He trained some church members to play selected indigenous musical instruments like Thai drums, cymbals, bells, flutes, the bamboo mouth organ and Thai wooden marimbas (*ranats*). The group made and painted their backdrops and stage props, appropriately in Thai style. They practiced for hours until they were ready for public shows. They named their troupe, in Thai, "Creation." Then they committed two or more months in the hot dry season each year to perform in villages and townships. During three consecutive nights they presented the message from creation to the resurrection. The people came out by the hundreds and even thousands to see the gospel performed in Thai style drama and song. Families and individuals were converted and new churches started. In 1996, one of his daughters, a leading actress in the troupe, became a cross-cultural missionary. The Li-kae man died a few years ago. But recently, the younger generation of that family, the children and grandchildren, have revived the troupe. Using indigenous forms for communicating the gospel makes a strong impact on family networks and local communities.

MISSIOLOGICAL SUGGESTIONS ON STRATEGY

A deliberate focus on evangelizing families and their networks is a vital strategy, grounded on sound principles for communicating the gospel. It is good missiology. In his lectures, Donald McGavran frequently reiterated the case for trying to win whole families, like the New Testament pattern, family by family, rather than pulling someone out of the family to join the church. In his classic textbook, McGavran wrote:

> "One-by-one against the tide" is a mode of conversion that pries a single person out this social matrix and leads him to become a Christian or an Evangelical. It encourages him to renounce his people. It assumes—often with good reason—that the tribe, the family, will be hard against the Christian religion. The family gathers on the tenth day to eat the funeral feast and "feed the ancestors." Since this is forbidden to the Christian (on the ground that the ancestors are godlings and hence "feeding them" is "worship of other gods"), he is conspicuous by his absence. Frequently the very people who will not hear his testimony are "those of his own household." They regard him as a traitor and the missionary as one who goes about snatching individuals out of families. Once this image has been firmly planted in any population, the church grows very slowly (1970:321).

Decades earlier in 1885, John L. Nevius argued similarly for letting each new believer abide in his or her old calling, based on First Corinthians 7:20-24. He wrote of this universal principle, "This Apostolic injunction, we are further told was ordained "for all the churches." It teaches most emphatically that Christianity should not disturb the social relations of its adherents, but requires them to be content with their lot, and to illustrate the gospel in the spheres of life in which they are called." (1958:19).

To work in harmony within the social and family structures provided the best opportunity for witness across normal relationships. Extracting believers from their social environment and family networks was detrimental to their witness and breached their regular routes of communication. Nevius was advocating another way of dealing with converts. By the old way missionaries pulled them individually out of their native way of life and family contexts. They put them into training schools for evangelism and ministry. From here they were frequently employed as hired workers under the missionary or paid agents of the mission. Their jobs included evangelists, pastors, teachers, station heads, colporteurs and others

(1958:8f). This approach isolated believers even further from their normal patterns of life within their regular extended families. It disrupted ordinary familial communication. Nevius made a potent observation of this disruption, "Take a man laboring on the plane of his ordinary life as an earnest Christian and make him a paid laborer, and you deprive him of half his influence" (1958:22). The new way that Nevius advocated kept converts in their self-supporting roles of farming or laboring or whatever. Instead of a hierarchy of paid professionals ministering in the churches, there were volunteer workers and unpaid elders serving the churches. Adequate training was still given locally, but the believers were not pulled away from their natural surroundings, familiar settings, family networks, and natural bridges of communication. A renewed examination and application of Nevius' book and wisdom is worth the effort.

Here are some practical strategies for consideration. Using them will assist in maintaining the spotlight on family networks as the basic context for communication. Brainstorm together as to what specific steps might be followed to do this:

First, teach believers, pastors and missionaries to pray strategically for outreach to whole family networks. Praying expectantly for whole families and their networks to respond to the gospel transforms intercession into a powerful and hopeful exercise.

Second, plan evangelistic work centered on reaching couples, families and extended family networks. Set clear and measurable goals to this end.

Third, design particular approaches into a cohesive plan to accomplish this. Include mobilizing existing believers to rebuild bridges to their own and new family networks. Train them for witness through their own familial connections and to families within their spheres of influence.

Fourth, collect stories of family conversions and publish them through literature, radio, and mass media. Observe that the story of the prodigal son focuses on the family context, not on the son (Luke 11:15-32).

Fifth, while conducting student ministries, follow up the parents and families of interested students as early as possible. Build relationships with the whole family not just the student. In order to reach the whole family it is essential to concentrate sensitively on the parents more than on the children or youth alone.

Sixth, when new believers—singles, couples or families—convert, encourage them to maintain normal social contact with relatives, their societal neighborhood and even their temple community.

Seventh, teach them from the start to pray for their family networks, to witness to whole families and to follow up family lines and networks. Even though seekers may not yet fully accept the gospel, encourage them to discuss the Good News with relatives and friends as best they can.

Eighth, gently suggest that they consider this matter and decide together as families what they will do about it. When opportunity arises as appropriate, rather than calling for an individual to accept the message, carefully include the whole family or group in the decision process. Sometimes it is wise to delay isolated decisions so as to get the whole family or group involved with the process. This gives time for the permeation and saturation of the family network with the message. I remember a missionary telling me of the Akha tribal village leader who suggested waiting for the group to be more ready to convert. The village leader said, "Next year we will become Christians, but we must wait till next time for the demon festival to make that break as a village."

Ninth, always remember to evaluate programs and strategies on the basic criteria of the goal of reaching family networks, not on the numbers of individuals who respond, nor on the number of people who heard the gospel proclaimed.

Consider doing an experiment or two. Maintain repeated contact with one or two interested Buddhist families over a period of three or more months. Visit them, build relationships with them and share life genuinely with them for an hour or two each week. Do not call for any family decision until after the end of the three months. Even then, the decision may not be to accept the gospel, depending on their level of understanding and receptivity. It may simply be, for example, an agreement to read and discuss the book of John together. Be available to answer any questions or concerns they may have during another three months. Be patient and sensitive always. Train any new believers in family devotional times of Bible reading, prayer and service related to family network concerns at home and in the church. One helpful resource in doing this is my book on *Multiplying Churches Through Prayer Cell Evangelism: A Manual for Church Planting Movements* (2003; Thai:1970). I also recommend studying the life and work of J. O. Fraser among the Lisu in China. This powerful model is entitled *Beyond the Ranges* (Taylor 1998) and was first published in 1944. His story shows how strategic prayer and wise approaches stimulated family movements among the Lisu, who today are almost ninety percent Christian. In 2009 OMF developed a docudrama on this story on DVD, now available.

CONCLUSION

This limited attempt to investigate briefly the anthropological, theological, historical, cultural, and missiological dimensions of this theme leads to the conclusion that family networks must be considered seriously in any effective attempt to communicate the gospel effectively. Family networks provide the context for communication. Anthropology helps define these networks. Theology verifies the biblical validity of this approach. Church history endorses it as a major contributor to the growth of the church. Communication theory reinforces that these networks provide an efficient means for effective and lasting propagation. Experience also endorses the success through implementing this strategy. Honing communications to a sharp edge, and applying the communicational process to the natural and primary societal structures of family networks, is likely to produce stronger movements than a focus largely on isolated individuals. A summary of several practical suggestions may help towards accomplishing this. Together the following form a grid for strategic missiological advance.

First is the need to understand family networks and research them in the specific people group among whom the cross-cultural worker ministers. This requires considerable time, concentrated thought and much patience. It is an essential initial step.

Second is the requirement of a new mentality or a changed

view. A deliberate change and wrenching shift must be made from an "individual" evangelistic mentality to a "family network" focused one.

Third, this will also demand a change in the way prayer and intercession are conducted. It is easy to pray for individual contacts, but much more complex and difficult to intercede for whole family networks to be reached and converted.

Fourth, a more strategic forward-looking family approach must be initiated. This will not neglect or ignore the individual seeker, but will build a strategy from the individual to reach out to the whole family network that surrounds the individual. Thus all specific individuals showing interest in the gospel will become potential bridges and catalysts in helping communicate the Good News promptly and effectively to their whole family networks as defined by their culture.

Fifth, a renewed focus on house or home churches will help accelerate the growth. New believers, especially in pioneer settings, are the primary elements of the embryonic church and are to be mobilized immediately to function as the body of Christ locally. These cutting edge household fellowships will supersede and be given priority over expensive buildings and large congregations, at least in the early years of the movement.

Sixth, seekers and new believers are encouraged to maintain contact with their old familial structures and networks, rather than withdraw from them or be isolated from them. Believers will stay in communication with the extended family and their broader networks. As long as they are able, they will maintain natural contact with the communities of their society, their temple companions and their regular work or employment colleagues. Thus they will live out Christ as salt and light through their lives in the midst of family and society. In time, the members of these communities may reject or expel the Christ-followers from their associations. But let us not prematurely precipitate that possible eventuality. Keeping societal contact in tact may also effectively penetrate the groups with the living Jesus and influence them towards a Christ-ward movement.

Seventh is the need for the creative development of new and

appropriate tools for evangelizing and for training new Christians, in keeping with the philosophy and strategy of the family network approach. Stories of family conversions, historical sketches of church growth through family networks, and media presentations of these family models as well as indigenous dramatic plays will likely be required.

Eighth, a pattern of itineration from house to house (family to family and house church to house church) by laypersons, church workers and missionaries will replace or at least strongly supplement the centralized concentration on one congregation in a visible, substantial building. Also a renewed pattern of training believers and seekers locally to do the work of ministry in reaching out to their own family networks will be a priority task.

Ninth is a vision implemented by deliberate actions to extend churches always, not to merely expand them. This calls for the follow up of new marriages, which give opportunity for bridging to new family networks. Believers need training to build relationships with the extended family structure and to communicate the ongoing mission of Christ to the new family network and beyond.

Tenth ways of respecting family leadership and honoring the ancestors appropriately must be developed and taught. Ancestral veneration is a major concern and often a serious barrier to becoming Christian in many Asian and Buddhist societies. More input is discussed in separate chapters later in this book.

By implementing these ten principles, powerful communication of the gospel will produce strong movements of lasting conversions and cohesive communities that will raise up enduring churches to transform whole family networks. Communication flows easiest along natural routes of contacts, relationships and networks. It crosses more speedily over bridges of normal relationships of familiarity already in place through established family networks. Family networks provide the crucial context for the most effective communication of Christ.

4

Duty, Obligation and Prostitution: How Family Matters in Entry into and Exit from Prostitution in Thailand

Christa Foster Crawford

"Whoever wanted to be a prostitute because they thought selling sex was fun and profitable? Just ask Samorn and Prasert. And even you, too, Reun. Do you like living here? Of course you don't. You all do it because you have to. Everyone has their own duties to perform." (Surangkhanang 1994:22)

Several years ago, my husband and I worked to help rescue children from prostitution in Thailand. In one particularly heinous case we helped Dee,[1] a young girl who had been sold into prostitution by her abusive mother. After months of repeated rape and abuse in a brothel, Dee was free and living in a Christian aftercare center. There she received opportunities for a successful future that she would never have received at home. She had all of her physical, emotional and spiritual needs met, was happy, and even thriving. Yet after a few months she left. She returned home, back to the same abusive situation, because she felt obligated to her family. Although Dee hated her mother for what she had done to her, she was the only mother Dee had ever known.

"Home" was located in an area with very limited jobs, especially for an uneducated girl. Dee got married when her mother tried to

---

1. Not her real name.

sell her again, and by the time she was 17 she had two young kids. She was expected to support herself, her children, her husband, her mother, her sister, her sister's kids, and her two brothers, and never seemed to question this overwhelmingly burdensome responsibility. Most of the time she was able to make enough to support them day-to-day, but whenever she faced financial difficulties her first thought was to sell her body for money, often times encouraged by her mother. She resisted, and for several years we worked with her to find sustainable work. We mentored and discipled her and she was growing as a Christian. She was able to make a healthy break with her mother, her husband found a job in another city to support their kids, and though she still helped her sister and her children, she was no longer the sole provider for her entire family system. Her story was very much a success.

Fast forward to the present. Despite the care and support offered by us and our team, Dee had decided to leave our program. Like many young adults, she felt that she knew what was best, even as she acknowledged she was making bad decisions. Our team kept in touch with her and offered unconditional love and continued support, even as they watched her make choices that caused her life to go down the drain. Unfortunately, one of those choices was to enter "voluntary" prostitution. Late one night I met up with Dee again after almost a year of this life. She took me to where she was living—at a karaoke that doubled as a brothel. I knew what to expect—a small, sparse room where she both lived and slept with customers. However, what I was not prepared for was who I saw inside. Lying on the floor taking up every available space were her mom, her sister, her sister's kids and her youngest brother. (Her husband was caring for their children in another city.)

What could cause a young woman who had been trapped in one of the worst brothels in Thailand to later choose to go into prostitution? What could cause her to literally sacrifice her body to care for a mother who had never helped, and only abused her? What could cause her to say "no" to all of the growth she had made and the future she was building and say "yes" to the never-ending needs of her siblings? Certainly economics played an important part. Surely trauma clouded her thinking. Obviously lack of education and opportunities mattered. We had worked on these issues, but I had underestimated the role of her family. As a Westerner, I had no idea of the strength of family duty and obligation, even when the family relationship is ambivalent. I had never been so disappointed and devastated by the fact that Dee's mother was back in her life, and never been so hopeless that Dee could really find lasting change. But unfortunately, while Dee's story is tragic, it is not unique. Understanding why this is so, and how to address it, is the purpose of this article.

Prostitution in Thailand and its surrounding countries has many complex and interrelated causes. Most of these causes not only lead to entry into prostitution, but also make it hard to leave. This article seeks to analyze one contributing factor, namely filial obligation, to determine its impact on entry into and ability to exit from prostitution. The article will first examine the roots of filial obligation found in Buddhist teachings and in Thai culture (specifically, the obligation arising out of the *bunkhun* relationship that often demands a stance of indebted goodness between parent and child). Second, the article will examine the possible connections observed by both Thai and non-Thai scholars between prostitution and filial obligation (especially of daughters), including the gender dynamics and distortions of obligations in play. Finally, the article will examine what the Bible teaches about responsibilities of children to their parents, and will explore how the power of God in application of these biblical concepts can bring transformation not only of this social problem, but also in Thai families for His glory.

Filial Obligations of Thai Children to Parents

Childhood in Thailand must be understood in the context of relationship with parents. Thai society is relationship-based, and this most basic relationship of parent-child is no different. A child in Thai society is not, and never will be, independent of or separate from her parents as children are in the West. Instead, the child has obligations to her parents that extend into adulthood, and even throughout the adult child's entire life.

One of the most basic obligations is that of filial duty,"The concepts of gratitude and obedience towards parents are pervasive in Thai society. It is the duty of children to support their parents as soon as they are able, and to repay the care that has been given to them" (Montgomery 2001:82-3). What is the nature of this duty towards parents? Where does this duty come from? And can it ever be met? It is hard to identify the exact source of this filial duty. It is rooted simultaneously in Buddhist religion and in Thai culture, which in the Thai context are inextricably interwoven and yet distinct. (Nguyen n.d.:2). This section will examine filial duty from both of these interrelated roots.

Filial Piety in Buddhist Teachings

"Filial piety is an important virtue throughout Asia, one that was articulated in many Buddhist texts" (Young 2004:44). The Buddhist teaching on filial piety is found in the Sutra, "The Buddha Speaks about the Deep Kindness of Parents and the Difficulty in Repaying It" which contains the following conversation between the Buddha and Ananda:

> The Buddha answered Ananda, "If when men are in the world, they enter temples, listen to explanations of Sutras and Vinaya texts, make obeisance to the Triple Gem, and recite the Buddha's names, then when they die, their bones will be heavy and white in color. Most women in the world have little wisdom and are saturated with emotion. They give birth to and raise children, feeling that this is their duty. Each child relies on its mother's milk for life and nourishment, and that milk is a transformation of the mother's blood. Each child can drink up to one thousand two hundred gallons of its mother's milk. Because of this drain on the mother's body whereby the child takes milk for its nourishment, the mother becomes worn and haggard and so her bones turn black in color and are light in weight" (BDEA & BuddhaNet n.d.).

This need to "pay back the mother's breast milk" is also found in the *Purnavaddana* and the concept is present in Thai society today where it is known as *ka namnom mae* (Young 2004:44).

Not only is the kindness of parents (especially of mothers) physically costly, its virtue is deep beyond measure and extremely difficult to repay. The Filial Piety Sutra explains:

> When Ananda heard these words, he felt a pain in his heart as if he had been stabbed and wept silently. He said to the World Honored One, "How can one repay one's mother's kindness and virtue?"
>
> The Buddha told Ananda, "Listen well, and I will explain it for you in detail…."The virtue of one's parents' kindness is boundless and limitless. If one has made the mistake of being unfilial, how difficult it is to repay that kindness!"
>
> [Upon hearing about the unfilial child, the Great Assembly cried out] "Please tell us how we can repay the deep kindness of our parents!"
>
> [To which the Buddha replied:] "If there were a person who carries his father on his left shoulder and his mother on his right shoulder until his bones were ground to powder by their weight as they bore through to the marrow, and if that person were to circumambulate Mount Sumeru for a hundred thousand kalpas until the blood that flowed out covered his ankles, that person would still not have repaid the deep kindness of his parents."
>
> [And after listing six other types of self-flagellation, all of which were insufficient to repay, the Buddha continued:] "Disciples of the Buddha, if you wish to repay your parents' kindness, write out this Sutra on their behalf. Recite this Sutra on their behalf. Repent of transgressions and offenses on their behalf. For the sake of your parents, make offerings

to the Triple Gem. For the sake of your parents, hold the precept of pure eating. For the sake of your parents, practice giving and cultivate blessings. If you are able to do these things, you are being a filial child. If you do not do these things, you are a person destined for the hells." (BDEA & BuddhaNet n.d.).

This Sutra is not just a Buddhist ideal, but also finds expression in Thai Buddhist society today. Anthropologist Niels Mulder observes:

In Thai education, the idea is inculcated that mother is the most important of persons. She has given life to the child, suffering for and feeding it at great psychological and physical cost to herself. What's more, she is the source of love and care, and she gives all freely. This tide of goodness results in a moral debt on the side of her child, a debt that it is never able to repay (2000:70).

Instead, "[t]he only thing that the child can do to reciprocate is to love its mother. This love is expressed in being obedient to her, in considering and anticipating her feelings, and in showing gratitude and respect" (Mulder 2000:70).

Filial Piety in Thai Culture

Filial piety in Thailand is also rooted in the Thai cultural concept of *bunkhun*. *Bunkhun* is "a deeply ingrained relational pattern with ancient roots in Thai society" that is fundamental to understanding interpersonal relationships in Thailand (Persons 2008:138). A compound word consisting of *bun* (merit) and *khun* (good or virtue), *bunkhun* can be understood simply as "indebted goodness" (Haas 1964:93, 292; Komin 1991:139). Suntaree Komin defines *bunkhun* as "a psychological bond between someone who, out of sheer kindness and sincerity, renders another person the needed helps and favors, and the latter's remembering of the goodness done and his ever-readiness to reciprocate the kindness" (Komin 1991:139).

Larry Persons explains the *bunkhun* relationship as a cycle of "generosity and gratitude" consisting of two parts (Persons 2008:115). The first part is an act of *bunkhun* in which the benefactor (the *phuu mii phra khun* or "person with benevolence") "performs a genuine, altruistic act of kindness for another person in need" (2008:114). In "true" *bunkhun* this act of kindness is done without any expectation of repayment, but results in feelings of "loving indebtedness" (*ruuseuk katanyuu*) on the part of the beneficiary (2008:114). "This feeling of indebtedness generates a response that completes the *bunkhun* cycle" (2008:115). According to Komin, this second part of the cycle requires the beneficiary to do two things: 1) *ruu bunkhun* ("know *bunkhun*") or acknowledge and be "constantly conscious" of the act of kindness and 2) *tab thaen bunkhun* ("return *bunkhun*") or repay and reciprocate the act of kindness whenever possible (Komin 1991:139). The result of this cycle is a lasting bond, "The cycle of generosity and gratitude causes both parties to feel close to one another, and this feeling can last for a lifetime" (Persons 2008:115). An act of *bunkhun* also results in a debt that cannot be extinguished.

The notion of *bunkhun* "occupies a prominent place in Thai interpersonal relationships" (Knutson n.d). It is an important aspect of "Grateful Relationship Orientation" which is one of the nine key values of Thai society identified by Komin (1991:139). According to Komin, "being *Grateful* to *Bunkhun* constitutes the root of any deep, meaningful relationship and friendship—be it grateful bond towards one's parents, or to a relative who supports one through school, or a teacher who provides one with knowledge, or a good friend who helps one out at times of troubles, etc." (1991:139).

While the notion of *bunkhun* is not particular to the parent-child relationship, it is nevertheless "important to understanding the ways Thai parents interact with their children" (Peaceful Societies 2005). This is especially the case in the relationship between mothers and children whereby:

> [T]he primary symbol of moral goodness is the *phrakkun* or *bunkhun*, the pure devotion which a mother has for her children. She cannot help but be good, cannot but give and

care; she is always benevolent and forgiving. She feeds and loves without expectation of return; she gives without asking and does not punish. (Peaceful Societies 2005)

Usually the child is indebted to the *bunkhun* of the parent. "According to the Thai Buddhist moral scale, parents are entitled to be 'moral creditors' (*phuu mii phra khun*) because of their presumably self-sacrificing labor of bearing and rearing children… while children are moral debtors" (Montgomery 2001:82). On the other hand, "[a]lthough the notion of *bunkhun* gives paramount authority to parents, both parents and children are bounded with certain obligations" (Promphakping 2003:9). According to Buapun Promphakping:

> [T]he obligations of parents towards their children include:
> - Preventing children from committing wrong-doing
> - Encouraging children to commit good deeds and making merits
> - Supporting children in acquiring knowledge or qualification
> - Supporting them to marry good persons
> - Providing them with assets when they form new households.

In a similar vein, children are also bound with certain obligations, including:
- Caring for parents in their old age, to pay back *bunkhun*
- Helping parents in their work
- Maintaining the dignity of the clan
- Being 'good children' to be entitled to parents assets
- Performing and dedicating merits (*tum bun*) to parents after their death (:9).

The filial piety arising from the *bunkhun* relationship between a parent and a child has significant similarities to the concept of filial piety found in Buddhist teachings discussed in the previous section.

First, both obligations arise from the basic fact of the parent giving the child life, "By the mere fact that they brought them into the world, parents gain enough *bunkhun* to make it obligatory upon their children to support them" (Rabibhadana 1984). Second, like the filial duty found in Buddhist teachings, "the *bun khun* of parents can never be completely repaid by their children" (Peaceful Societies 2005). There is a Thai saying *nii bunkhun gin mai mod*, which means, "Debt to *bunkhun* cannot be consumed" (Persons 2008:127). This holds true for children's debt to their parents, "Bunkhun of parents over their children, particularly that of mother, is so great that whatever favors the children do for their mothers, they will be never sufficient to repay bunkhun" (Promphakping 2003:9).

It is impossible to determine whether the filial duty of children to parents in Thai society arises purely from the *bunkhun* relationship or purely from the teachings of Buddhism. In fact, this may be a false dichotomy to the extent that the notion of *bunkhun* is "derived from the Buddhist concept of karma" (Peaceful Societies 2005). It is likely that filial piety finds its source in both Buddhist religion and Thai culture. In fact, those in whom I have observed filial piety do not call it as such, nor do they identify their obligation with any specific source be it Buddhism or *bunkhun*. It is taken for granted, and is unquestioned. It "just is." As such, the remainder of this article will focus on the obligation of Thai children to parents generally, except where the literature specifies a difference. And even in that case, the distinction drawn between Buddhist teachings and *bunkhun* may not be completely precise or accurate.

POSSIBLE CONNECTIONS BETWEEN PROSTITUTION AND FILIAL OBLIGATION

My parents have six children. I am the oldest daughter. My role as the oldest daughter is to care for my aging parents and I must also support and help my younger sisters and brothers to find a beautiful future. School is not for me. Only the rich people go to school…

My mother is not very well. We have no money to take her to the doctor. We do not have any free hospitals. I see my family suffer, and I want to help them. I must go to the city to earn money with my friends.

> *My friends and I are looking for work. We are thinking we will work in a restaurant, but we cannot find work. Bangkok is not safe for women like us. We don't know anybody to help us. We are very hungry, and we have no money. We feel we have no choice but to sell our bodies. I sell my body to save my mother's life and so my five younger sisters and brothers can go to school* (Pusurinkham 1997:15).

Many girls and women cite taking care of their families as their reason for entering into prostitution. This has been documented extensively in research on prostitution in Thailand:[2]

> A number of researchers have drawn attention to the deeply rooted cultural expectation that Thai daughters contribute in any way they can to the support of their parents. Research by scholars like Yoddumnern—Attig, Bencha, et. al stresses the point that such expectation on part of parents represents a strong motivation for young women to enter prostitution. Similarly Pasuk Phongpaichit has emphasised the link between support for parents and prostitution in Thailand. (Ghosh 1996:29)

Traditionally, children fulfill their filial duty through working on the farm or in a factory. But this is not always the case. For example, where there is "no family land to farm and limited options available to uneducated children from the slums [and countryside] there are few ways to earn enough income to support a family [besides prostitution]". As a result "many children turn to prostitution as a way of fulfilling these obligations" (Montgomery 2001:83). How frequently this occurs is a matter of debate; however it certainly does take place. Obviously, not every family encourages (or is even aware of) their daughter's prostitution as a way of fulfilling filial obligation. Some families may directly send their children into prostitution through ignorance or greed. Others may turn a blind eye to the

---

2. The link between filial obligation and prostitution is not unique to Thailand. Similar dynamics exist in neighboring countries, including Cambodia, Laos, certain parts of Burma bordering Northern Thailand, and probably others as well.

source of funds. The satisfaction of a daughter's filial duty does not necessarily depend on prostitution. But all too often it is the case.

Why is this so? This section seeks to examine the apparent connection between filial obligation and prostitution. First, it will consider the gendered nature of filial obligation and its implications. Second, it will consider the impact of distortion and corruption of genuine filial obligation.

Gendered Difference of Filial Obligation

Some make the connection between prostitution and filial obligation due to the gendered nature of that obligation. The obligations of children to parents in Thai society have a gendered dimension. While both boys and girls have a filial duty to parents, satisfying that duty does not always look the same. Promphakping explains that boys repay their parents by making merit; girls, by making money:

> There are gender differences between son and daughter in rights, obligations and responsibilities which are predicated on the notion of *bunkhun*. The differences are largely manifested by the means through which son and daughter return *bunkhun* to their parents. There are two ways for son and daughter do to [sic] return *bunkhun* to their parents; caring (*liang du*) and making merits (*tum bun*) for them. The first involves with [sic] material resources, whereas the second involves non-material resources. (2003:6)

According to Promphakping, "[t]he most important non-material means to return *bunkhun* to parents is to ordain in the monkshood [sic]" (2003:6).[3] In terms of merit, the ordination of a son "generates a significant amount of karmic merit for his parents" (Matzner 2001). Having a son ordain as a monk is especially important to

---

3. On the other hand, Promphakping points out that "although becoming a monk is held as a means to return *bunkhun* to parents, the value given to this practice has declined, as witnessed by the small number of men ordaining and the short time they stay in the monastery service." (2003:6).

mothers in Thai society because under Thai Theravada Buddhism women are not allowed to be ordained yet "women are thought to gain tremendous merit by having a son ordained in the temple" (Mulder 2000:69). However, because girls cannot be ordained , they must repay their obligation in a different way:"As women are denied the right to ordain, the economic burdens of the household are likely to be on the shoulders of the daughter rather than the son" (Promphakping 2003:9).

This material repayment from girls is not only more burdensome, but also inferior to the spiritual repayment from boys. First, it is considered less valuable. "To ordain as a monk is to act like a bridge leading our mothers to heaven. This provides more merit than providing them care or material needs (*liang doo*). It is a duty of a man to become a monk to compensate for the *bunkhun* of his mother who raised him" (Promphakping 2003:9). Second, it is only temporary and does not discharge the debt. Even though the filial obligations arising out of Buddhist teachings and the *bunkhun* relationship are considered impossible debts, ordination is one way in which they can be satisfied. It is said that "[s]on's [sic] pay once—by being born—and a second time by being ordained" On the other hand, "[i]t is normal for daughters to continue to pay throughout their lives" (Pusurinkham 1997:26). It does not matter how long a son remains in the monkhood for his debt to be repaid. "Whether he is ordained for three days or three years, once a son has done this, his debt to his parents is paid. A daughter, on the other hand, is taught to be responsible for household chores. She is also expected to take care of her parents as they grow old. Accordingly, her obligation lasts for life" (Matzner 2001).

Some Thai scholars attribute prostitution to this gendered difference in filial obligation.[4] For instance, Akin Rabibhadana argues that:

> By allowing only sons to enter monkhood as a means of re-paying parents, the society places greater burden on daugh-ters by requiring them to provide financial support to par-

---

4. It is important to note that "Buddhism does not promote or encourage prostitution" (Kabilsingh 1991:41). Instead, "Buddhist texts say that being born a prostitute is the result of karma" (:42).

ents or earn bride price. Such an obligation on the part of daughters helps explain the greater degree of participation of Thai women in economic activities, and the prevalence of the institution of minor wives and even prostitution. (1984)

A number of other Thai Buddhist feminist writers also agree. Most notably, Dhammananda Bhikkhuni (known as Dr. Chatsumarn Kabilsingh before she became the first Thai woman to receive full ordination a Theravada Buddhist nun), writes in her book, *Thai Women in Buddhism*:

> Buddhist temples have traditionally served another "hidden" function as "half-way houses" for destitute people. But because there are only monks in Thailand, this social service is limited to men. Sulak Sivaraksa, a well-known Thai Buddhist social critic, has said that the lack of the Bhikkhuni Sangha [order of ordained Buddhist nuns] in Thailand is partly responsible for the high growth of prostitution. (Kabilsingh 1991:46)

Ouyporn Khuankaew concurs that "[t]he relatively equal number of monks and women prostitutes in Thailand suggests that monkhood and female prostitution may be closely related" (Khuankaew 2000:58). She argues that:

> [M]ost women who enter prostitution come from the same background as monks. Because they do not have another free choice like their fellow men, they often have a choice between a factory or a brothel.... For the poor young rural women [ordination] would become another choice in their lives for making their parents happy. They could decide on something other than being a wife and a mother or going to the factory or a brothel to earn money for the family. They could see that living an ordained life is another way to pay gratitude to their families and their community. (2000:59-60)

Putting aside the debate about women's ordination, it is clear that the link between gender and filial obligation plays a role in entry into prostitution not only in the eyes of outsiders researching prostitution, but also in the Thai Buddhist mind.

Distortions of Genuine Filial Obligation

Others claim that the connection between prostitution and family obligation is due to distortions and corruption of filial obligation rather than the result of genuine obligation. For instance, in her explanation of Grateful Relationship Orientation, Komin describes how distortion and exploitation of the *bunkhun* relationship can to lead to prostitution:

> Another example of this high attachment to family, and showing of gratitude, has to do with the sad but true stories of the rural poor daughters who, with the hope for city jobs, unfortunately end up in the trap of prostitution, but somehow always manage to send money home. (1991:141)

Promphakping describes another distortion of notion of *bunkhun*, "Parents have been increasingly using the notion of *bunkhun* to claim material support from both sons and daughters, as returns from agriculture are insufficient to satisfy their needs. But the expectations of parents on daughters are higher than on sons, because of the cultural notion of *bunkhun*" (2003:6).

In addition to distortion or exploitation, it may be that the imputed connection of filial obligation to prostitution does not actually involve genuine obligation but a counterfeit. According to Persons, "certain patterns of behavior in Thai society today are called *bunkhun* but are so far from the original essence of *bunkhun* that they do not deserve the label" (Persons 2008:124). For instance, Heather Montgomery connects child prostitution to the notion of *bunkhun*:

> They claim that they become and remain prostitutes out of duty and love to their parents, that they have a moral dept to their parents for bearing and raising them; a duty known in

Thai as *bun khun*. This is the debt of gratitude that children owe to their parents, and especially their mothers, for their existence.... [T]he sense of duties they have to their families is overwhelming, and is used by them to inform and contextualize what they do. The duties of kin towards one another are used by the children who work as prostitutes as a way of explaining and condoning what they do, and it is through the obligations that kinship entails that the public vice of prostitution is turned into the private virtue of support for the family. (2001:82)

But others, such as Siriporn Skrobanek, attribute the connection not to genuine *bunkhun* but to other factors such as "the superior claims of economics" (1997:75) or changing attitudes:

The expectation of parents that their daughter must contribute to enhancing the economic status of the family, even if that means working in prostitution, reflects a major change in attitude. When parents insist that children must pay them back with money for their upbringing, this suggests that the relationship has become commercialised. Many young women feel that their primary purpose is to provide material comfort to the rest of the family. (Skrobanek 1997:73)

THE POWER OF CHRIST TO TRANSFORM FAMILY OBLIGATION

Children have no choice in being prostituted; they are innocent and therefore victims of this foul trade. They obey their parents and yet, ironically, it is most often their parents—those whom children naturally trust—who in Thailand too often betray them by selling them, compounding the evil (Pusurinkham 1997:9).

While not every daughter in prostitution was sent there by her parent, and while it is certainly not common for Thai parents to sell their children into prostitution, some parents have—directly or indirectly, knowingly or unknowingly—done so. In any event, even in cases where the parent has not sold or otherwise caused the entry of the daughter into prostitution, we have seen that a daughter's desire and duty to care for her parents is an oft-cited reason for her entry and makes it difficult for her to leave.

What does the Bible have to say about the obligation of children to parents? How can the problem of prostitution in Thailand be transformed through the living out of God's intentions for families? And how can those families be transformed themselves?

In asking these questions it is important to note that the practice of Christianity does not always reach its ideals. First, though Thailand is a Buddhist society and the societies of the West are primarily Christian, it is by no means the case that the West is necessarily freer from prostitution or other exploitation and abuse of children. In fact, the United States has more women and children subject to commercial sexual abuse than Thailand. As we look at factors leading to prostitution in Buddhist Thailand, it is just as essential that we are aware of factors that lead to prostitution in the "Christian" West. Second, Buddhist societies have important values that Western societies should learn from—for instance, moderation of desire vs. being driven by greed and consumerism, or the importance of family and community vs. excessive individualism and disconnection. While these, and other, concerns about Western Christian practice are important and real, this section seeks to look at the ideal—the standard for families that God has set forth in Scripture—both as a guideline for behavior and as a goal to which to aspire.

Biblical Responsibilities of Children

"Scriptures reveal at least nine specific responsibilities children are expected to fulfill in relation to their parents" (Brewster n.d.:64). Roy Zuck in his book, *Precious in His Sight: Childhood and Children in the Bible* (1996:161-68), identifies them as:

1) Honor and Respect
2) Obey
3) Accept Discipline

4) Learn from Parental Instruction
5) Ask about Spiritual Things
6) Fear the Lord
7) Imitate
8) Care for
9) Work with and for

Many of these responsibilities are not unique to Christianity, and in fact, many of them appear in the Thai context as well. However, the specific application of these duties, when empowered by the Spirit of God, has the power to transform children, families and even whole societies. In this section we will look specifically at the teachings of Scripture about honor, obedience and care, and their application by Thai pastor Dr. Sirirat Pusurinkham to the issue of prostitution in Thailand in her dissertation, *Child Prostitution in Thailand: A Challenge to the World Christian Community* (1997).

The Powerful Fruit of Biblical Honor and Obedience: "The fifth commandment, 'Honor your father and your mother' (Exod. 20:12; Deut. 5:16), is the only one of the ten addressed specifically to children and the only one with a promise" (Zuck 1996:161). Jesus reaffirmed the call to honor in Matthew 15:4 and Mark 7:10 (1996:161). Similarly, in the New Testament, Paul instructs children to obedience (1996:164):"Children, obey your parents in the Lord, for this is right" (Eph. 6:1); "Children, obey your parents in everything, for this pleases the Lord" (Col. 3:20). This requirement of obedience "is also evident in the Mosaic law", for example Deuteronomy 21:18-21 (Zuck 1996:163).

While it is only a generalization, Asian children tend to do better at honor and obedience than Western children, being raised in a system which values "Asian ideals of obedience, loyalty, respect for authority, and respect for one's elders" (Chan n.d.). On the contrary, Western children are raised in a system that values "independence, critical thinking, and respect for individual rights" (Chan n.d.). These values, even among Christian families, tend not to lead children to give parents the biblical respect and honor they are due. On the other hand, while traditional Asian cultural values about honor and obedience are admirable, "[n]ot all the traditions and values of either culture are biblical" (Chan n.d.). We must hold them up to the standard of Scripture.

What do these Scriptures mean when it comes to addressing prostitution in the Thai context? Pusurinkham points out that in Thailand, "Children are considered the property of their parents and are sacrificed to the need or the greed of the family. They are taught that loving their parents means they must always obey their instructions and wishes" (1997:110). This is true even when it means entry into prostitution. Yet prostitution "destroys people both in mind and body. It destroys families and communities" (1997:142).

Biblical honor and obedience on the other hand results in promise. The result of honoring one's parents in the Old Testament is "that you may live long and that it will go well with you in the land the Lord your God is giving you" (Deut. 5:16) and in the New Testament is "that it may go well with you and that you may enjoy long life on the earth" (Eph. 6:2-3).

The challenge is to bring Thai practices relating to filial obligation in line with the biblical ideal of honor and obedience. An important step according to Pusurinkham is to:

> Teach people to love God and that to love God is to honor and care for all people.
>
> Teach that the family must care for and support their daughters, not dominate the children but prepare a beautiful future for them. Teach that children are precious gifts of God, costly and important in the family of God. (1997:162)

This must be done in Thai Buddhist and Christian families alike. It cannot be assumed that Christians have necessarily gotten this obligation right.

The Protection of Biblical Care: The Bible teaches that "[a]s parents care for children as they are growing up, so children should care for their elderly parents" (Zuck 1996:168). For example, in the Old Testament, children are told "do not despise your mother when she is old" (Prov. 23:22). In the New Testament, they are instructed to take care of elderly parents and grandparents, "But if a widow has children or grandchildren, these should learn first of all to put their religion into practice by caring for their own family and so repaying their parents and grandparents, for this is pleasing to God" (1 Tim. 5:4). In fact, 1 Tim 5:8 continues on to warn that, "If anyone does not provide for his relatives, and especially for his immediate family, he has denied the faith and is worse than an unbeliever."

The West, including the Western church, in its individualistic orientation has much to learn from the group and family orientation that is typically valued in Asian cultures. For instance, it is common for adult children in America to live hundreds if not thousands of miles away from their parents. In contrast, it is not unusual for my single adult Thai friends to live with their parents until they are married, and some continue to live with their parents even after they are married. Living on one's own is seen as the exception; living with family is seen as a sign of relational health. By contrast, an American who continues to live with his parents well into adulthood is looked down upon as not being a responsible adult.

Similarly, when American parents grow elderly or old, it is not uncommon for them to live apart from their children in senior-housing, known tellingly as "independent living." While my Asian friends may question how American children can be so "heartless," in many cases it is not so much about a child's willingness to care for her parents as it is a reflection about how strongly American parents value independence that they want to live independently until they are no longer capable of doing so. That being said, American and Western Christians must evaluate their drive to be independent from their children and from their parents against the standard of Scripture and be willing to make adjustments even when it goes against culture.

While "Asian values" promote the concept of care for elderly parents, we have seen how this godly responsibility can be distorted to obligate "dutiful daughters" in Thailand to sell their bodies to provide for the genuine needs and greedy desires of their parents and other family members. Yet the biblical concept of "repayment" is predicated on care that is "pleasing to God" (1 Tim. 5:4). Care for parents that fails to protect children is not pleasing to God. However, even though Thai notions of filial obligation (including the duty to return *bunkhun*) can be misused to entrap, I believe that God can and will use Thai values—brought into alignment with the biblical concept of repayment found in 1 Timothy 5:4—to bring freedom to daughters, and ultimately, transformation to society as a whole.

In addition, we have seen that much of the injustice related to the obligation of parental care stems from "the position of women in the Thai family and culture [and] the situation of women in Thai Buddhism" according to Pusurinkham (1997:11). For instance, the reason that *bunkhun* results in an unfair burden on girls and women is because "[i]n Thailand, as in numerous places, men still look down on women either because of cultural and economic factors or because of religious status" (1997:81-82). Instead, we need to look at what Bible says about gender, "It is time for the church to promote the liberation of men and women from ancient customs, to break down the barriers between the rich and poor, the powerful and powerless, and to change the society in Thailand" (1997:97).

Family and Societal Transformation

This call to change society must be seriously considered if girls and women like Dee are to remain free from prostitution. But first it is necessary to change families. If the connection between filial piety and entry into prostitution is based on faulty views of parenting and childhood, then those views themselves must be transformed. In our case, we worked hard to support Dee in her individual decision to follow Christ and in her ability to sustain herself, but we failed to address adequately the deeper underlying issues of family and obligation. It is not enough that a daughter believes and changes, but the whole system must also change in order to support and maintain her freedom.

This is especially true when biblical values of honor, obedience and care are played out in the context of Buddhist society. In a country where less than one percent of ethnic Thais are Christians, it will usually be the case that the daughter, even if she becomes a

Christian, will have Buddhist parents and family system. Furthermore, because of the strong link between Buddhism and Thai identity, the worldview even of Thai Christian families is often fundamentally Buddhist. Finally, just because families are taught about the biblical standards of honor, obedience and care does not mean they will be applied in a biblical manner—in Thailand, or in the West. I have often wondered, in a society that has so few Christians, how it is that I know a number of Christians who are in prostitution because of the need to support their families? I have always attributed it to a lack of discipleship or authentic personal conversion. That may very well be the case. Yet, when I consider that these are individual women who have become Christians without the surrounding religion, worldview, values or practices of their families changing, it should be no surprise at all.

So what can we do in the future to help Dee and the thousands of girls and women like her? First, we need to focus on the all-important individual level. Individual salvation is essential, even as we seek transformation at a broader level. We must also address the individual's holistic needs (including emotional and vocational as well spiritual), providing social services that are otherwise lacking to "the least of these" who are in need. This is not only an obligation, but also a tremendous opportunity. Second, we must address the familial level. Alex Smith advocates that effective evangelism in the Buddhist world takes place "with families in mind, rather than individuals" (2006:174). Where prostitution is a result of the role of daughters in the family, "whole family evangelism" is not just of strategic importance, but it is also essential for girls to remain free. Third, we must seek change at the societal level. For Christian individuals and families, maturity in the faith requires them to examine their views of filial obligation and to bring them in line with Scripture. This will involve, in part, holding fast to the aspects that reflect biblical teachings about honor, obedience and care, and shedding off the parts that do not. But reconceiving filial obligation is not just a requirement of Christians. The whole of Thai society must become aware of and examine the possible connections of filial obligation to prostitution and other abuses and injustices. Only as societal structure is changed can change be sustained in individual lives. At the same time, it is only the power of Christ in individuals and families seeking to live out biblical obligation that will result in transformation of whole communities, and ultimately Thai society as a whole.

Thankfully Dee's story is not over yet. There is still hope. And there is much that can be done. For instance, our program has begun working with the parents of children who are at risk of sexual exploitation while selling flowers in the red-light district. The children—as young as five years old—work unattended, late into the night to earn money to support their families. In the process, they are approached for sex. The kids have a saying, "Never go with a stranger.... But, if he offers you a few thousand Baht that is too much to turn down." One thousand baht is approximately US $30—usually one-third to one-fifth of the monthly income of the child's family. The pressure on children and parents alike is great. But, by educating parents about the risks their children face, and by helping them understand that their children's futures will be better if they stay in school instead of working, we have been able to make a difference in the lives of children and their families. In fact, all of the children in our program have been allowed to stop working and we are continuing to work with the parents to help them learn Godly parenting principles.

While Dee's mother is in another city and thus not part of this program, we know better the need to support Dee in the context of her entire family system, and to work with the family as a whole so that they too can learn about Christ and grow in their faith, even as Dee does. There is also hope for the future with respect to her own children. Dee has learned about biblical parenting. Her husband also became a Christian. While much work is left to be done, family transformation is happening in the next generation, in the same way that God promised lovingkindness for a thousand generations to those who love him and keep his commands (Exod. 20:6). It will be a while before we see transformation of entire communities, and of society as a whole, but by working together—one family, one daughter, one child at a time—we are starting to see change in the lives of many individuals.

CONCLUSION

As I was writing this article, I had a conversation with two female friends in their early twenties, one a Westerner, and the other Thai. My Western friend was moving back to the US after several years of living independently in Thailand. In order to save money, she was planning to drive from Los Angeles International Airport to her final destination five hours away. The money she would save would be less than US $300. Because her parents were worried about her safety, they insisted that she fly instead and purchased the ticket for her. An hour later, I was sitting with my Thai friend at the bar where she makes around 5000 Baht a month (approximately US $150). She was worried because her brother had gotten his girlfriend pregnant and my friend's parents were asking my friend to pay the bride price demanded by the girl's family. The amount my friend was expected to pay for the irresponsibility of her brother was 130,000 Baht (almost US $4000)—more than twice her *annual* salary. Since she entered prostitution at the age of fifteen, this friend has constantly been supporting her family with what she earns. She may be upset and worried about it, but she never questions whether it is her duty.

We have seen that among the multiple, intertwined causes of prostitution, the obligation to parents arising from Thai Buddhist and cultural concepts of filial piety, wrongly applied, can result in the practice of ensnaring and trapping girls and women in prostitution. We have also looked at the biblical teachings on duty to parents and seen how godly application of the obligation to honor, obey and care can address the problem of prostitution through transforming families and society. Finally, we are reminded that as we seek to bring the power of the gospel to the issues of Thai society, "church members [must] look at their own relationships with family members and consider how these relationships compare with the love, care, and forgiveness that the life of Jesus shows" (Pusurinkham 1997:143). It is only as we do these things that we can ever hope to see Thai family matters become as they really matter to God.

5

The Ritual of Reconciliation in Thai Culture: Discipling New Converts

Ubolwan Mejudhon

A Thai pastor complains, "When our church gets one weak Christian, we get two hundred strong enemies from the new convert's social networks."

What this Thai pastor says is a plain fact. In Thailand, a Thai becomes a Christian in secret. The church and the seeker do not let the parents know about the searching, being afraid that the parents will stop the seeker from attending the church. Then, one day, out of the blue, their son or daughter announces his or her conversion to Christ. Having no emotional shock absorber, the parents are enraged. The conversion brings shame to them. The neighbors gossip that they did not bring their child up well. The convert challenges their authority by making an important decision without acknowledging them or asking for advice. The parents worry for their child. They have no idea about the new social network their son or daughter is having fellowship with. They know nothing about Christ. The announcement brings bewilderment to the parents and relatives.

Moreover, the church trains the new convert to witness aggressively to their parents and relatives. The aggressive witness causes anger because the convert violates the values of hierarchy and smooth relationships, as well as accepted social roles and status. The parents and relatives listen to the new convert's testimony, patiently, until they reach a boiling point. Then they hit back, hard. As a result, the new convert takes refuge in the church community. Yet, the missing relationship is too great. Though the church community is strong, it cannot provide the support the convert needs. The church has thus gained one weak Christian while, through the convert's angry relatives, it has gained many strong enemies.

It can be seen from its history that Thai culture is very kind and generous to all religions. Thailand has accepted primal religion, Hinduism, and Buddhism for more than two thousand years. The believers of these faiths lived in peace. King Rama V (1868-1919) issued a law out of love toward missionaries that they were free to preach the gospel. At the present time, the government gives money to missionaries to preach the gospel to the Thai (Mejudhon 1994:1). It is a myth among Christians that Thais are against other religions. Usually, parents allow their children to learn about other faiths. Religion is good, from the Thai's viewpoint. The Thai learn about other faiths from primary school to high school.

The royal academy of Thailand records that the king is the protector of all religions (The Royal Academy 1995:783). This evidence should rid Christians of the fear they have of the seekers' parents. In fact, Christians should get to know them because Thai culture is a relationship-based culture. A relationship provides a shock absorber and lessens anxiety for the parents when they know about the conversion of their children.

Suntaree Komin, a Thai scholar, conducted empirical research among the Thai. She found nine Thai value clusters: ego orientation, grateful relationship orientation, smooth interpersonal relationship orientation, flexibility and adjustment orientation, religio-psychical orientation, fun making, education and competence orientation, interdependence orientation, and achievement-task orientation (Komin 1993:133). Christians violate the grateful relationship orientation, smooth interpersonal relationship orientation, flexibility and adjustment orientation, and the interdependence orientation when the new converts abruptly tell their parents of their conversion. The Thai like the proverb, "slowly but surely." They hate abrupt changes. Change is a slow process for them. They have a saying, "slowly, slowly change" (*koy pen koy pai*), "I need time to prepare my heart and my mind" (*tong tiam toi tiam jai*). The Thai concept of time is cyclical (Feig 1989:23-24).

When new converts witness aggressively to their parents and relatives they violate their value of confrontation avoidance, as well as their culture's value of hierarchy, which Feig considers as an important characteristic of the Thai (Feig 1989:37,76). While doing so, the new converts are usually under the spell of the "theology of redemption," according to which their parents and relatives are lost and will be in hell. Out of love, they are even more aggressive as their parents and relatives respond to their witness kindly and in quietness, or even with teasing remarks out of humor. As days pass by, new converts are more aggressive in witnessing. They overlook the ego-orientation value of their parents, who have strong self-esteem and strong self-identity as Thais. In order to keep their children meek and quiet, the parents fight back by scolding and criticizing. When the children talk back, their parents are enraged and ignore them, acting as if the children do not exist. Then the new converts withdraw into Christian communities and their other relational ties are broken.

As a result, these new converts lose their identity as Thais, which inhibits their spiritual growth. It seems to me that if converts were to remain bonded to their natural community—that is, to Thai culture—it would affect their identity as well as their bonding to Christian meaning. Because this does not happen, I believe that Christian churches in Thailand have many weak Christians.

As for the parents of the new converts, although they ignore their children completely, as Thai parents, they love them dearly. They long to bond with their own children and know what is going on in their lives so that they can help. This is an important duty of Thai parents, but they cannot do so as long as they feel that the church is stealing their children away. According to the parents, they invested their lives into their children, yet their children now belong to Christian churches which have invested nothing in them. The result leaves an open wound for the Thai families because Christians violate Thai values and break the family's relational ties. The letter recorded below is from Nantachai Mejudhon's mother, written to him from Thailand when she learned of his conversion while he was living in the States.

May 22, 1972
My Dearest Son,

Your last letter is the most important letter of my life. I read your letter at the office and in the bus and then at home in secret, afraid your younger brother would know about it. Usually, I allow him to read your letters as they inspire him. I have read your letter more than ten times now. I am glad that you have found peace and joy. Now that you are grown up and have a good education, you can think and make decisions on your own. I have tried to analyze your comment "I am still a good Buddhist in the way that I practice his teaching. I still respect and love Lord Buddha." I am trying to use this statement to comfort myself and put myself in the Buddhist middle way. Yet, I am confused and I ask myself, "Can he enter the monkhood again as he once did? Can my son still make merit as he once did? Does he have to give up all these rituals when he accepts Christianity?"

Why do you write to me, "Please don't be sorry?" What about this religion could change the deep relational love between mother and son? I accept that I am too stupid to study and make experiments to find the truth like others. Even in the religion in which I worship and which I have respected from birth for more than sixty years I cannot find the truth yet. How could I find the truth in another religion? It is impossible.

I now accept this suffering because I have a lot of bad karma. I can no longer find peace and joy in my life. I have fought against all kinds of fate and shed my tears many times. I will try to quench my suffering, saying to myself, "It's my karma." The fate of karma predestines our life. Through suffering and pain, I will accept my karma and try my best to do good. I will try my best to do the mother's duty in this life, so that I don't have to suffer in another life. I think in my humble capacity. This world, this life is uncertain. That is the truth of truth.

Anyhow, I congratulate you, my son. Yet, I would like to plead and beg of you not to announce your new religion to any relatives. I plead with you not to be baptized like some others until you return and meet me, because I need your help in solving some problems. Please heed my requests in this matter. Good luck, my son. May you have peace and joy in our Lord Buddha's teaching. May you think about the grace of Buddha, Dharma, and Sangha, if you can?

From Mother,
Tipparat Mejudhon

P.S. I am frustrated and wonder how far this religion sets limitations and disciplines for other religions. Is it possible for this religion to get along with Buddhism in worship and rituals or is absolute separation the only possibility?

The wounds caused by broken relationships can no longer be ignored. I believe the ritual of reconciliation in the Thai culture provides an answer for the dilemma mentioned above. This paper presents, in four parts, Thai culture's ritual of reconciliation as a discipling tool for new converts. The first part has been introductory. The second part is a theoretical framework for the ritual of reconciliation. The third part deals directly with critical contextualization proposing a way of creating a Christian ritual of reconciliation for bonding new Christian converts with their families. The last part is the conclusion.

Theoretical Framework

In order to understand this paper, we need to understand three important definitions: the definition of "reconciliation," the definition of "ritual," and the definition of "critical contextualization." I will present "reconciliation" as it is defined by Robert Schreiter. I will explain "ritual" (within the context of rites of passage) using A. H. Mathias Zahniser's thought as a framework. I will use the theoretical frameworks of Schreiter and Zahniser to analyze the Thai ritual of reconciliation. Finally, Paul G.

Hiebert's theory of critical contextualization and Suntaree Komin's nine Thai value clusters will serve as a guideline for inventing a Thai Christian ritual of reconciliation. They are authorities in contextualization.

Robert Schreiter's Definition of Reconciliation

Robert Schreiter is an eminent Catholic scholar who has written many books about social reconciliation. He presents his idea about the definition of reconciliation as follows:

> There are at least three understandings of reconciliation that come close to the genuine meaning of reconciliation but distort and even falsify its true sense. These three are reconciliation as hasty peace, reconciliation instead of liberation, and reconciliation as a managed process. (1997:18)

Many people misunderstand "reconciliation" as hasty peace. They perform reconciliation to cover over problems. We need to understand the real meaning of "reconciliation." Robert Schreiter explains that reconciliation is a long process. Reconciliation does not require victims to quickly forget their pain and suppress their memory of a history of violence. Schreiter thinks that to trivialize and ignore the memory of victims is to trivialize and ignore human identity. To trivialize and ignore human identity is to trivialize and ignore human dignity. In this long process of reconciliation Schreiter believes that only certain people have the moral authority to issue the call for reconciliation. Reconciliation demands special grace and kindness from victims. Oppressors cannot initiate it. Therefore, reconciliation is more likely to come from the victims in the situations, not from the wrongdoers. Reconciliation requires time for starting a new life for both victims and oppressors if reconciliation really takes place between them.

Moreover, Schreiter affirms that reconciliation goes hand in hand with liberation—without liberation, there will be no reconciliation. Schreiter states, "If the sources of conflict are not named, examined, and taken away, reconciliation will not come about. What we will have is a truce, not a peace" (1997:23). He believes that true reconciliation must meet conflict and confront its cause. Schreiter points out that reconciliation is not a managed process. Reconciliation is spiritual. It is God who reconciles. It is God's grace welling up in one's life. Reconciliation is more of an attitude than an acquired skill or strategy. Schreiter implicitly suggests that forms of reconciliation should be designed to fit various cultural contexts. He explains, "By making reconciliation a skill it is accorded the highest (read: most scientific) form of rationality. But to reduce reconciliation to the technical-rational is to devalue it in other cultures" (1997:27). Robert Schreiter's framework for the definition of reconciliation is summarized in a schematic representation below.

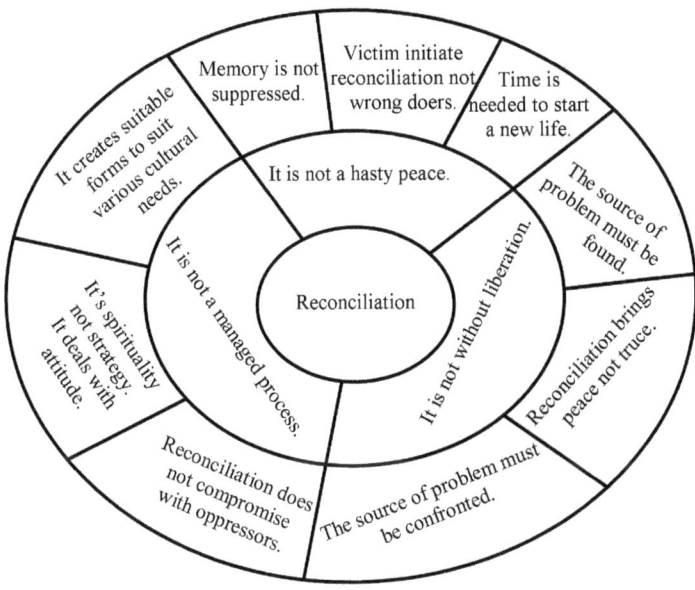

Figure 1: Schematic Representation of Schreiter's Definition of Reconciliation

A.H. MATHIAS ZAHNISER'S THEORY

A. H. Mathias Zahniser, the John Wesley Beeson Professor of Christian Missions, firmly believes that Christians can utilize symbols and ceremonies in making disciples across cultures, especially in times of crisis and transition. He points out four reasons for his belief:

> (1) at times of crisis and transition people revert to traditional religious practices; (2) at times of crisis and transition people are ripe for bonding to meaning; (3) the discipling done at times of crisis and transition will help individuals, families, and their communities deal with daily, more ordinary needs in Christ; and (4) at times of crisis and transition outsiders need the loving service of the Christian community of faith. (1997:107)

In order to understand Zahniser's ideas, we should look closely at some definitions: the definitions of "ritual," "symbol," "rites of passage" and "liminality."

Scholars and anthropologists define "ritual" differently. Victor Turner, a renowned anthropologist, defines ritual as an aggregation of symbols (1968:2). I think any ritual is rich with symbolic objects, symbolic actions, symbolic time and place. Victor Turner views rituals as performances. These rituals transform lives of ritual participants. Moreover, rituals reveal major classification, categories and contradictions of cultural process (Grimes 1995:148).

As rituals are an aggregation of symbols, Turner also recognizes that symbols are the "molecules of ritual" (1969:14). Of the many definitions of "symbol," I personally like Paul Tillich's. He says, "Symbols point beyond themselves, in the power of that to which they point (1997:77)." Tillich recognizes that symbols are powerful—that the forms of symbols contain powerful, important and deep meanings. These deep meanings justify the use of symbols. The national flags and national anthems of our countries are just such symbols, and they powerfully affect the hearts and minds of people.

Rites of passage are important rituals in all culture. Victor Turner explains rites of passage as follows:

> Van Gennep himself defined rites de passage as "rites which accompany every change of place, state, social position and age".... Van Gennep has shown that all rites of passage or

"transition" are marked by three phases: separation, margin (or limen, signifying "threshold" in Latin), and aggregation. The first phase (of separation) comprises symbolic behavior signifying the detachment of the individual or group either from an earlier fixed point in the social structure, from a set of cultural conditions ("a state"), or from both. During the intervening "liminal" period, the characteristics of the ritual subject (the "passenger") are ambiguous; he passes through a cultural realm that has few or none of the attributes of the past or coming state. In the third phase (reaggregation or re-incorporation), the passage is consummated. (1969:94-95)

A. H. Mathias Zahniser puts the explanation about rites of passage of Gennep and Turner into the schematic diagram below (1997:92)

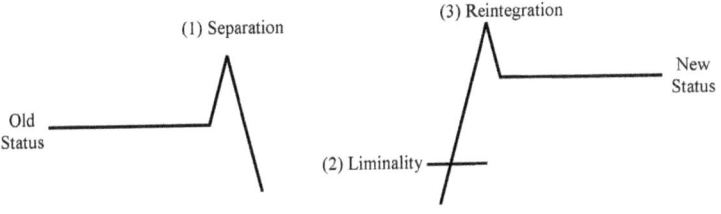

Figure 2: Zahniser's Structure of a Rite of Passage

According to Zahniser,

A rite of passage enables initiates to make a transition from one clearly defined position in society to another. These rites usually accompany the change from nonbeing to being in birth, from childhood to adulthood in puberty rites, from the single to the married state in marriage, and from life to the status of ancestor in the funeral. (1997:92)

In rites of passage, liminality or "threshold" is very important. Initiates are in a gray area of life that causes them to deeply think and feel. This experience encourages them to grow spiritually and socially. Many Buddhist novices weep in the ritual process of monk ordination and many Christians experience God's presence when they are baptized. Zahniser also advocates anthropologist Kenneth Tollefson's saying about the power of the rite-of-passage structure as a "pedagogical opportunity for promoting personal development and spiritual growth" (1990:315). Tollefson believes that liminality provides educational opportunity. The initiates experience the state of marginality which helps them reflect on the past and the future. The process of reflection encourages cognitive dissonance which stimulates the initiates' reorientation of self-understanding and perception of suitable social obligation and behavior. The state of liminality is very important for the structure of the rites of passage.

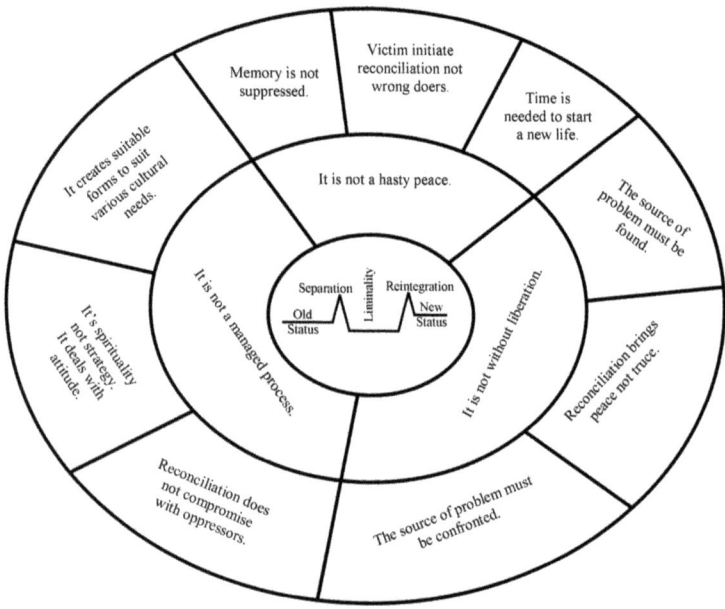

Figure 3: The Schematic Presentation of the Ritual of Reconciliation

Figure 3 is a schematic presentation of my theoretical framework concerning the ritual of reconciliation. Here, I utilize Schreiter's theory about the definition of reconciliation, and Zahniser's schematic presentation of rites of passage abstracted from Arnold Van Gennep and Victor Turner.

CRITICAL CONTEXTUALIZATION

Now, I will elucidate a concept of "critical contextualization." Paul G. Hiebert makes many suggestions in his book Anthropological Reflections on Missiological Issues (1994). I will discuss their bearing on contextualization as follows: (1) exegesis of the culture; (2) exegesis of Scripture and the hermeneutical bridge; (3) critical contextualization's demand for a critical response; (4) new contextualized practices; and (5) checks against syncretism.

Hiebert explains exegesis of culture:

> The first step in critical contextualization is to study the local culture phenomenologically. Local church leaders and the missionary lead the congregation in uncritically gathering and analyzing the traditional beliefs and customs associated with some question at hand. (1994:88)

He also describes exegesis of Scripture and the hermeneutical bridge:

> The leader must also have a meta-cultural framework that enables him or her to translate the biblical message into the cognitive, affective, and evaluative dimensions of another culture. This step is crucial, for if the people do not clearly grasp the biblical message as originally intended, they will have distorted view of the gospel. (1994:89)

Hiebert explains that critical contextualization requires a critical response from local Christians in the light of their new biblical understanding. They should make decisions toward the new found truths; then Christian leaders will be able to help locals practice a new ritual that expresses the Christian meaning of the event. Hiebert suggests four criteria for checking against syncretism: that critical contextualization be biblically based; that believers be guided by the Holy Spirit; that the church acts as a hermeneutical community in contextualization; and that evangelical theologians from different cultures participate in discussion.

Using Paul G. Hiebert's theory of critical contextualization I will proceed to exegete the Thai ritual of reconciliation. Then I will present the exegesis of Scripture and the hermeneutical bridge of etic and emic Christians concerning the biblical meaning of "reconciliation." After this, I will briefly present a critical response to the ritual of reconciliation among Christian communities in Thailand. Following this, a Thai Christian ritual of reconciliation will be illustrated. My new contextualized practice will then be ready for checks against syncretism. Exegesis of the Thai Ritual of Reconciliation:

The Thai naturally participate in rituals of reconciliation through rites of passage: e.g. through monk ordination, funeral rites, conflict solving process, eloping and a lot more. With the help of Schreiter and Zahniser's theory of the ritual of reconciliation, in order to find out its meaning and structure, I will analyze an example of the Thai ritual of reconciliation as it is recorded in a famous novel "A Child of the Northeast." Recorded below is an event concerning a couple in the Northeast of Thailand who committed fornication:

*   *   *

Early the next morning, when it was still dark as midnight, Koon awoke to hear a woman yelling at the top of her voice, right outside their house.

"Put down your ladder, Koon's papa!"

It was Auntie Kao, who was the wife of Uncle Yai and the mother of Kamgong. "Open your door," she yelled.

"The water buffalo?" Koon's mother called out, opening the door and leaning out.

"Where is it now?" Koon's father asked.

"Still in Kamgong's bedroom," she said. "And her Papa is standing outside the door with his long knife."

His parents leaned out the doorway, and there was a hasty discussion. Koon soon understood that the water buffalo was Tid-Joon, son of Uncle Mek, and that he had been in Pi Kamgong's bedroom the whole night. Just before dawn, at the hour when the rooster was about to hop from his perch, Pi Kamgong had called to her mother that Tid-Joon was in there, and had been with her the whole night.

At once, her father had jumped up and grabbed his long knife to stand guard in front of his daughter's door, so that Tid-Joon could not jump down from the house, leaving Kamgong up there, as daughters sometimes were left.

Koon's father sent Auntie Kao off to fetch Tid-Joon's mother and father. Then he dressed and went to tell Auntie Bua-si and Uncle Kem. They were more distant relatives, but in any important family matter, all of the family gathered—which was to say, almost the whole village.

"Mama, will Tid-Joon live with Pi Kamgong now?"

"Yes, son."

"Why don't they have a wedding, and invite people to eat lop and drink whiskey?"

"Because they are so poor. When two people marry this way, it is called chu sao. Kamgong's Papa says that he does not like Tid-Joon, and that Tid-Joon has no money. But that is not really true. The important thing is that Kamgong is the only child in the family who still lives at home and can help Uncle Yai and Auntie Kao. That's why Kamgong needs a little help herself . . ."

"So Tid-Joon went over there last night and sneaked into her bedroom and helped her?"

"Er . . ."

The sun still had not risen when they reached Uncle Yai's house, but Koon could see the dim shapes of many people clustered in the yard. Four of five of the oldest people in the village were up on the porch, chatting quietly with Koon's grandmother.

When they climbed into the house, Koon was very

relieved to see that Uncle Yai was not standing in front of Pi Kamgong's door with a long knife, but sitting calmly enough on the kitchen floor and smoking a cigarette. And he was amazed to see that Tid-Joon's father had arrived already, and was sitting and smoking with Uncle Yai. He did not see Tid-Joon's mother.

And there was Pi Kamgong, the cause of all the trouble, sitting next to her mother, sitting hunched over and staring miserably at the floor.

"All right, everyone is here now," Koon's father said. "It is time for Tid-Joon to come out of the bedroom."

The door opened slowly and Tid-Joon crept forward. He crawled to his father's side on his hands and knees, and sat hunched over just like Kamgong, staring at the floor.

Koon was astonished. The swaggering young man he had seen at the well was not swaggering now!

"What do you all say to our mother speaking first?" Koon's father asked. No one replied. They all turned toward the old woman, and waited respectfully for her to speak. Koon's grandmother looked at Kamgong and Tid-Joon for a moment, then at the others. She said,

"A man and a woman become husband and wife in one of three ways. One, the man asks for her, and there is a wedding ceremony. Two, they run away together. Three, chu sao . . ."

"So what is to be done now?" Uncle Yai asked angrily.

Koon's grandmother raised her hand.

"If Tid-Joon asks forgiveness of our family, and of the spirits of our ancestors, that is enough."

She looked sternly at Uncle Yai and said; "Everybody in the village knows that Tid-Joon does not have a thing to offer but his apology, so that will have to be enough!"

"Our family accepts the whole blame," Uncle Mek said, "because Tid-Joon is our son, and he did wrong. But if the other family calls for some payment, I do not know what we will do, because we do not have anything, and that is the truth. There is nothing of value in our whole place but three bahts and a chicken."

They talked until the sun began to rise, and it was then that Tid-Joon's mother appeared, carrying a tray on which she had placed one folded pakomah, some flowers, and the family's three baht. Tid-Joon sat up straight, for the first time, and Koon noticed the movement of the powerful muscles in his shoulders, arms and chest as he took the tray from his mother and crept on his knees toward the elders. He bent low before Uncle Yai, and before Auntie Kao; then he crawled toward Koon's mother and father, and bowed before them.

"And before our grandmother!" Uncle Yai said gruffly, and Tid-Joon quickly crawled to Koon's grandmother, and touched his head to the floor before her.

Koon's grandmother smiled down at him, and dabbed at her eyes with a square of red and black cloth.

"This Tid-Joon is a good boy," she said. "This boy has gone to the temple to be a monk in his time, and he will be a good husband and a father until he is an old man.

"Tid-Joon, listen to me. If you are a poor man, then you make merit with your good heart, and with the strength of your body."

Tid-Joon looked up, smiling gratefully at these sweet words from his bride's grandmother, and it was at the moment that Tid-Hod, the drunk, came struggling up the house ladder with the chicken under one arm, and stood steadily on the porch.

"Kamgong! What is this, letting that big water buffalo into the garden? Ha ha ha!"

"It is my karma, Tid-Hod," said Kamgong in a small shaky voice, not raising her head.

Tid-Hod sat down, leaned back on one elbow, and said

that as soon as he had heard about this bad water buffalo, he had gone out and gotten a chicken for Tid-Joon to cook for his bride's ancestors. "After we make some lop from the chicken," he said, "and after the ancestors have had their share, we will all take a few bites ourselves."

Tid-Hod picked himself up and went off with Uncle Sang, Auntie Si-nin's husband, to kill the chicken and make the lop. It took them only a few minutes, and soon Koon's grandmother was lading chicken lop into a tiny bowl.

She put this bowl into a tray with some betel leaves, prettily folded and sprinkled with water, and the three baht from Tid-Joon's family. She carried the tray from the kitchen, and called Tid-Joon and Kamgong to follow her into Kamgong's bedroom, where she made them kneel down and ask forgiveness of Kamgong's ancestors, so that they could have a happy life together, and then she led them out to sit facing the people who by now filled the house, and also the porch.

"Tid-Hod brought a chicken for lop," she told them.

"Will there be enough rice for all these people?" one old woman asked.

"There will be enough," said Auntie Kao, Tid-Joon's mother. "Our neighbors have come, bringing four boxes."

Koon sat beside his father, sniffing the air hungrily. When six small bowls of chicken lop were set down between four boxes of rice, the people all reached forward politely, quickly rolling balls of rice and dipping them into the delicious food. (Boontawee 1994:84-90)

* * *

The Ritual of Reconciliation in Thai Culture

The events portrayed here illustrate a transition in the lives of Kamgong and Tid-Joon from the status of single to the status of married, through fornication. They separated themselves to secretly enjoy their desire. The first state of separation was abruptly ended when Kamgong called at dawn to her mother acknowledging Tid-Joon's presence in her bedroom.

Then the liminality elucidates itself driving Kamgong and Tid-Joon into "threshold." They were not single; yet they were not married either. They brought shame to both families and relatives. Kamgong's parents became victims. Tid-Joon polluted their virgin daughter without paying a dowry. Both Kamgong and Tid-Joon committed a cultural sin. They also committed a religious sin, breaking the third precept of Buddha. The spirits of Kamgong's ancestors were violated. The spirits could punish the whole clan of Kamgong and Tid-Joon. In liminality, Kamgong and Tid-Joon lost their old status. However, during, betwixt and between in these events, both of them probably learned about the difference between pollution and purity, as well as the importance of community. They probably reflected a lot about their past and future as they were confronted publicly by the victims of their sins.

Note that the victims initiated the process of reconciliation. It was a long process because the victims did not suppress their pain and anger. They pointed out the cause of the problem. The father wanted to liberate himself from shame, the loss of identity and the loss of dignity. Grandmother was the authority of the ritual of reconciliation. I believe that through God's image left in each victim, they could forgive Kamgong and Tid-Joon. Yet, they also humiliated both oppressors. Thai culture demanded that both oppressors bow down to their victims' feet—the most humiliating of actions—signifying the submission of ego and oneself to the victim.

The ritual objects are humble and simple: a piece of cloth, a small amount of money and flowers. A piece of cloth is a gift the Thai give to elderly people in sacred times such as festivals and ceremonies. Money represents a dowry. Tid-Joon's dowry, three baht, was all that his family had. Flowers represent friendship. Liminality ended when the victims forgave their oppressors and grandma blessed them. Then Tid-Joon and Kamgong were reintegrated into a new status as a married couple. They reconciled to the victims and to the Buddhist precept of purity. They also apologized to Kamgong's ancestors' spirits. After that, celebration of the new status quickly followed.

This analysis reveals that the Thai ritual of reconciliation follows Schreiter's definition of reconciliation as well as the structure of rites of passage. The only superfluous action from the Christian perspective is the reconciliation to the ancestor's spirits. Apart from that, most of the ritual can be participated in by Thai Christians.

Some more information about the ritual can be helpful. This ritual of reconciliation is called the *kama* and *ahosikarma* Ritual. *Kama* and *ahosikarma* are archaic words which come from Pali. *Kama* means "to ask for pardon; to humbly apologize." *Ahosikarma* means "forgiveness of the offence is granted" (Thai Royal Academy 1995:128, 925).

Perhaps these concepts come from myths in primal religion, Hinduism, and/or Buddhism, being that these are the main strands of Thai syncretistic religion (Sataanandha and Boonyanate 1993:6-12). Hinduism provides many myths about humans who offended gods and, thus, had to be reconciled to gods through sacrifices. Buddhism emphasizes reconciliation for broken human relationships. The Buddhist myth of Buddha's life tells about the great thief, Ongkulimand, who asked for pardon from Buddha, whom he wanted to kill. Buddha forgave him. Primal religionists in Thailand worship spirits both good and bad. When Thai people offend these spirits, they have to ask for forgiveness (*kama*) and make an offering to suspend the offended spirits' chastisement.

Nowadays, the words *kama* and *ahosikarma* are frequently used in Thai language when relationships between persons are being challenged. The word *ahosikarma* is shortened to *hosi*, being a vernacular expression. This demonstrates that the concept of reconciliation is still very important in Thai culture.

EXEGESIS OF THE BIBLICAL CONCEPT OF RECONCILIATION

I will present here a meta-cultural exegesis of the biblical concept of reconciliation. I will employ the theological work of Robert S. Schreiter, a C.P.P.S. American Theologian, William Barclay, a Scottish New Testament interpreter, Clarence B. Bass, an American Professor of Systematic Theology, and my own work, that of a Thai missiologist and theologian. Schreiter also references a German theologian of New Testament, Cilliers Breytenbach:

> Cilliers Breytenbach has argued recently that the usages in the authentic Pauline passages in Romans 5 and 2 Corinthians 5 are not connected with the older biblical ideas of atonement, but reflect a more secular usage, namely, a making of peace after a time of war (1992:42).

I think Breytenbach's idea elucidates human reconciliation in a way which can be easily understood by non-Christians. Making reference to Latin American liberation theologian Jose Comblin, Schreiter notes:

> Combining the references in Romans and 2 Corinthians with the usages in Colossians and Ephesians, Jose Comblin has suggested that a theology of reconciliation can be discerned on three levels: a christological level, in which Christ is the mediator through whom God reconciles the world to God's self; an ecclesiological level, in which Christ reconciles Jew and Gentile; and a cosmic level, in which Christ reconciles all the powers in heaven and on earth. (1992:42)

Robert J. Schreiter condenses the exegesis of the New Testament texts regarding reconciliation into five points: (1) it is God who initiates and brings about reconciliation; (2) reconciliation is more a spirituality than a strategy; (3) reconciliation makes both victim and oppressor a new creation; (4) the new narrative that overcomes the narrative of the lie is the story of passion, death and resurrection of Jesus Christ; (5) reconciliation is a multidimensional reality.

I have clarified the first three points in the "Theoretical Framework" section of this paper, but have not touched on the fourth and fifth. Schreiter beautifully interprets the meaning of passion, cross, death and the resurrection of Jesus Christ. God illustrated his passion when He incarnated Himself into the suffering, violence and death of humanity through his death on the cross. Human blood brings death; God's blood brings life. Jesus' resurrection heralds "new status" for all mankind, both victims and oppressors.

Schreiter also notes that reconciliation goes beyond problem solving. Reconciliation heals otherness and alienation, as stated in Romans 9-11,God reconciles Jews and Gentiles. Reconciliation includes all things in heaven and on earth (Colossians 1:19-20, Ephesians 1:9-10). Reconciliation, therefore, takes on a cosmic dimension. I think Schreiter has given us a cornerstone for the exegesis of the biblical concept of reconciliation.

William Barclay's exegesis confirms the first four points of Schreiter's conclusion. Barclay believes that God initiates reconciliation. It is completely by grace. The death of Christ changes our status with God. Christ's resurrection changes our state. Christ's justification puts us into a right relationship with God. Christ's sanctification affects our state. We can experience God's continuous saving grace (1975:75-77). Barclay's exegesis seems to emphasize a specific dimension of reconciliation, that of God-man relationship.

Clarence B. Bass exegetes terminology regarding reconciliation. The exegesis is much more detailed than that of Barclay. However, the conclusion is the same in its lack of reference to social reconciliation, individual reconciliation and cosmic reconciliation.

I, myself, exegete "reconciliation" differently. As a believer from Asia, I prefer to exegete the deep meaning of "reconciliation" from life stories. In this paper, I want to explore the reconciliation process recorded in the story of Joseph and his brothers in Genesis 37-47 and the story of Peter's reconciliation with Jesus in John 21. I see in these two incidents some structures similar to Schreiter's exegesis of "reconciliation:"

1) It is God who initiated the reconciliation. Probably, Joseph met God on the road to Egypt. He was a changed man while in Egypt; God was with him (Gen. 39:3, 5, 21, 23). Jesus is God who incarnated Himself into Jewish culture.
2) Reconciliation is more a spirituality than a strategy. Joseph and Jesus encountered betrayal from someone whom they loved. Both of them experienced pain, violence and injustice. However, they forgave. They took initiative in the reconciliation process. They confronted their oppressors. The causes of problems were clarified.
3) Reconciliation makes both victims and oppressors a new creation. Joseph's brothers were changed. Joseph was changed. Peter became a pillar of the early church. Jesus, the Victim, became the Victor.
4) The new narrative that overcomes the narrative of betrayal is the narrative of atonement. Suffering begets life and liberation. Death brings life.
5) Reconciliation is a multidimensional reality. Individual reconciliation between Joseph and his brothers affects the clan and the nation. Peter's reconciliation affects the community, various nations, the world and the cosmos as the gospel spreads out. Reconciliation is holistic. It affects the material world, relational world and spiritual world.
6) Reconciliation confirms that God's image remains in all cultures (Gen. 1:27). People had reconciled through God's image before Christ came.

It seems to me that the exegesis of meta-cultural theologians provides strong ground for the claim that the Thai ritual of reconciliation is biblical.

A Critical Response

Through various seminars I have discussed the concepts involved in the Thai ritual of reconciliation with approximately one hundred missionaries to Thailand. Most agree that the Thai ritual of reconciliation is biblical and it can be contextualized. Thai Buddhists unanimously suggest that Christians use this ritual in discipling. Most Thai Christian leaders like the Thai ritual of reconciliation. Though few missionaries express concern about the use of symbolic objects, their use remains the only area of question. We are now ready to look at the contextualization of the ritual of reconciliation and its ability to bond new converts to their families.

NEW CONTEXTUALIZED PRACTICE

On the basis of the frameworks and exegesis of Scripture, I believe that the concepts of reconciliation in the Thai *kama* and *ahosikarma* ritual can be stepping stones in Thai culture for the understanding of Christ as the Reconciler. I also believe that it can heal the broken relationship between new Buddhist converts (as well as old Buddhist converts) and their social networks. The contextualization of this ritual into a Christian *kama* and *ahosikarma* ritual must, therefore, be designed to help the new converts bond to their natural social networks and Christ, the Reconciler. This study will now lay out a Christian *kama* and *ahosikarma* ritual.

THE CHRISTIAN RITUAL OF RECONCILIATION, KAMA AND AHOSIKARMA

As a rite of passage, the Christian ritual of *kama* and *ahosikarma* is divided into three stages: (1) separation, (2) liminality, and (3) reincorporation.

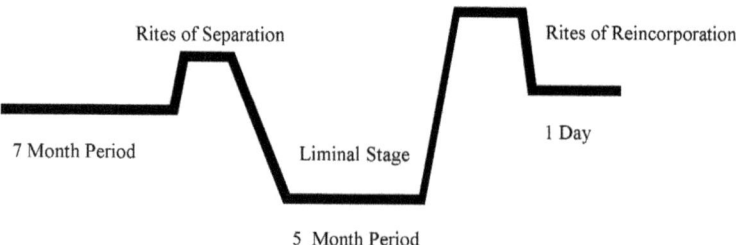

Figure 4: The Rites of Passage Structure of the Christian Ritual of Reconciliation

According to the figure above, the rite of separation and the liminal stage take one year. Due to the Thai's value of grateful relationships and smooth interpersonal relationships, and the Thai's flexibility and adjustment orientation, the prolonged time provides a shock-absorber, allowing the new converts to throw away their idols and to tell their parents of their conversion to Christianity. These are acts of separation from Buddhism. At the same time, the prolonged time provides a shock absorber for the parents when informed by their children of this important separation. During the liminal stage, the prolonged time allows the initiates to be bonded to the meaning of reconciliation to other persons, to God, to cultural communities, and to Christian communities, thus allowing them to be both Thais and Christians. This will result in a good identity for the new converts. They will grow as Thais and Christians because they will have good relational ties with their natural and cultural social networks, as well as with their Christian communities. They will have sound identity and good roots.

Due to the importance of this issue, I would like to concentrate on the bonding of the new converts to their relatives in each phase of the rite of passage in the *kama* and *ahosikarma* ritual. I will discuss this bonding within the context of the ritual of *kama* and *ahosikarma* as recorded in the event mentioned above. Moreover, I will use the nine value clusters of the Thai, their concepts of hierarchy, cyclical time and being, and their activity as a framework for the stages of separation, liminality and reincorporation.

The Rites of Separation in the Christian Ritual of Reconciliation, *kama* and *ahosikarma*:

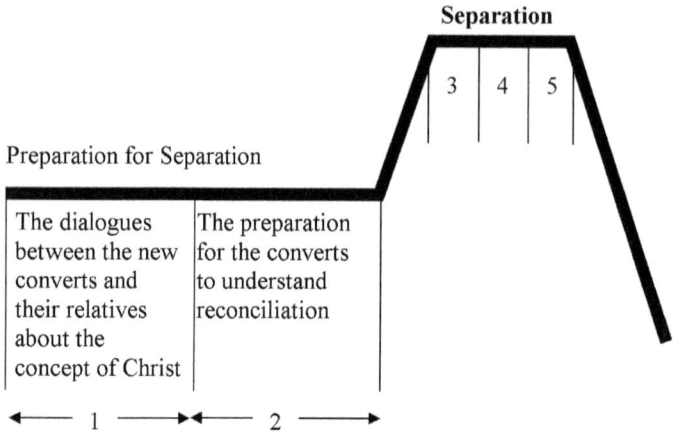

Figure 5: The Rites of Separation

There are five steps in the rite of separation: (1) the religious dialogues between the new converts and their relatives about Christ and the church, (2) the preparation for the new converts to understand the concept of reconciliation, (3) putting away idols, (4) informing the families of the conversion and (5) negotiating for confession and forgiveness. The religious dialogue between the new converts and their relatives is an important foundation for the Christian ritual of reconciliation, *kama* and *ahosikarma*.

Religious dialogue demands trust, respect and love for parents on the part of the new converts. According to the apostle John,

There is no fear in love; but perfect love casts out fear, because fear involves punishment, and the one who fears is not perfected in love. We love because He first loved us. (John 4:18-20)

This kind of attitude will help the new converts to communicate their contact with Christianity to their parents from the very beginning. This style of the communication will be effective only when it fits Thai cultural values. The parents will feel respected, trusted and loved if the new converts ask for permission to go to the church and report what they learn from the church. The parents are willing to discuss religion with their children because the children's behavior indicates that they cherish the parents' identity, their concept of hierarchy, grateful relationship orientation, smooth interpersonal relationship orientation and interdependence orientations.

The new converts should also encourage Christians who are well aware of Thai culture to get to know their social networks. This will ease the fear and anxiety of Thai parents and help them to have a clearer view of Christians. They have various myths about Christians and churches. These myths should be corrected through the Christians' goodness.

The new converts must pay attention to their family's problems and needs. They must co-operate with their relatives to solve these problems because collectivism is very important for the Thai. These behaviors will prevent new converts from alienating themselves from their relatives. They will also help bonding with relatives, and both sides will be prepared for the religious separation. The meekness and the vulnerability on the parts of the new converts will prepare their social networks to negotiate in the liminal stage, as well as the rite of reincorporation. The Liminal Stage of the Christian Ritual of Reconciliation: *kama* and *ahosikarma*:

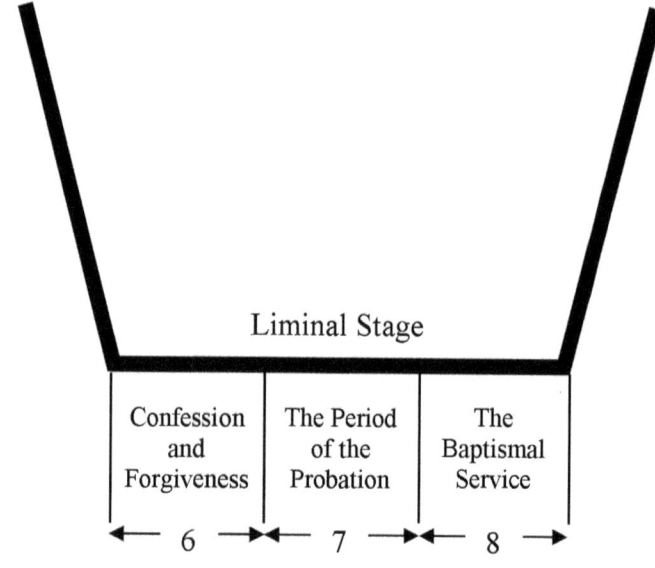

Figure 6: The Liminal Stage

The liminal stage creates deeper bonding between the new converts and their social networks. The bonding is divided into three steps: (6) confession and forgiveness, (7) the period of the probation, and (8) the baptismal service.

The first step is the formal act of confession, in which the new converts who bring shame to their immediate families and relatives ask for forgiveness and bow down at the feet or their parents. The meekness in communication, the sacred indigenous objects, and the sacred ceremony speak to the hearts and minds of the Thai, allowing them to respond positively to the new converts.

This ritual of confession and forgiveness provides ways for the parents and relatives to vent their anguish, anger, frustration, disappointment, and concern before they proceed further to truly grant forgiveness to the new converts. Their forgiveness is the action of reciprocity. When the new converts take the initiative to value the interdependent orientation in Thai culture by asking for forgiveness, they show respect for Thai culture and their parents' pain. As a result, the parents respect their decision to convert. A Thai poem states clearly the importance of interdependency in Thai culture.

> Tigers are tigers because of jungles;
> Jungles are jungles because of tigers.
> Soil is soil because of good grasses;
> Grasses are grasses because of good soil.
> (Praya Sri Sunthorn Woharn 1962)

Respecting interdependency creates bonds between new converts and their social networks. The bonding will go deeper in the periods of probation and baptismal service.

In the period of probation (Fig 6, No. 7), the families receive back their authority over the new converts. They will set criteria together with the local churches for the new converts to prove their accountability in preparation for their baptism. Thai culture perceives and defines 'activity' as *being* rather than *doing*. Therefore, the families will require the accountability of being from the new converts, and will be very happy that they can maintain their authority over them. If the new converts submit themselves to the families' authority, there will be deeper bonding because Thai culture requires the authority to be merciful to the submissive. As a famous Thai proverb suggests:

> The meek bow down with burden;
> They shall be blessed at the end. (Ngamdee 1993:36)

This bonding will prepare the parents and relatives for the baptismal service. This is one of the most difficult times for the convert and their families (Fig. 6, No. 8).

At this stage, liminality will soon end for the new converts, but suffering is at its peak for the new converts' parents and relatives. The bonding will go deepest if the new converts are sensitive to the pain of the parents because, from their viewpoint, the baptismal service signifies a complete separation from Buddhism and a full identification with Christianity. The children can comfort the parents in attitude and in action according to the Thai value of grateful relationship orientation. In Thai culture, gratitude is expressed through obedience, serving and giving.

As the baptismal service approaches, the new converts should dialog with their social networks about the concept of death and resurrection. In doing so, they should use stepping-stones, such as familiar experiences in daily living and familiar concepts in Buddhism. Eliade suggests that the moon symbolizes death and resurrection (1987:156-157). Wit Wissawate lectured that, in Buddhism, life is a continuous death and rebirth like electricity (1967). This will help social networks to understand the deep religious meaning of the ritual and they will be more appreciative because the Thai are religiously oriented. They should be led to understand the ritual not as a departure from Buddhism but as a fulfillment of Buddhist self-emptying. The baptismal service should symbolize the perfect bonding to the concept of self-emptying in Buddhism through Christ. The families should be invited officially to attend the ritual. Now the process of this Christian ritual of reconciliation takes us to the rites of reincorporation.

The Rites of Reincorporation of the Christian Ritual of Reconciliation, *kama* and *ahosikarma*:

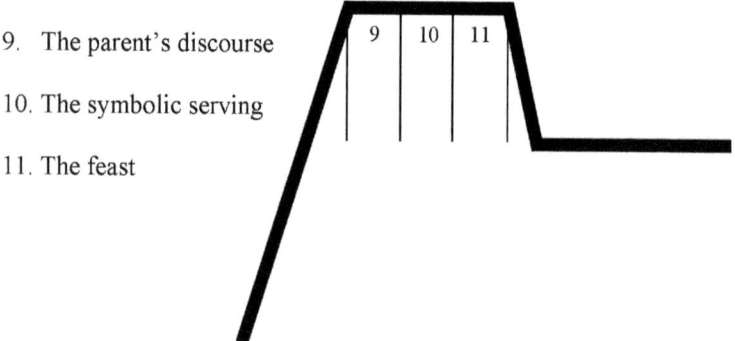

9. The parent's discourse

10. The symbolic serving

11. The feast

Figure 7: The Rites of Reincorporation

The rites of reincorporation are divided into three steps: (9) the parents' discourse, (10) the symbolic serving, and (11) the feast.

The bonding between the social networks and the new converts takes place in the first step. The parents are invited to give words of wisdom, which urge their children to fulfill their Christian duties to their families, communities and nation. The Thai like participating in formal ceremonies because of their value of hierarchy. If invited officially, they will usually agree to participate in religious ceremonies.

The feast provides another chance for bonding. The parents should be sat at the head of the table with their children, the other elderly relatives and the church elders. The food being served should symbolize bonding and blessings. The rites of reincorporation end in joy and fellowship, but the bonding continues, as well as the discipling of the new converts.

The bonding between the new converts and their social networks is not a sideline. It is their lifeline and it lasts as long as their life. If the bonding is life-long, the discipling of the new converts will last, and the church will have both strong Christians and good friends who are candidates for the kingdom. This indicates the effectiveness of the ritual.

The Effectiveness of the Christian Ritual of Reconciliation, *Kama* and *Ahosikarma*

The ritual is likely to be effective because it creates bonding between the new converts and their social networks throughout the whole process. As a result, the new converts are not cut off from their cultural roots. The problem of their crisis in self-identity is solved and discipling becomes possible.

The ritual trusts God, the parents and the relatives of the new converts. Thais value ego orientation very highly, making respect and trust very important ethical issues for them. Christians cherish the Thai self-identity, self-esteem and self-respect.

This ritual accentuates six of the nine Thai value clusters: ego orientation, grateful relationship orientation, smooth interpersonal relationship orientation, flexibility and adjustment orientation, and interdependence orientation, as well as fun-pleasure orientation.

The Thai will respond to this much more than to the old model of aggressive evangelism.

This Christian ritual of reconciliation, *kama* and *ahosikarma*, fits the Thai's concept of time and hierarchy, allowing Christians to be viewed as humble, meek, gentle and vulnerable, each of which is a religious model for Jesus' disciples. This is an effective way to win Thai hearts. As an ancient Thai poem says, "Be soft as a silk thread and tie a tiger down" (anonymous).

This ritual of reconciliation has been tested in at least three local churches. The results have been positive. People did not detect syncretism in the contextualization of the Christian ritual of reconciliation. I believe this ritual can be effectively used to heal memories of pain, violence, injustice and oppression in war-torn countries like Laos, Cambodia and Vietnam.

Conclusion

This study presents what is perhaps the core problem for Christianity in Thailand: the relational bonds between new converts and their natural social networks are broken; as a result, the new converts lose their identity as Thais and become weak Christians; the parents and relatives thus turn against the church and become strong enemies of Christian conversion. This study has determined the cause of this problem to be the violation of Thai cultural values. It has pointed out that Thai culture uses the ritual *kama* and *ahosikarma* to heal such broken relationships. This Thai ritual can be contextualized to become a Christian ritual of reconciliation and resolve the problem mentioned above. The study has demonstrated that the ritual is a rite of passage and has given the ritual's respect for Thai values as evidence for its potential effectiveness. The study thus concludes that the Christian ritual of reconciliation, *kama* and *ahosikarma*, can be a means to solve the problem of the church gaining one weak Christian, yet many strong enemies, with each new convert. It will provide an effective means for helping new converts to be reconciled to their culture and to understand "reconciliation" itself.

6

A Day in the Life of a Sinhala Buddhist Family and its Relevance for the Evangelical Christian

G.P.V. Somaratna

Buddhism in Sri Lanka is primarily of the Theravada school, and constitutes the religious faith of about seventy percent of the population. According to Sri Lankan chronicles, Venerable Mahinda introduced Buddhism into Sri Lanka in the third century BC from North India (Geiger 1993:68). The Buddhists believe that the Buddha visited Sri Lanka three times in his life time to bless the nation (Geiger 1993:5). Ever since, Buddhism has been the main driving force of the culture of the Sinhala people.

Buddhists express their faith in different ways. The popular Buddhism and intellectual Buddhism take two different paths in their religious practices. The core of their faith, however, remains the same. One can also notice local differences in the practice of religion in the various districts of the country. However, for the majority, it is more of a way of life than a philosophical understanding as expressed in Buddhist texts. Some Buddhists wish to restrict the designation "Buddhism" exclusively to the teachings of the Buddhist scriptures, which are usually interpreted in an intellectual manner (Kantipala 1982:20-24). On the other hand, the practices and observances of popular Buddhism claim an integral place in the practices of the majority of its adherents.

Side by side with the intellectually sophisticated Buddhism of the texts, we find in Sri Lanka a warm current of devotional Buddhism, mixed with Hinduism and animism. A complex of ceremonies, rituals, and devotional practices that are not be found in the canonical texts bridges the average person's world of everyday experience.

The Sinhala Buddhist lay community has accumulated a large body of popular beliefs and religious rituals that are tolerated by Buddhist monks and integrated into their belief system. Many of the features of this popular religion have come both from Hindu practices and from ancient local traditions of regional deities and demons. Sinhalese Buddhism is thus a syncretistic fusion of various religious elements forming into a unique cultural system. Since its introduction in the sixteenth century, the Roman Catholic faith has also had an influence on the day-to-day practices of popular Buddhism. Similarly since the nineteenth century Protestant Christianity also has had an impact on Buddhist practices. All such inputs have enriched the popular expression of Buddhism (Perera 1988:100).

The Buddhist monastic community is divided into a number of orders with different styles of discipline. It is interesting to note that divisions of the order do not in anyway hinder the religious practices of the laity. They freely move from one temple to another without regard for sectarian differences of the monks.

There are many aids to practice Buddhism for the lay people in Sri Lanka. The daily practice of Buddhism has a large component of exterior forms. There are numerous practices popular among Sri Lankan Buddhist families in their daily religious life. However, there are some rituals which are common to everyone. One would notice that the popular Buddhism with its shamanistic associations is oriented more towards healing and prosperity while the canonical Buddhism teaches salvation, morals and ethics. These two arms of Buddhism are visible in the worldview of the Sinhala Buddhist (Huxley, 1995:47-95).

This paper will confine its subject matter to some aspects of daily Buddhist practices with a view to finding their relevance to Christian evangelism. Although many other practices of Buddhism may be useful to the evangelist we have been forced to limit our discussion strictly to the common daily religious activities of the Sinhala Buddhist. Therefore, we have left out life cycle events, feasts

A Day in the Life of a Sinhala Buddhist Family

and festivals and occasional religious rituals such as pilgrimages. In the first part of this paper, we shall identify the Buddhist practices we find in contemporary society. In the second part, our attention will be drawn to analyzing their usability to the evangelist.

FAMILY

The vast majority of Buddhists are lay people who live in and maintain close relations with immediate and extended families (Weeraratne 1996:220). The Buddhist family has, in general, common values, which are prescribed by their common faith. They also have many of the same goals such as living a pious life and endeavoring to attain nirvana and to avoid bad *karma* (Malalasekera 1999:22; Weeraratne 1996:218). The common religion establishes a broad base of commonalities and doctrines called *dharma* to guide the religious behavior of the Buddhist. All of them believe the concepts of *karma* and *samsara*. Likewise, they perceive moral and ethical conditions in the same way by benchmarking them against the *dharma* (Jones 1989:61).

Canonical Buddhism does not espouse any particular form of the family or family relationships. The traditional Sinhalese Buddhist family is patriarchal and there are clearly defined familial roles. The Buddha even emphasizes that the order of nuns should be subject to the authority of monks. The degrees of relationships, which govern marriage, are clearly defined in the Sinhala vocabulary of kinship.

Buddhism's primary contribution to the family consists of five ethical prescriptions known as the Five Precepts. They are binding ethical mandates promoting personal virtues. These precepts govern social and interpersonal relationships and provide an ethical framework for family life. They are chanted in family devotions and public ceremonies. The Buddhists feel affection for their families and maintains close contact with a broad range of relatives, especially on occasions of major religious festivals and family celebrations.

In the *Sigalovada Sutra* (teaching) the Buddha described social relationships in terms of six directions; the four compass directions being East defined as parents, South as teachers, West as wife, and

North as friends and colleagues, and the two vertical directions being: Up as Brahmins and ascetics and Down as the servants. This text elaborated on how one should respect and support the six categories of persons and, in turn, the manner in which the six would return the kindness and support. Apart from this, the Buddha or Buddhist texts give no specific instructions on marriage and family life. There is, however, a great deal of Buddhist commentaries offering advice on how marital and family life can be lived happily (Ediriweera 2000:64; Narada 1984:4; Weeraratne 1996:220). The *Maha-mangala Sutra*, which is chanted by Buddhist media every morning, also encourages the duty to support one's parents, wife, children and relatives as noble. From the beginning of the twentieth century, the Buddhist leaders through the *daham pasal* system, which is explained later, have encouraged Buddhists to read and follow the instructions given in this *Sutra*.

Father and mother take upon themselves the responsibility to teach their children the religion of their ancestors. However, in practice the fathers may take a lesser role or no role at all, very often giving the excuse of being hard at work. But they give every encouragement to the wife to perform the rituals. However, the entire family may not take part in the religious rituals simultaneously (Kariyawasam, 1995:10).

Mothers train girls and boys in their childhood to attend to religious rituals. One may find boys more enthusiastic in their tender age than girls, but most boys eventually become less active in the religious rituals of the home environment. Yet they help the females and also resort to religious rituals in times of crisis.

Learning of Religion

In our interviews of people from very old age to youth in various parts of the island we have noticed that the majority of them have had some form of institutional instruction of Buddhism. It is no exaggeration to say that none of them can be considered ignorant of the basics tenets of their religion. Broadly speaking most Buddhists learn their religion in several ways from childhood.

A Day in the Life of a Sinhala Buddhist Family

The first source of learning is the Buddhist family, which usually takes the responsibility to transmit the message of Buddhist religion to the next generation. The second is the *daham pasala*, which is usually held on Sundays. The third is the regular school where Buddhism is taught at elementary and secondary levels to prepare students for national examinations. The fourth is the cultural milieu and mass media which impress the religious consciousness in the people. In addition to these four ways the religious festivals and ceremonies conducted by the Buddhist monastery (*viharas*) always act as communicating religious rituals to the people. The people's religious awareness enables them to distinguish popular Buddhism from the intellectual Buddhism. Nevertheless, they typically subscribe to both areas of Buddhism.

The religious educational establishment known as *Daham pasala* is a new innovation. It became a national level institution after the setting up of the ministry of Buddhism in 1990, and has contributed to the coordination of teaching, ceremonies and maintenance of Buddhist temples. Most of the religious practices found today owe their origin to this period. The older generation of Buddhists did not practice the daily worship of parents or chant so many stanzas (*gathas*) and Buddhist chants (*pirit*) as they do now. The watchword of the All Ceylon Buddhist Congress has been, "Let us restore Buddhism to its rightful place." Therefore, the conscious effort on the part of Buddhist leaders has raised the awareness of Buddhism of the population to a very high level.

Daham pasala, *sil* (or morality), *pirit*, and *bana* (or preaching) ceremonies are social events that help the families to teach their children Buddhist rituals. In addition radio, TV, and newspapers also contribute to the enhancement of knowledge of Buddhism.

The Buddhist environment of the country comprising of monks, temples, *vihara* monuments and tradition encourages the practice of Buddhism. There are many books published by numerous organizations and individuals to help Buddhists to practice their religion daily. There are several radio stations which chant *pirit* and preach short and long sermons every day. The TV stations also contribute in the same manner. There is a Buddhist channel where Buddhist teaching is done in the Sinhala and English languages.

Buddhist education demands large amount of their beliefs to be committed to memory. This is done through chanting of *gatha, pirit* and liturgy. It is constantly reminded by repeated usage. Therefore, the Buddhist of any educational background is aware of the basic teachings of the religion.

The times of getting up for the Sinhala Buddhist varied, although average Buddhist begins the day before the daybreak. There is unanimity with regard to certain actions they do in the morning before embarking on any other important event of the day. Some people utter an expression like *namo buddhaya* ("I salute the Buddha") as they get out of bed. One of the important religious acts that they do in the morning, as they wake up, is to go to the household shrine which is either inside or outside the house. Some families have the shrine with the statue of the Buddha inside the house while the one for gods is placed outside. In these altars the most prominent is the statue or a picture of the Buddha. Buddhists begin their day with religious devotion. Most of the religious activities in the home take place around the household shrine.

HOUSEHOLD SHRINE

Most common in all Buddhist traditions is the household shrine. It is found among almost every Buddhist home in Sri Lanka irrespective of social class. It plays a pivotal role in their daily devotions. The appearance of the shrine differs from house to house. The well-to-do may have a separate building adjoining the house as the place of worship. Some have a separate room inside the house set aside for their daily devotions or an area curtained off from the rest of the room for religious worship. Average people have a special shelf high on the wall where an image of the Buddha or a picture is placed. Most families have a small place set aside for it in the sitting room area on a place higher than the level of a person's head as they sit facing it. On this shelf they place their offerings.

The primary place in the shrine is given to the Buddha statue. If unable to acquire a statue a picture of the Buddha is used. The Buddhist offers the highest seat in the house to the Buddha,

A Day in the Life of a Sinhala Buddhist Family

therefore it is placed high on the wall or on an elevated pedestal. The Buddha statue is always an object of worship and never treated as an ornament. Nothing noticeable is placed above the shrine. In case the shrine is in a room where people sleep people always place their head towards the shrine. The Buddhist children are taught to treat Buddha images as one would the Buddha himself.

If there are other images in the shrine the image of the Buddha takes the central place. The others are treated as lower than the Buddha. Other Buddhist personalities, which would be displayed in the shrine, would be Sariputta and Moggallana[1] who were two chief disciples of the Buddha. The shrine is intended for household devotions. There is space in front of the shrine for the family to kneel down to worship. It is where the family members chant stanzas in the posture of kneeling. When they meditate they have a special sitting posture.

Beside the shrine they use pictures of famous *stupas* (bell-shaped masonry monument designed as a Buddhist shrine or reliquary), the Temple of the Tooth at Kandy or the sacred *Bodhi*-tree at Anuradhapura as a focus of veneration. A picture of Seevali *Thera* (venerable senior monks) also may be found in many houses. His picture or statue is seen in many a house, trade stall and work place. It is placed above the front door because of the belief that it would safeguard the supply of food to the house.

Many people have pictures of gods on either side of the Buddha statue. Normally, they do not have statues of gods. Some families keep the pictures of gods somewhat below the statue of the Buddha. Among the Theravada Buddhists female deities, such as Lakshmi, Saraswathi, Kali and Pattini receive homage (Obeyesekere 1984:59-60). Their favors are sought daily for prosperity as well as in times of adversity.

The Buddhists worship gods who are in the Buddhist pantheon. Their four guardian deities are Vishnu, Kataragama, Saman and Pattini. Kataragama is more popular as he is believed to bring prosperity to the family. In addition to the national gods of the

---

1. Sariputta and Moggallana were the two chief disciples of the Buddha.

Buddhist pantheon there are local deities of the village level. Some people worship local gods who are regarded as guardian deities of the village. Some families have pictures of such gods in the household shrine usually outside the house. People also believe that these gods can be vindictive if a person does not keep his promises to them. There are homes where the shrine includes a row of pictures of gods. Saraswathi, Pulleyar, Aiyanayake, Natha, and Kali are among gods and goddesses who are popular in various districts of the Island (Wickremeratne, 2006:227).

Besides the household shrine, almost all Buddhist business premises have a shrine. Rituals performed in such places would not be as elaborate as that of home. There are shrines in schools, hospitals, and government department offices and so on where some kind of religious observance would take place. Public buses and trains also have Buddhists shrines. Some Buddhists have a statue of the Buddha and picture of a god in their vehicles. While travelling in a vehicle some devotees rise from their seats as a mark of respect to a Buddha statue or a *Bodhi*-tree (Kornfield 1996:113). Today, there is a proliferation of statues in public places. Therefore this habit is limited to the main shrines. If it is a long journey there are places where travelers may get down from their vehicles and offer coins or other offerings known as *panduru*.

None of these shrines can be regarded as ornaments. All of them receive veneration. The Buddhists claim that shrines placed even in public transport vehicles give them a sense of security.

WORSHIP AT THE HOUSEHOLD SHRINE

Families conduct daily religious services before their Buddha shrine. It is customary to wash at least one's face before approaching the altar to worship and make offerings. This is regarded as a sign of respect for the objects represented there. During the worship, members of the family make devotional offerings of food, flowers, candles, and incense to the Buddha. The rituals may vary from simply placing a glass of water to offering a host of other items (Khantipalo 1982:6-

7). These pious activities may continue as acts of ritual and with great religious enthusiasm and respect. Many devotees believe that they will be successful in their daily work by worshiping in this manner at the family altar. Chanting of the three refuges and the five precepts would complete the religious ritual. The day of the Buddhist begin early in the morning very much like their Hindu neighbor. The religious devotions take place very often before they have breakfast.

Various people conduct personal devotions according to their preference. Usually the three refuges and five precepts are chanted at the beginning. The average Buddhist chants the five precepts every morning. Some people chant *pirit* for five to ten minutes. There are others who meditate for about five minutes in the morning after worshipping the Buddha. After everything is over they end it with a blessing saying 'May all beings be healthy, healed and without pain.' In addition they also recite several stanzas. One stanza is used for worshiping the Buddha, another for offering flowers, and yet another to transfer merit to dead relatives and gods. All these rituals take place in front of the household shrine.

According to tradition it is customary to offer a bowl of water, flowers, candles or oil lamps, and incense to the Buddha image in the shrine. In rare instances it is customary in some families to offer food and drink at the shrine on a daily basis. Some devotees stated that they do not do this ritual everyday as the inability to do it one day would bring about ill fortune to the family. All of them, however, stated that they make food and drink offering on special occasions. The purpose of making offerings is not merely to accumulate merit. It is a way of obtaining protection for the day.

The collection of flowers in the morning is an important act in a typical Buddhist home. Some people plant flower plants mainly for offering. Other goes out in the street to collect them from neighboring gardens. Taking flowers from other people's gardens without permission is not regarded as theft in the Buddhist society as it is done for a pious purpose. The person who planted them would also receive merit from the *puja* (offering of items).

Worship of Parents

Buddhists worship their parents. Most children do it every day. Others do it when the parents come to their home or they visit the parents. There are two separate *gatha* they use to worship the mother and father. This ritual receives the encouragement of radio broadcast and television display everyday.

The worship of parents takes an important place in the daily activities of Buddhists. The children worship their parents in the morning before they go to school. A lesser number worship their parents when they return home. In addition, some worship their parents before going to bed. This habit is promoted by *daham pasala* schools and temples. The children get a satisfaction by worshiping their parents. They have indicated that they have missed something if they are unable to do it on a particular day. The parents in return lay hands and bless the children by saying "may the triple gem be with you" or "may the gods protect you." Some parents kiss their children after they worship them. These rituals are continued even after school-going age is passed.

Other occasions where parents are worshipped would be religious or national festival days. When there is a family ceremony in addition to the parents the other elders present are also worshipped. A newly married couple would worship their parents first, then the elder members of the family and other relatives. The worship of the parents is the most important. When a younger brother visits with his family of a home of an elder brother the younger one would worship his brother and his wife. If the father and mother in law are present they also would receive similar treatment. When a person kneels before an elder, there is a practice of blessing by laying hands. The blessing will be continued with the words "*budu saranayi*" (May the Buddha be your refuge).

The tradition of worshipping one's parents is an old one. However, the frequency of worshipping parents has increased recently. The generation who are sixty years old and above did not have the habit of worshipping the parents daily unless in rare instances where the parents were extremely pious. But today parents teach the children from their tender age to worship them.

The tradition of worship of parents and one's elders clearly teaches the younger generation to respect the elders. Because they also worship schoolteachers there is a respect to their teachers. Such respect enables the elders to discipline the younger generation. There are numerous instances within the Buddhist scriptures where the Buddha enjoins his disciples to honor father and mother.

REVERENCE

The honor and respect to elders regulated the general norm of the varied relationships between different members of the family. Reverence is a part of Buddhist teaching found in the *Dharmapada* (Thanissaro 1997:31). The *Mahamangala Sutra* (Narada 2007:160-161), which is often chanted by way of a *pirit*, inculcates these habits. Reverence is offered to the Buddhist monks, parents, teachers and elders of the family. Therefore, the students stand when the teacher comes to the class. When the parents, teachers, elders or monks come to their presence the students get up from the seat in order to respect them. Neglect of these practices would cause offence. Honoring the elders of honorable positions is a practice that the Buddhists regularly adhere to.

Buddhist culture makes a clear distinction between the sacred and the profane. This is mirrored in the language referring to sacred personalities and institutions. They use the most honorable language to refer to the Buddha. Disregard of such language conveying honor would be offensive and may even provoke anger. Buddhists have a different vocabulary when it comes to religious establishments and personalities. For example, an ordinary man's eating is called '*kanava*'; but the same action by a Buddhist monk's is '*valandanava*.' Offering food to monks it is done respectfully using both hands.

Similarly, they respect their elders, teachers and other dignitaries. They have different words in addressing such people. Buddhist monks, nuns, parents and elder brothers and sisters are treated with honor and respect by offering their veneration. These members were treated with honor and respect even though they were on the periphery of the proper family. If something is given to an elder it is always with the right hand, with the left hand clasping the right elbow. Elders were treated with high esteem and received respect depending on their relative seniority.

In the ritualistic form of worship the flowers are respectfully placed on the altar in front of a statue of the Buddha or any place of religious significance. The devotees clasp their hands in a respectful gesture of worship. They solemnly repeat various stanzas and formulas. When they refer to Buddhist scripture or objects of worship like a *Bodhi* tree or a statue they add the honorific epithet '*vahanse*' (venerable). Religious establishments such as a Buddhist temple or Hindu temple (called *devale*) would be approached with utmost respect (De Silva 1974:127). The *Dharmapada*, a post-canonical commentary, elaborating on the canonically identified meritorious triad of *dana-sila-bhavana* states that lay devotees can make merit by honoring others (Thanissaro 1997:29).

Beliefs and Practices Concerning Food

After religious rituals in the morning the Buddhists take their breakfast. There is no special law governing food in Buddhism. However, the extremely pious Buddhists do not take meat or eggs. There are others who do not consume these items only on the days that they observe *sil*. There are some who have special dislike of pork and beef.

Since the first precept of Buddhism prohibits killing of any being they have been averse to killing animals for food. In recent times, there is a strong movement within the Buddhist populace against the consumption of beef. Pious Buddhists even go to the extent of redeeming the cattle brought in for slaughter. The rearing of animals for food is treated as something sordid.

Since there are other traditions regarding the intake of food Buddhists do not like to consume food in public. They do not like outsiders to see them eating as they fear that it would cause stomach ailments if it is witnessed by a person who had not been able to have food that day. Children are asked to consume their food inside the house. For this reason nursing-mothers do not feed their babies for others to see.

A Day in the Life of a Sinhala Buddhist Family

PRETA

There are taboos and ideas of pollution with regard to the intake of food. Preta is a ghost associated with hunger, described in Buddhist texts as a being that undergoes more than human suffering, particularly extreme degree of hunger and thirst (Obeyesekere 1984:40). The *Buddha puja* offered at the family shrine are normally given to Preta after it is removed from the altar. Some people regularly set aside a very small part of their meal to Preta in order to avoid any ailment arising from the food they partake. A small portion of food is set-aside for Preta on special occasions such as *dana* (or donation) ceremony or a wedding feast. When the first rice is prepared from a new harvest some cooked rice is placed on a tray with a coconut oil lamp for Preta. It will be placed on a higher elevation for the crows and other birds to eat. Food offered to demons and *spirits* is placed on a special tray made out of coconut leaves. The tray would have rice, fried items and other food. Sometimes, a raw egg also will be placed.

There are three ways that lay Buddhists offer food to religious objects. The *Buddha puja* is always done at home. The second is the offering to the gods of Buddhist pantheon. They are done only at the temples dedicated to a particular god. Normally the tray of fruits is taken to offer to gods. No cooked rice or meat will be offered to gods.

The third is the offering made to *spirits*. They can be malevolent or benevolent. They are offered fried items, meat, cooked rice, eggs and occasionally blood of a fowl. These trays are placed at public junctions early morning before day break. If there are flowers offered in the tray they would normally be red flowers.

GOOD AND BAD OMENS

The Sinhala Buddhists have clear-cut beliefs regarding good and bad omens. But more attention is given to bad ones, as they have to be avoided. There are traditionally accepted items and creatures, which are portent.

Leaving home for work is also an important daily activity where some religious ritual may be found. The household gecko is also treated as a bad omen. The Sinhala almanac gives a special attention to the behavior of a gecko. They would not normally go out of the house if a gecko makes a noise at the time of departure. Similarly, the sound of a woodpecker is a considered a bad omen. If a dog howls at a time of a special event, the people consider it a bad omen. The hoot of a night owl is regarded as bad. Therefore, they are chased away. There is a long list of things that are considered bad. The acceptance of these omens will differ from person to person.

The first person one would see in the morning or one would meet first as he goes out of the house is regarded as a good or bad omen. Bad are Buddhist monks, nuns, barren women, widows or any other person who is regarded by the society as bad omen. Similarly, the first person who comes to a boutique to purchase something is important. Vendors would be displeased if the person is considered to be an inauspicious. A person carrying an empty pot, hoe or any other working tool is also regarded as bad omen in some parts of the country.

No matter how silly these may sound, they are realities to many Buddhists in villages and even in cities. There are numerous ways to avert these bad omens. In the case of meeting an inauspicious person first on the road, the party would return home and restart the journey. The same thing will be done with regard to the noise of a gecko. There are other ways to avoid an expected misfortune. Therefore, an important work or journey would be kept secret even under questioning.

Another mechanism that people adopt in order to avoid bad omens is purposely bring about good omens in order to achieve success. There are people who are considered to be good omens. Good omens such as married women with children, a person carrying a pot of water; the man who brings milk would be purposely introduced to meet the person embarking on an important project.

The evil eye is something they fear. For an example a new building still under construction can be seen carrying an effigy prominently placed in order to ward off evil.

Astrology

Astrology plays an important part in the daily life of a Buddhist. The Buddha himself, however, taught that one's future is conditioned primarily by one's karma, not by the stars. He condemned astrology and expressly forbade his monks and nuns to practice it. Despite this, astrology is widely believed and practiced by Buddhists in Sri Lanka and even some monks act as astrologers (Gombrich and Obeyesekere 1984:311). The Buddhists have overcome Buddha's injunction by treating the planets as a set of gods who are intimately connected with sicknesses and epidemics (Perera 2000:108).

Many Buddhists believe that the positions of celestial bodies and their movements either directly influence life on earth or correspond somehow to events experienced on a human scale. They consult astrologers for special activities. They carefully cast astrological chart or horoscope for each child based on the time of birth and consult it at times of difficulties and before marriage to check the astrological suitability of the partner. Some check their horoscope in the daily newspapers. Astrology lays down various rules for finding good days and times. The rules also specify which days to avoid. If an event is to be planned and done at an inauspicious time, then the astrologer gives remedial measures.

They avoid certain days for important work branding them as bad days. The good days of the week according to many of them are Thursdays and Fridays. Normally, Monday is regarded as an inauspicious day.

Every important activity is undertaken at an auspicious time with the help of the village astrologer. In addition, the almanac, which is found in every house, would also be used as a guide. When building a house they consult an astrologer for laying the foundation, or placement of the door and window frames, to come into occupation and so on. Auspicious times are now calculated to the exact minute. However, calculation to the exact minute was not possible before the introduction of the clock in the twentieth century.

Each day has a ninety-minute period called *Rahu Kaalam* which is believed to be an ill-omened time period of the day. During this time, one should avoid any auspicious action such as investments, business transactions, asset purchases, journeys, relationships, meetings and medical treatments. It is believed that work done during this period does not bring successful results.

Besides the general periods like *Rahu Kaalam* there are inauspicious times affecting individuals. They resort to Buddhist ritual practices to ward off ill effects of such bad times. They invite a monk to the house and offer a *dane*, get them to chant *pirit* (Perera 2000:93). Some would resort to performing *Bodhi* puja (Gombrich and Obeyesekere 1990:384-389). Some even go to a *devale* and seek the help of gods by making vows requesting gods to avert these dangers.

RITUALS AT THE END OF A NORMAL DAY

The majority of Buddhists perform some religious ritual before they go to bed. The rituals done in the morning may be repeated in the evening in some families. There is a habit of chanting five precepts and the stanza used for worshipping the Buddha at the end of the day. Various individuals have numerous rituals. Chanting of *Mahamangala Sutra*, *Maitri Bhavana* (meditation of compassion), stanzas and offering merit to deceased relatives are some of them. Some have the habit of worshipping the parents in addition to worshipping the Buddha.

When there are days that they are unable to do all these things the most important item will be given attention. Often they will worship the Buddha through a special chant called *Itipiso Gatha*. There are some Buddhists who meditate and chant the *gatha* while resting in bed.

DREAMS

The Buddhists sometimes see their deceased relatives in their dreams. Their reaction to such an event depends on their view of dreams. Some interpret it as a deceased person's way of asking for merit. On such occasions, in order to help the departed ones, they perform some meritorious deeds in memory of the departed ones. Such acts as giving alms to others, building schools, temples, orphanages, libraries, hospitals, printing religious books for free distribution and similar charitable deeds are considered meritorious. The belief is that they can transfer these merits to their beloved ones for their well-being.

The Buddhists believe that the greatest gift one can confer on one's dead ancestors is to perform 'acts of merit' and to transfer the acquired merits. The belief is that the departed one might have gone to the world of the departed spirits. The beings in these lower forms of existence cannot generate fresh merit, and have to live on with the merit earned from this world. Friends and relatives could release those who are reborn in an unfortunate spirit form from their adverse condition through the transferring of merit to them.

FEAR

Buddhist society is full of superstitious ideas regarding their security. They believe that there are evil spirits or *bhuta* powers all around them. Popular Buddhist rituals have several ways of handling fear. The fear of darkness, ghosts, and cemeteries are handled mostly by chanting *Itipiso Gatha* or chanting a *pirit* known as *Ratana Sutra*, which relates the banishment of demons by the power of the word (Perera 2000:113-115). In order to avoid terrifying dreams which produce feelings of extreme fear and anxiety some families encourage the chanting of *pirit* before going to bed. If the fear persists, they would resort to other rituals. Most of them would invite monks to their homes to chant *pirit* and offer a *dana* to appease the evil powers. The services of a shaman also may be sought. There is a host of ceremonies performed in such situations. The simplest will be a shaman chanting a mantra and tying a thread around the neck or the hand of the client. The most elaborate and expensive ritual in the Sri Lankan low country would be the *tovil* ceremony, which is known as "devil dancing." There are several other ceremonies in between these two. These shamans are heavily influenced by Buddhism because they use eulogies of the Buddha in the mantra to heal the sick.

Purpose of Daily Buddhist Rituals

The purpose of practicing Buddhism may be more or less common among most people except in the case of mavericks. Life after death, security from ill effects and bad karma, personal satisfaction and tradition have been the most prominent reasons for practicing Buddhism. Many respondents have stated that it is their ancestral religion, therefore, they should follow it. When they do good things they expect to be reborn in a good life. But many of them engage in religious activities primarily to make this present life more prosperous and secure. In Buddha's words, all the items offered as *pinkama* (ritualized meritorious acts) are equally efficacious bridges of offerings in the road to Nirvana.

Despite the fact that their understanding of Buddhism varied every Buddhist who was interviewed considered themselves to be good Buddhists without any *Akusal Karma*. Buddhism is deeply rooted in the life of the Sinhala Buddhists. Their religion affects their life-style from birth to death. One day's religious behavior would roughly depict the Buddhist life-style in Sri Lanka. The day's activity of Sinhala Buddhist shows how these principles influence their life every day. They begin the day with religious observances and end the day also in the same manner. There is hardly any area left untouched by Buddhist teaching morals and ethics in the course of the day.

Sacred and Profane

Buddhism clearly separates the things of the Buddha and that of the popular religion. Buddhist devotees are very much aware of this. There are some Buddhists who refuse to have anything to do with shamanism, astrology, *deva* (or god) worship and devil worship. At the same time those who seek the help of these animist forms of Buddhism do it in a way that it does not hinder their faith in the Buddha as their savior. The services that they get from these beings of the popular religion are paid for by way of *bali*, *panduru* (offering), *baara* (vows), *puja* and cash payments. In the case of cash payments they are offered to shamans (*yakadura*), and the priest of the Hindu temples (*kapuwa*) for the service rendered.

The real worship of the day is offered to the Buddha. Chanting, bowing, prostrating, and meditation are done to the Buddha (Kornfield 1996:151; Soma Thera 1967). The gods are offered merit at the end of the daily devotions. These merits come from the personally accumulated merits of the devotee. Buddhists believe that gods need these merits in order to remain in the state of *deva*. The belief is that all other beings are subject to the authority of the Buddha.

CHRISTIANITY

This research was done with a view to seeing ways and means to conceptualize evangelical Christianity among the Buddhists in Sri Lanka. We have found out that there are serious cultural flaws in the Christian camp, which needs attention (*Report of the Presidential Commission* 2002:39). However, one would find these lacunae to be least among the Roman Catholics. The evangelicals on the other hand have disregarded the cultural norms of the country and are therefore at the other end of the spectrum.

There are three types of Christianity in Sri Lanka. The oldest is Roman Catholicism with close to ninety percent of the total Christian population in the country. The second is the traditional Protestant body divided in to several branches. Among them the Anglican, Methodist, Reformed, Baptist and Presbyterian Churches are prominent. Their numbers have been dwindling and very little conversion growth is noticed in the recent past. Third are the newly emerging evangelical groups. Our attention in this article will be on them because of their expansion amongst the Buddhist community in various parts of the island. The activities of the evangelical churches have affected the other Christian bodies as well, since the Buddhists treat all of them alike as Christian.

The Christians, unlike the Buddhists, are divided and suspicious of each other. Almost all Christian denominations are of foreign origin and bear the imprint of foreignness. Most of the Sinhala-speaking converts come from the Buddhist society. Their defense mechanisms are formed within that belief system. They come from traditional societies where they have been taught these rituals for generations. The evangelical churches have to bear in mind that the converts they receive are from this background.

Many of them come for reasons of healing and other answers to prayer. This is, as noted above, the domain traditionally covered by popular Buddhism, rather than the intellectual Buddhism. Converts to evangelical churches have hardly changed either their value system or their worldview. When they come to Christianity they bring their cultural bag and baggage. However when they embrace Christianity, the cultural pattern that they are used to is taken away; the wall of protection that governs morals, ethics, social behavior and family relationships has now been altered. Our attention in this paper is to enquire if the church has been successful in offering to the converts a system to compensate for what they have lost.

Froth and Bubble

Evangelical Christianity in its western origin was a flowering of the already existing Christian culture where the basic ethics are taught and established by the Church. The basics of Christianity have been already ascertained in the minds of the people. Evangelicals and charismatics introduced what they thought was lacking in their church. Therefore, whatever they introduced was on top of what existed in the existing Christian culture. Their teachings and doctrines explained what was lacking in the established church. Paul Hiebert called this the excluded middle (1982:35-47). When evangelicals and charismatic evangelists introduced their teaching to the Buddhist in Sri Lanka they introduced it to a society where the basic Christian background was lacking. They introduced the froth and bubble without the main content thus making Christianity almost a miraculous performance similar to Buddhist shamanism.

A Day in the Life of a Sinhala Buddhist Family

EDUCATION AND INSTRUCTION

The converts who come from the Buddhist background naturally tend to compare Christian religious practices with their Buddhist heritage. Their knowledge of Christianity is minimal. Most of them, being adults, have had a thorough training of Buddhist rituals and culture. Therefore, these converts have to be taught the basics of Christianity. They have taken the decision to change their allegiance from the Buddha to Christ. They have decided to give up manifestation of their old religion including its value system. Therefore they are willing to learn. What is lacking is a proper method of teaching basics of Christian ethics.

It is helpful to know the reasons for conversions. Research indicates that majority of new converts embrace Christianity on account of some tangible experience. It could be a healing experience or an answer to a prayer. Most new evangelical and charismatic churches lack facilities to train new believers. As a matter of fact, the majority of their pastors are themselves converts and have had very little Christian learning.

We have already indicated that there are four main methods of imparting Buddhist knowledge to the devotees. The first is the home. The converts being first generation Christian are ill-equipped to perform this task because they themselves lack training. In this process Buddhists learn basics through memorization. Many of them are able to chant all the stanzas required for worship, some amount of *pirit* and basic quotes from the Buddhist scripture. There is nothing similar to this in Evangelical Christianity. The summary of Christian belief is taught in the Nicene Creed. But these churches do not use it. The majority of the people in these churches have not even heard of a thing called Nicene Creed.

Basic teaching regarding prayer is taught in the Lord's Prayer. The Christian church has used it for centuries. But the new churches do not use it. Therefore, basic concepts of Christianity are unfamiliar to them.

The constant chanting of five precepts keeps Buddhists in control of their ethical behavior. The equivalent to that in Christianity are the Ten Commandments. New believers who come from Buddhist background seem to be unaware of these commandments, as Evangelicals do not systematically teach them. The absence of an ethical anchor makes the new believer vulnerable and opens the door to behaviors which are not acceptable as Christian. Even if they are taught, there is no emphasis on them in the sermons. On the other hand, the Buddhist temples show in the frescoes, murals and sermons the dangers of hell and need to be faithful to ethical teachings. The teaching that a person once saved cannot loose his salvation is also prevalent among evangelical circles.

All practicing Buddhists are well aware of the five precepts. By contrast the new believer in the evangelical camp is ignorant of the Ten Commandments. The convert has decided to give up the old traditions when he made the decision to cross the line. The evangelicals have failed to invest the Christian ethics in the place where the former Buddhist precepts were honored. The churches should realize this danger and address it in a systematic and unified way. The new converts lack anything similar to Buddhist way of training. They lack the parents' teaching of religion and religious ethics. The ritual and liturgy, which can be taught by parents, is absent in evangelical churches. The result is discontinuity of cultural and religious values without a substitute.

Buddhists have a well-organized Sunday school system. The Christians do not have anything compared to that today. Each Christian denomination or the church has its own program of teaching but there is no systematic contextualized teaching. Most of the teaching material available is translation of the English originals. They are not specially prepared for the Sri Lankan pupil. The sectarian bias has made it very difficult to coordinate any Sunday school teaching among the Christian churches. There has to be a vision for a clear cut, coordinated and well informed teaching program in the evangelical churches.

The teaching of religion is compulsory in elementary and secondary Sri Lankan schools. Buddhist, Hindu and Muslim children get a proper training and education in their religion in the national school system. Out of the Christian denominations Roman Catholics and some Protestants in urban areas are able to learn Christianity as a subject in the school curriculum. The evangelical Christians who are scattered throughout the island and live in predominantly Buddhist areas have found it hard to benefit from this provision. Most of the children of new Christian parents have been forced to study Buddhism, as it is a requirement of the government for school children to learn a religion. The children who sought Christianity have either been punished or informed of the inability to find teachers. Therefore, the new Christian is at a disadvantage. In addition, the Christian pupil who learns Buddhism has to take part in Buddhist rituals by way of practical training. According to the available reports those who have refused have been punished, at times severely.

Any Buddhist who somehow does not have any of the above three avenues of learning nevertheless get a great dosage of it from the society and the mass media. They hear *pirit* and *pansil* in public places, morning and evening radio and television broadcasts and so on. The majority being Buddhist, they use a Buddhist vocabulary, which is filled with ethical teachings, concepts, rituals and rites of Buddhism. The new converts may be bombarded with these ideas from morning to evening. The evangelical Christian would not have any comparable means to sustain his faith.

The Christian churches are far behind the Buddhists in educating their children. The Buddhist Sunday schools are well equipped for the task. Every Buddhist temple has a *daham pasala* where they train children for examinations conducted by the government. They offer a progressively advancing systematic knowledge of Buddhism. They have well trained groups of teachers who are familiar with the main teachings of Buddhism. Christian churches do not have anything comparable. Each church has its own program of teaching. Frequently many churches do not have Sunday schools for children. The fact that majority of Evangelical Christians are first generation converts means that more serious attention needs to be given to adult education.

The attendance at Sunday worship service is mandatory for Christians. The evangelical churches can utilize this opportunity to impart Christian knowledge if they have a unified and coordinated system to do it. This is one area where the Christian church is ahead of the Buddhist because the whole family comes to the church to worship on Sundays. The church does not seem to utilize it in the full potential.

MEMORIZATION

Buddhist learning has been transmitted from generation to generation by committing it to memory. Children from their childhood memorize *gatha*, *pirit* and scripture portions. They chant it when they worship, in times of trouble or even to comfort them in solicitude. This tradition of committing to memory is in the Sri Lankan culture. The evangelical churches have failed to utilize this valuable practice.

Evangelicals use songs and the sermon in their worship services. Any evangelical function would have songs and a sermon. The Sunday sermon may be the only teaching of religion to most evangelical Christians. But it is often inadequate as the pastors who preach are inadequately trained. Even the songs they sing are often meaningless as they are word-to-word rather than idea-to-idea translations of English songs.

Education is the primary area where religious knowledge is transmitted from one generation to the other. There has to be a well thought-out plan to achieve this purpose. What exists today is an ad hoc program at best. Some churches neglect education altogether. The necessity is more conspicuous against the challenge of Buddhist educational activities.

RESPECT FOR RELIGIOUS THINGS

As we have already mentioned the Buddhists make a clear distinction between the holy and the profane. Things of religion will be offered highest honor and respect (Korkfield 1992:199). They use the highest vocabulary of terms to refer to the Buddha, the Dharma and the *Sangha* (Buddhist monastic community). The books they use, the *Bodhi* trees they worship and the monks they associate with are given respect in their forms of address. They even extend this vocabulary of respect to Christianity.

The evangelical Christians have totally failed in this area. The distinction between the holy and profane has been completely missed. This failure springs from the fact that they have adopted a neo-Protestant model that has no specific demarcation between these two. This is eye-catching in a culture like Sri Lanka and has been a hindrance to introduce the Christian faith.

Moving down to the specific areas one can point out the use of non-honorific language for the holy in the evangelical circles. Reference to Christ without any honorific title in a culture where the Buddha is offered veneration, the highest honor and respect in the use of the language could amount to proof of the Buddhist belief that Christ is far below the Buddha. On the other hand, the Buddhists use the honorific titles when they refer to Christ. The evangelicals have to realize that they have created a language block, which is detrimental to evangelism. They have forgotten the fact that the Ancient Christian church had taken possession of pagan practices and transformed them in order to enrich Christianity within a local culture.

The *Mahamangala Sutra* clearly indicates that Buddhists should honor those who deserve respect (Narada 2007:160). A constant complaint is that conversion to Christianity eliminates all this expression of respect. The Christians sadly lack this kind of respect in their use of Sinhala language for God, Christ, the disciples of Christ or the saints.

As we indicated earlier the Buddha statue is always venerated. The evangelical's disrespectful behavior towards them is strongly resisted by the Buddhists. There are a number of occasions where evangelical pastors have beaten severely for destroying Buddhist statues or desecrating *Bodhi* trees. Over-exuberant public acts of this nature have already created an enmity towards the evangelical community.

Respect to religious personnel, parents, teachers and elders are embodied in the Sinhala Buddhist culture. The worship of parents is a part of their every day life. But the evangelical Christian leadership has found it difficult to approve it because of their adherence to a western cultural model. Respect for family and filial piety can be taken as a way of fulfillment of the fifth commandment without treating it as paganism (Richardson 2000:119-128).

Honoring our father and mother is an important commandment. It has been said that the fifth commandment is pivotal, for it is between the commandments teaching us to love our Creator, and those admonishing us to love our fellow man. As we have seen earlier the Buddhist children respect their parents by bowing down and prostrating themselves before them. They get up from their seats in the presence of their parents. Many of them do not even argue with parents out of respect. Many converts have informed us that the inability to worship the parents when they went home to visit them was the most harrowing experience. Some Christians who had this experience even fifty years ago still remember with regret the pain that they caused to their parents. Pastors have instructed them that worship is due only to God therefore bowing down before their mother and father amounts to idolatry. Therefore, Buddhists see Christianity as an antisocial and anti-Sinhala movement. Some critics have even stated that Christian evangelicals are agents of foreign imperialists who have come to destroy the Sinhala Buddhist culture. The prohibition of Christian churches on honoring parents in the traditional manner has to be seriously reconsidered. Many evangelicals do not understand that the introduction of the gospel does not mean the destruction of local cultures. They believe that the Evangelical Christianity flavored with American culture is beneficial to the Sri Lanka church, while others see it as cultural imperialism and a threat to national identity.

The respectful attitude is expressed in the way the Sinhala people use their language. There are specific terms on filial relationships and social relationships. One can notice that the vocabulary used in this context by the converts suddenly change from the Sinhala to English. Therefore any elder person becomes uncle or aunt; whether it is regarding the family circle or an outsider when it comes to social addressing one would see the total disregard to age factor and family relationships. The result would be the inevitable weakening of family ties.

A Day in the Life of a Sinhala Buddhist Family

Buddhist monks are venerated by calling them '*sanghaya vahanse.*' Lay people get up from their seats when a monk is in their presence. The monks also have to endeavor to live a life that deserves respect. From among Christians Roman Catholic and Anglican priests come close to this tradition. The evangelicals who dress like ordinary people have found it hard to receive that respect. The words used in regard to evangelical leaders are English terms such as pastor, brother and sister. To address religious leaders in this manner is counter culture, which the evangelicals have failed to recognize.

PUNCTUALITY

Buddhists are punctual in attending to their religious duties. The astrological charts give the time to the minute to perform religious and social ceremonies. The *Buddha puja* at the household altar is offered at the correct time. Monks have to be given food before twelve noon. Buddhist sermons conducted in village temples are conducted at the correct time without waiting for the arrival of a sufficient crowd. On the other hand, the evangelical Christians do not start their meetings at the correct time expecting more people to arrive later. Their leaders have learned from foreign missiologists that the Sri Lankans are task oriented and not time oriented. They have used it to justify this action. At marriage, the Buddhist couple would set their foot on the *poruwa* at the exact auspicious time. By contrast the Evangelical Christian couple often fails to arrive at the church at the time mentioned in their invitation cards. The congregations at times wait over one hour before the bride arrives. The converts see this as a weakness and total irresponsibility. Once again, the responsibility lies in the evangelical leadership who fail to address this weakness.

LACK OF RESPECT FOR NATIONAL HERITAGE

The inability of some evangelical Christians to get along with neighbors is another problem. Many of them have not attended social functions such as *pirit* and *dana* ceremonies in the neighborhood stating, that they are Buddhist activities. They have refused to contribute to functions organized by Buddhists. This would bring about alienation, suspicion and even hostility.

Sri Lanka has a very old civilization. The Buddhists are proud of it. Most of the ancient monuments are Buddhist and some Hindu. Christians have failed to appreciate the achievements of the Sri Lankan heritage before the arrival of Christianity. This imperialistic and self-centered attitude of many Christians in the past is no longer appropriate today. What does seem clear is that Christians are called upon to witness to Christ before the whole world, and that an essential element of this witness is serving the world which is full of different cultures.

Conclusion

Christian religion is a living expression of one's faith. It has to be communicated in the particular situation we live and must be expressed in a culturally relevant form taking traditional beliefs and expressions of faith. It is a human activity that takes place in a culture. We have imported methods of evangelism and theological expressions that do not make sense in the context in which we are living in Sri Lanka. There are deep insights in Buddhism, which can enrich the expression of the Christian faith in the Sri Lanka culture. However, there is a reluctance of having anything savoring of Buddhism among the evangelicals. The old Buddhist forms can be reinvested with new meaning (Davis 1993:83) while giving attention to transform the non Christian worldviews and values.

Sri Lankan Buddhist culture is very rich in religious expressions. It has a very high estimation of religion and this respect is extended even to other religions. The appreciation of religion is closely associated with the respect it shows to those who deserve respect. This includes personalities and objects of Buddhist religion and the parents and elders. They have a well-developed system of educating the believers so that the religion becomes embedded in the total life of the Buddhist. A Buddhist family, irrespective of their social standing, makes every attempt to start and end the day with religious devotion. They constantly remind themselves of the basics of their faith by repeatedly chanting the main precepts of their religion. They memorize the most important teachings of their religion and resort to it in times of necessity. Evangelical Christians also should make an attempt to use memorization of basic teachings as a mode of instruction.

The evangelical Christian has failed to appreciate this tradition. Their model of religious expression is devoid of respect to religious personnel and objects, and the lack of a proper system of educating the believer can be detrimental to the sustenance of the religion. The evangelicals who receive Buddhist converts for reason of healing and answer to prayer are actually dealing with those who are interested in popular practices of Buddhism (Hiebert 1999:47). The Buddhists do not have a respect for the personalities of popular Buddhism. The latter are sought in times of difficulty and neglected after the purpose is achieved. Buddhists make offerings and fulfill vows by way of payment to these forces of animism. But the latter have no power to save them. In fact they need the help of the Buddhists to give merit either to maintain them in that position or redeem them. The Buddhist does not remain within the domain of popular Buddhism. Their morning and evening worship is to the Buddha whose *dharma* alone is able to save them. The strength of Buddhism lies there. Buddhist ethics and values emanate from it.

Thus, the evangelical Christians who attract people on account of healing and answer to prayer will have to go deeper. They will have to have a proper system of teaching their new believers and the young generation in the solid grounding of Christianity. They also need to learn from Buddhists to respect their religious personnel and objects so that the believer would be able to feel that the religion speaks to their heart every day.

7

The Struggle of Asian Ancestor Veneration

Alex G. Smith

Recently in Mongolia the long-standing power of ancestral veneration in Asia was clearly highlighted. Almost eight hundred years after his warring exploits that cut a swath through the nations of his day, Genghis Khan is still revered as the legendary hero of the Mongolians. After successfully uniting warring tribes, the great Khan took over half the known world of his time. In two short decades, he built an empire that was larger than Rome's—from Korea to the Black Sea. In August 1227, Genghis fell from his horse and died. He was buried in a secret location. All traces of it were erased as thousands of horses raced over the area around his final resting place. Those attending his funeral were massacred to keep the site secure—not uncommon practice in ancient Asia.

Finding Genghis Khan's gravesite baffled archeologists for centuries until 2001 when a team headed by a University of Chicago professor believed they had located the Khan's burial area. Associated Press revealed how deeply ancestral veneration can permeate a nation. The archeological work was brought to a halt after Mongolia's former Prime Minister, Dashiin Byambasuren, wrote to the current President, Natsagiin Bagabandi, accusing the archeological team of desecrating and defiling the remains of the dead. He wrote, "I regret that our ancestors' golden tomb has been disturbed and the purity of our burial places tainted for a few dollars." Earlier in 1993,

Japanese archeologists ended the search for Khan's tomb because of the unpopularity of the project among the general populace in Ulan Bator, the capital. "According to Mongolian tradition, violating ancestral tombs destroys the soul that serves as protector." A local student summed it up poignantly, "Genghis was the greatest khan of them all, and I pray that his soul will protect Mongolia" (Oregonian, August 14, 2002). Ancestral practices and influence are powerfully perpetuating.

This paper will follow three approaches for investigating ancestor practices: first, comprehending and understanding concepts underlying ancestor rites, second analyzing and evaluating data concerning them, and third applying and experimenting with practical approaches towards solving problems encountered.

A Phenomenon of Universal Value

One widespread belief that affects many Asian peoples is ancestral cults with various forms of overt or covert worship. This is more engrained and commonly practiced than most westerners realize. Offering to ancestors was a central tradition that predated formal systemized religions. Herbert Spencer suggested, "Ancestor worship is the origin of religion," processed through reverence to ancestors or their ghosts. This worldwide phenomenon is deeply rooted in many Asian peoples. It was a prevalent practice down through the historic ages in many sophisticated societies, including the former empires of Greece and Rome. Ancestor worship is performed at special sites, in temples, at shrines and on home altars. Rites, sacrifices, prayers and offerings are usually involved in a myriad of expressions of ancestral veneration. Professor Hwang declared, "There are perhaps more people who practice ancestor cult than people who live the Christian faith" (1977:340).

Most ancestral practices arose around the concepts of death and the afterlife. Bronislaw Malinowski calls death "the supreme and final crisis of life." Death is the last turning point every human must face. The general belief in the immortality of the soul, and the subsequent belief in social interaction between the living and the dead, especially in monistic worldviews, helps to develop practices of ancestral cults. While death brings normal social relations to an end, vivid memories of the deceased continue. Death rites are universal. Ancestral worship and ritual practices are common in Asia.

THE CONCEPT OF ANCESTRAL VENERATION

Veneration covers two aspects: respect and worship. Christians only accept the first as biblically legitimate. Ancestor worship is worship directed to deceased parents or forefathers based on the belief of the immaterial and immortal part of humanity, along with the belief that these ancestors continue to have the same kindly interest in the affairs of the living as when they were alive.

Many believe that their ancestors uphold family tradition, provide family survival and protect the family. Therefore it is right for the living members of the family to remember the ancestors and make offerings to them. Since, when alive on the earth the ancestors ruled the family, functioned as head over it, protected it and rewarded or punished the family members as needed, these ancestors are therefore seen as continuing to carry out these functions after death. The Chinese believe that the spirits of the ancestors fly above and around the house of the living relatives. The ancestors may provide protection, blessings and prosperity or if neglected, bring misfortune.

The initiation of ancestral deification has a long history. Anthropologist E. B. Tylor (1889) describes how the dead ancestors are deified as ghosts or saints and are consequently worshipped. In ancient Rome's religion, this developed as manes worship. In other societies and tribes arose a belief that the members were all descendants from a common non-human ancestor. This may be a god, spirit, animal or person of myth. This prime ancestor then became the clan's totem. One expression of this kind of thinking was found in Japan where, under State Shintoism, the Emperor was ardently believed to be the incarnation of the Sun goddess.

John V. Taylor noted that ancestors are considered part of the social group and are not cut off at death (1963:103-105). In the minds of relatives, these "living dead" still exert a powerful influence, recognized as very real and intimate. The belief that the souls of dead ancestors may become ghosts is also strongly held. These ghosts exercise power over current situations and are involved in many forms and functions among the currently living relatives. The ancestors take up residence in some abode of souls. This is like a parallel kingdom to earth. That similarity is viewed as a counterpart reflection of it. As an expression of this the Chinese, Vietnamese and others burn paper offerings of money, cars, houses and other items to the ancestors. These are meant to help comfort them in the abode of dead souls and also to keep them kindly disposed towards the living. In some cultures the ancestors may be regarded as guardian spirits over the family, clan or tribe.

The cohesive continuity in worldview reinforces the ancestral cult. Since this perception is learned early from the cradle, its perspectives, perceptions and values continue persistently on till the grave. The permeation of education, thinking and daily life produces a comprehensive and continuing connection with the ancestors, so much so that the dead are seen as having an ongoing, intimate relationship with the generations of the living. In Sri Lanka the "rice-name" ceremony is performed usually about seven months after the birth of a child. An auspicious date is calculated and all the relatives gather. The grandfather places a handful of rice in the child's mouth and gives his grandchild its name. This reinforces the perpetuation of ancestral continuity (Peiris 1956:226; Weerasingha 1989:93).

The pervasive control of cultural tradition also fosters ancestral cults. One example is the Damal tribe in the Indonesian jungles of central Irian Jaya. Damals view the spiritual world as more real than the physical realm. Their ancestor worship is consequently most vital to them, and they offer many items to their ancestors including stone axes, dogs and pigs. For Vietnamese Mahayana Buddhists ancestor worship and shamanism are more essential to daily living than tenets that direct them towards countering their *karma* to overcome suffering, ignorance and illusion.

The Importance of Ancestor Worship in Asian Thinking

The experience of ancestors is highly valued and respected. Ancestors founded many things in the family lineage, both methodological and moral. They have experienced common problems in the past and so can empathize with living relatives now facing similar difficulties. The knowledge and achievements of the ancestors provide a rich pool of resources from which to draw. Their priority of headship provided experienced leadership in decision-making in bygone days.

Ancestors' presence in the dreams of the living also points to reminders of their importance. These are to be noted, not ignored. Keeping ancestors alive in the memory by frequent reminders through visions fosters a feeling of continuity and connection with the deceased. It is not uncommon for Asians to interpret dreaming about ancestors as warnings from them of some impending danger. Dreams are taken seriously.

The ancestors' perpetuity in living memory is powerful. Often only ancestors known from memory are venerated—usually back to grandparents. In some cases statistical ancestral lines are recognized to seven or more former generations. Names are usually recorded on some kind of ancestral tablet or lineage record. Ancestral founders of clans or tribes initiated much leaving legacies of learning. Cult and totem practices are maintained in almost endless perpetuity.

Ancestors are recognized as part of the current social group and identified as "the living dead." Deceased forebears live in a spiritual world but they are believed to have an ongoing interest in the material world. Normally there are locations or sites where the ancestors are accessible and can be contacted or consulted. This may be a high mountain, a body of water, or some centralized ancestral shrine. Gravesites are also chosen carefully, usually through some form of geomancy such as *feng shui*. This includes peoples such as the Chinese and Vietnamese (Reimer 1975:158; Hickey 1964:38f).

Ancestral powers are believed to be available to the living who may invoke them. Ancestors have already trod life's path, experienced its problems, faced and surmounted its difficulties, and made important decisions. Therefore they possess a wealth of knowledge, achievement and power that the living family believes it may draw upon. These are at the disposal of the family provided they are accessed correctly—through offerings, sacrifices, libations, prayers, incantations or other appropriate forms of ancestral worship.

The Motivations Behind Ancestor Worship

Filial piety or respect and affection for deceased ancestors have a high value among peoples such as Chinese, Japanese, Korean and Vietnamese. The motivation for this veneration has strong ethical and social implications. It includes gratefulness to the ancestors for their care, training and provision for the family. Usually filial piety is expressed in three primary ways:

1) Proper burial and funeral rites for the deceased
2) Offerings before the ancestral tablets
3) Correct care of the ancestral graves

First, culturally acceptable decorum and appropriate ceremony with the rightful administration by the eldest son and/or priests and shamans are required. This is both a public social event and a private family affair. Due respect and correct procedure dignify the final rites of passage for the deceased, sometimes accompanied by professional mourners as well as feasts and other activities.

Second is the worship at family altars, known in Japan as *butsudan*, set up in each family home. This entails some form of ancestral tablets inscribed with the names of forebears going back a number of generations. These are placed on the altar. Generally these tablets are wooden, stone or occasionally paper. Often a photograph of the ancestor is placed at the shrine. Living family members make daily offerings of food, drink, fruit, flowers and other items, before the ancestral tablets or the altar. Incense is burned. Candles are lit. Often a perpetual light is kept burning. These offerings allow the ancestors "to eat" and so preclude the deceased from becoming hungry, unhappy, miserable and unfortunate ghosts (Hung 1983:32). Where deceased kinsmen are deemed to possess enough interest and power over human affairs they may be regarded as deities and often are worshipped (Taylor 1973:392). Family members direct prayer requests for their current problems to the ancestors and also plead for their assistance in any difficulties that the family may be facing. This kind of worship is maintained daily or weekly. After the sacrificial rituals are completed and the ancestors have partaken, the living members then eat the food from before the altar. In this manner they also partake in a communal sense with the ancestors (Lowe 2001:4f).

A third way of showing filial piety is the ritual ceremony of visiting the ancestral graves at least annually at special times of the year to honor the dead. The graves are cleaned and spruced up at this time. This is known as "sweeping the graves." Special offerings are made and veneration of the ancestors is performed. In China, this festival on April fifth, is known as *ching ming*. In similar fashion the Japanese celebrate *bon* festivals in summer, as well as popular *boson*—frequent visiting of family graves (Shibata 1985:247).

Another dominant motivation behind ancestral worship is fear of ancestral ghosts. Death is a serious event in Asia because of the dread of ghosts and spirits. If not treated properly the disembodied entities may cause all sorts of havoc, trouble and even curses for the living thus the departed ancestors are viewed with terror. Consequently the living meticulously provide for the recently departed by offering money, houses, possessions and means of transportation to help them in the abode of the dead. Usually these are only models made of paper or perishable materials, which are burned as offerings along with joss sticks. Fulfilling these duties is like insurance for the family, even if due respect and true love for the departed are absent. Thus selfish desires may be at the true root of some ancestral practices. The proper rites of passage, appropriate funeral, and adequate sendoff are deemed essential for the efficient transportation of the dead to their spiritual resting place. This is also necessary to protect the living relatives and their families. Daniel Hung lucidly described the fear behind ancestral cults, "Failure to worship ancestors is not only considered to be a great sin and an act of rebellion against one's ancestors, but is also believed to result in disasters and misfortune for the living" (1983:33).

A third motivation reinforcing the ancestral system is conformity to social customs. Confucian teaching established and institutionalized prescribed forms, expectations and ceremonial rituals. To neglect the ancestors produced strong social stigma. Among many peoples, especially in North and East Asia, not following the prescribed patterns for honoring ancestors is considered a major disgrace, a most despicable sin. This posed a dilemma for Christian converts, criticized as deviants for disrespecting their own ancestors. Abstaining from society's ancestral rites brought persecution. In Vietnam, Christianity is ridiculed as "the religion that is ungrateful to the ancestors" (Reimer 1975:156).

A fourth motivation for ancestral practices is maintaining the bonding of the family. The ancestral celebrations and rites give the relatives an opportunity for family gatherings and provide a sense of togetherness. This reinforces the strength and unity of the extended family. Often help for field labor, aid in financial crises, and assistance and advice in major decisions comes first from immediate family members and relatives. This is true both in rural and urban communities. Gatherings for ancestral veneration not only show the value of communal respect but also remind families of these close bonds, their common unity and the obligation for interrelated dependence on each other and the ancestors.

So far the focus has been on comprehending and understanding the concepts underlying ancestor rites. Now we turn to some analysis and evaluation of contexts and data.

The Comparison of Two Differing Worldviews

It is crucial to comprehend the divergent perceptions of two outlooks—that from a biblical analysis and that from a culture developed around ancestors. The general biblical view describing the flow and process of life simply is summarized in diagram 1 below. This shows a duality separating the spiritual from the physical realms. God as Creator is outside the process but works within it. He is not part of the creation itself. Not neglecting the human physical factors in the process, one can grasp a biblical answer to the question "Where do babies come from?" In scripture it seems clear that the unborn come from the blessing of a sovereign Creator God, the source of all life. According to considerable illustrations and verses in the Bible, the Lord is the One who opens or closes the womb (Gen. 29:31, 1 Sam.1 1:6). So babies are recognized as a gift from God. They come into the world of the living by the blessing of God through His command for humankind to procreate and multiply (Gen. 1:27-28).

Normally each person has an allotted lifespan of "three score years and ten" (Ps. 90:10). At the end of each life it is then appointed "once to die" (Heb. 9:27). This is a radical break with life, with a fixed state of no returning (Job 10:21; Luke 16:13).

The terms *sheol* (Hebrew) or *hades* (Greek) are similar in their focus as the abode of the dead. Like most religions, there is also a sense of final accountability. The future state of the dead seems to be either paradise (Abraham's bosom) or *hades/sheol* (a place of discomfort and pain). Afterwards, at the appointed time of the end comes the climactic judgment, followed by assignments in heaven or hell. Commentators have differing views of what these terms mean, ranging from literal to allegorical, physical to spiritual, or figurative to actual.

Figure 1: A Biblical Worldview

This somewhat simple explanation of the process and flow of life from a biblical perspective is in considerable contrast to that of the cult of the ancestors, diagramed in figure 2 below.

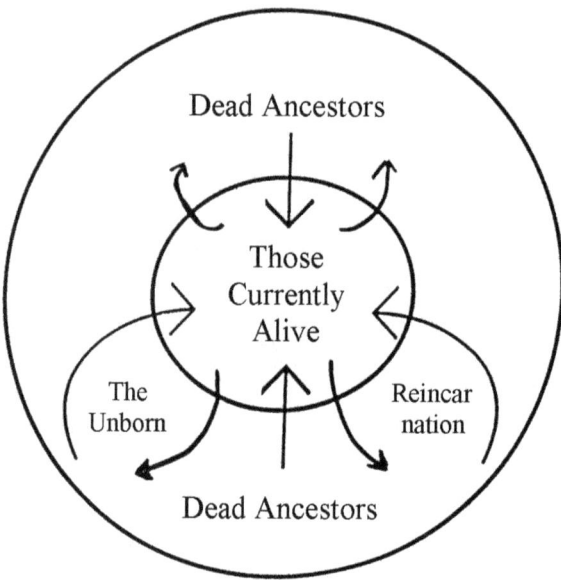

Figure 2: Asian Worldview: Ancestor Related

Generally the Asian worldview is monistic rather than dualistic in its orientation, where all is part of the whole. In this view dead ancestors are believed to be part of the sphere of life that includes those currently alive as well as the departed ("living dead"), and even the "not-yet-born." Berentsen analyses the relationship between the performers of rites and their ancestors under three interrelated aspects of cosmic-monism:1) The community of obligation, 2) The community of interdependence, and 3) The community of cosmic continuity (1985:264-269). So the outer circle above contains the broader pool of relationships recognized as true viable life where interaction and communication take place, not just the inner circle of those actually alive on the earth. Even where Buddhist concepts reject the entity of human soul, this view of the world recognizes that the ancestors are living entities who can affect the affairs on earth for good or evil. In their spiritual state the ancestors still are intimately related to the material world and integrated with it. These "living dead" still have an influence on the current live family. When humans die they go to the abode of the ancestors, awaiting reincarnation, depending on their accumulated *karma*. As shown in figure 2, the newborn come from the pool of the ancestors by means of reincarnation or rebirth. This recycling motif indicates more of a cyclical life process than the linear one common to the orientation of the West.

THE MEANS AND CAUSES FOR CONSULTING ANCESTORS

Where ancestral cults are prevalent, established patterns of approach to the deceased must be followed. These include a kind of priesthood or mediators. Frequently the head of the household as family mediator performs the rituals in the home. In other situations the eldest son in the extended family acts in this prescribed function. Where Buddhism became dominant through its cultural accommodation of integrating ancestral and animistic practices, Buddhist priests also took on similar roles in performing some of those ritualistic tasks.

The main reasons ancestors are consulted include:

1) *Biological concerns for human fertility.* This relates to the physical extension of the tribe or family line. Infertility or barrenness becomes a cause to consult the ancestors. One example is the Kaguru tribe of East Africa, who illustrate this belief clearly. First, the Kaguru marriage rites

affirm that the ties of marriage "will continue beyond the life span of the couple involved." Second, if a woman has difficulty conceiving or retaining a pregnancy, a diviner is consulted in order to identify the cause of the difficulty. Usually the problem is diagnosed as "disruptive forces associated with the ghosts of the ancestors who do not want the unborn to leave the land of the ghosts of ancestors and go to the land of the living" (Grunlan 1981:50-51).

2) *Fertility and fruitfulness of the land.* Since the land is inherited from the ancestors, they still have an interest in helping preserve it for the current family and causing the harvests to produce prodigiously.

3) *Personal relationship between the living and the dead.* There is high affection for the ancestors and/or a considerable fear of them - usually a combination of both. This ambivalence of the ancestors being predictable and unpredictable, exhibits something quite human about them. Like a mirror, the ancestral cult reflects the kind of dynamics found in the living family. A mediator with special knowledge, aptitude and experience considers how to approach the ancestors in ways that are like human to human, in order to placate them, plead with them or trick them on behalf of the living.

4) *Sickness and disease.* The deep reason or hidden cause divined behind illness is usually identified as neglect of the ancestors. Because he was angry or dissatisfied, the ancestor failed to protect the living. The family examines themselves to see why the ancestor disapproved of their behavior. A similar process and cause is traced in cases of drought, famine or natural calamity. Where these or an epidemic is widespread throughout the tribe or people, it is often interpreted as a matter of national significance. The cause is usually determined that all in the group neglected their religious duty to the ancestors, so renewed ceremony and ritual is called for so as to correct the general neglect of ancestors.

AN EVALUATION OF BIBLICAL PRINCIPLES

First, the problem of idolatry in ancestor worship is raised in the first Commandment. "You shall have no other gods before Me" (Ex. 20:3). The question is, "Do ancestral cults worship their forebears as gods and thereby violate this primary command?" (Kraft 1991:309). On the other hand one must also ask, "Is all sincere reverence of ancestors, with their practices and rites, necessarily elevating their position to that of gods, thereby competing with Jehovah?" How does one distinguish between the two? In what ways can one discern when the fine line has been crossed from valid respectful veneration to veritable idolatrous worship? These are most difficult missiological questions.

The belief, common in China, Japan, Korea and Vietnam, is that after death the ancestor's spirit actually returns to enter the ancestral tablet. Sometimes a hole or a slit is made in the tablet for this purpose. After a short time the deceased soul is located in three places simultaneously: in the abode of the dead in "heaven," at the coffin or gravesite, and in the ancestral tablet in the home (Liaw 1985:186). The living relatives worship the ancestors with incense, candles, flowers, spirit money, prayers and offerings before the ancestral tablet and altar. This can contravene the second commandment "You shall not make yourself an idol, or any likeness... You shall not worship them or serve them" (Ex. 20:4-5). This is a notable concern, especially where incense is burned, for in North Asia joss sticks and incense automatically indicates worship to a deity (Tan 1985:221-223; Hung 1983:36).

Reginald Reimer points out that the Vietnamese cult of the ancestors is founded on their complex "beliefs concerning the soul" (1975:155-156). This is likely true of other Asian peoples also. Interestingly the Hebrew word for soul, *nephesh*, does not distinguish clearly between soul and body. In cultures where ancestors are venerated, it could be argued that though the physical body has died, the spiritual soul lives on and is thereby potentially accessible for communication with the living. Most ancient nations and waves of civilizations believed in life continuing after death. Consequently humans developed elaborate systems to provide for their ancestors and to assure harmony for the afterlife. The nation of Israel did not establish any formal practice of ancestral worship, though they highly respected their ancestral forebears as frequently commanded in scripture. Israel was strictly to worship only one God, Jehovah.

A second problem concerns adequate respect following the fifth Commandment. "Honor your father and your mother, so that you may live long in the land the Lord your God is giving you" (Ex. 20:12). Here Asians might rightly ask local Christians and especially those in the West, "Do Christians neglect respecting their ancestors? Is the first commandment more important than the fifth? Or is the fifth less inspired?" Western theology relegates little attention to ancestors, though a large volume of scripture talks about them (Hiebert 1985:210). The repeated ancestral maxim, "The God of Abraham, Isaac and Jacob," is a vital statement of ancestral veneration and continuity. What of the West's lack of showing true filial piety to the forebears used of God to prepare the heritage we have today? Christians should excel in respecting parents, in caring for their elderly relatives, as well as in nurturing their own families.

Furthermore, the only one of the Ten Commandments that was given with a promise of blessing was the fifth, calling for us to respect our parents, despite their weakness, inadequacies and sinfulness. In fact being classed in the first five, which seem to relate God-ward, the fifth commandment also reflects the honor due unto God.

THE MISSIOLOGICAL CHALLENGES OF ANCESTRAL PRACTICES

When the gospel entered North and East Asia, cult practices for the ancestors were among "the most critical problems, which Christianity had to face" (Ro 1985:4). Like "a giant rock blocking the flow of water in a river," Hung wrote, "Ancestor worship is the greatest obstacle to the Christian mission among the Chinese" (1983:32).

The complex, eclectic stewpot of Chinese religion contains a broad list of deities including "Heaven" (*Shang Ti*). "The great mass of Chinese worship Buddha, the bodhisattvas, the Taoist immortals, Confucius and their own ancestors, with equal vigour" (Samagalski

1984:69). A similar though modified consensus could describe Korea, Japan, and Vietnam, as well as most other parts of South East Asia.

Significantly in Japan, Buddhist sects such as Nichiren, and "new religions" like Tenryko, have incorporated ancestor worship (Shibata 1985:253). Similarly in Vietnam the Hoa Hao, Cao Dai and Coconut religions have a heavy focus on ancestor veneration (Reimer 1975:165). Actually, most religions of Asia are neither "pure" nor "pristine." They are mostly conglomerates of Buddhism, Hinduism or Islam, their dominant components, with various forms of animistic mixtures, including the cults of the ancestors.

Ancestral practices among other Asian peoples are not always as obvious as those of the Chinese or Japanese. For example, except for those of Chinese extraction, the Thai do not appear to have codified ancestral cults. But when significant adversity strikes a family, their first reaction is to make sacrifice and obeisance to their angry ancestors. Similarly, though nominally Christian, the Filipinos pay homage, make sacrifices and offer prayers to their dead ancestors "so they would respond favorably to the needs of living family members" (Henry 1986:8). In Cambodia the festival of *Pchum Ben* is held for fifteen days in the autumn. During the celebrations all families are expected to travel around to seven Buddhist temples (*wats*) to gather together and make balls of sticky rice, which they throw around the *wats* to feed the famished spirits of ancestors. For rural Cambodians, ancestral ghosts are among "the spirits they most fear, and with whom they are concerned on a day-to-day basis" (Bowers 2003:48). In Laos and nearby lands, when a death occurs in a *Taidam* family, animal sacrifices are made to provide offerings to the spirit of the deceased ancestor. The corpse is placed on a stand in the house. Then in communal fashion the living attendees at the funeral partake of the sacrificed food. One could multiply scores of examples from other people groups of Asia, but this is sufficient.

These illustrations identify the heart of the problem concerning ancestral practices. The worldviews affected by ancestral influences are so deeply engrained in the psyche of many Asian peoples that a simple dismissal of the issues is not only inadequate but also ineffective. In the war torn devastation of South East Asia during the 1970s, ancestral sites and altars in homes were destroyed and the people forced to flee across borders. Yet within a few weeks, ancestral altars reappeared in the refugee camps of east Thailand (Reimer 1975:163). The powerful, persistent influence of the ancestors permeates the hearts of many Asians and penetrates their deepest culture. Meeting these deep felt-needs requires considerable research and understanding.

ANCESTRAL CULTS INCORPORATED INTO BUDDHISM

In Buddhism, rites for the deceased have a long tradition from earliest times. Once King Bimbisara invited the Buddha and some priests to a meal at his palace and offered robes to the Bhikkus. The king dedicated "his merit to his deceased kinsmen." The Buddha announced that the offerings "will go to benefit the deceased" and assured the king, "A great merit you have done in performing your duties as their relatives, in worshipping the deceased through this fruitful kind of worship and in strengthening the Bhikkus in doing so." In Brahmanism ancestral offerings were limited "only to three former generations," but Buddhism sets no limit for transferring merit to all previous generations. The Brahmin practices of using lumps of rice and pouring water oblations for the deceased were incorporated into Buddhist rites for the deceased in Thailand and elsewhere. Buddhism set three qualifying conditions for effective transfer of merit to ancestors: (1) While giving charity, donors must make a mental note to dedicate their merit to the deceased. (2) Only deceased ancestors who have taken their place in the planes of hungry ghosts can appreciate and share this merit. (3) The acts of merit are effective when dispensed towards those who are worthy, namely first, Buddhist priests and second, others in need (Nyanasamvara 1993:125-133; Berentsen 1985:267).

Professor Wei's excellent historical analysis of Chinese ancestor worship traced its roots back to primitive animism and totemism. In the Hsia (Xia) dynasty 2,000 years before the entry of Buddhism, worship of ancestors was only a little less important than the worship of Heaven. The heart of ancient rites was the belief that "all things originated from Heaven; people originated from their ancestors" (1985:119-125). Over time changes transformed ancestor worship. Though China's contact with Buddhism started from 200 B.C., the most significant changes came with its official introduction during the Han dynasty (65-73 A.D.), around the time of the destruction of the Temple in Jerusalem. Wei reports the Chinese classics had no recorded use of incense. "The practices of burning incense, candles and paper money were added to the ancestor worship ceremonies after the introduction of Buddhism to China." Originally the meaning of ancestor worship was "to revere Heaven, to enlighten moral virtues, to edify filial piety, and to show gratitude to the ancestors." Buddhism also encouraged "the worship of the deceased" so as to help them enter the western Paradise (1985:128-130).

While fundamentally rejecting all spiritual entities as inconsequential, Buddhism is most accommodating and highly syncretistic, strongly influencing Asian cultures at the grass roots. From a historical perspective, Arnold Toynbee stated, "Buddhism has transformed every culture as it has entered, and Buddhism has been transformed by its entry into that culture" (Maguire 2001:207). Consequently the majority of Folk Buddhists views their ancestral cults as part of their Buddhism, whether in China, Korea, Japan, Taiwan, Vietnam and elsewhere.

After understanding the concepts related to ancestral veneration, and evaluating their contexts, we finally suggest practical approaches for applications and experimentation, towards solving problems encountered in ancestral rites.

The Need for Functional Substitutes

Historical controversies in the church over this sensitive issue have been well documented (Ro 1985:149-160). Generally church and missionary responses to ancestral veneration have been either to condemn all or to condone all. The first results in isolating Christians from society as outsider aliens to the culture. The second is so accommodating that syncretism takes over in the church. The first can be too ethnocentric, unfeeling and unaware of the deep felt needs of Asians. The second is compromising, confusing and lacking understanding of both scripture and culture. The goal is to find solutions that are both thoroughly biblical without compromise, and truly cultural while satisfying deeply felt needs of Asians.

Current scholars encourage a middle way that demands determined development of adequate functional substitutes, specifically appropriate for each people's ancestral practices. Functional substitutes overcome blocking barriers by building bridges. It is safer to take old forms and transform them with new meanings, than to bring in new forms, which tend to transfer and retain old meanings. Discarding key elements may also leave frustrating voids. Discernment is surely needed for three actions: (1) Retaining things which one can follow, (2) Rejecting things one cannot practice, and (3) Recognizing things that can be transformed and adapted through functional substitutes. Serious experiments and evaluation are required on the third, so that efficient solutions are implemented. Past examples on these were made in Liao (1972:130f), Hwang (1977:353f), Hung (1983:36f), and Ro (1985 part IV). Crucial solutions find answers, which do not leave empty voids in the hearts of believers, and still keep the church in close cultural proximity to society. It is futile to continue denying the depths of the emotional grip that ancestral practices hold on Asians. Below are some ideas for functional substitutes that may provide models for experimenting, testing and evaluating. Since each cultural situation is different, we offer only possibilities. Creativity is required.

1. Funerals and disposal of the body. All proceedings related to the coffin, and the services for funeral, burial or cremation must be dignified, solemn and sober. They are also to uplift the attendees with comfort, peace, hope and joy. The best of local forms should be used rather than outside imports. Make them cultural not western, Christian not cultic. Setting up a memorial altar with items such as a large photo of the deceased, a family Bible and tastefully arranged flowers is helpful. Display large banners with fitting Scriptural texts or words of appreciation for the deceased. Wear proper cultural dress and symbols of grief. Though not offering joss sticks, Christians should first pay respects to the dead and give condolences to the family before helping with meals, drinks or refreshments. Where culturally appropriate, church bands or choirs should perform, eulogies honoring the deceased delivered, and a history of his/her accomplishments, provision, care, giftedness and value to the family given by various attendees. Other cultural trimmings and practices that are not proscribed can be added. All should fit as thoroughly as possible with the culture of the local society, within biblical bounds. Non-judgmental attitudes are important, as some will probably perform practices unacceptable to believers. Here is a chance to show acceptance and love to them. Be patient, not unkind. Tasteful tombs, grave markers or headstones honoring the ancestor should be set up afterward.

2. Memorials to the deceased. These are held at different times and places. Initial memorials and death anniversaries call for much creativity in expressing honor and thanksgiving for the ancestor's nurture and good for the family. Make provision for memorial meals and for sharing feelings and appreciation for the deceased. These are times for families to show their solidarity and mutual love and concern. Play cultural games, music or drama, as deemed proper. Togetherness and unity are the watchwords. Give donations to charities in the name of the deceased towards needy projects of community and church. Plant trees or shrubs in honor of ancestors, adding memorial plaques. It is important to maintain fellowship with those who are not believers at family or clan gatherings and anniversaries. Remembering ancestors at annual, lunar or New Year festivals stretches one's imagination for ways to show respect. Where relatives still insist on ancient rites for unbelieving ancestors, Christian families can hold a final ceremony. On that occasion they tell the ancestors before all relatives that this is a respectful, final, special celebration of veneration to the ancestors. As God's children Christians are giving the deceased the highest honor now by entrusting them to Creator God, and committing them to His power and eternal care. The family should express much sincere gratefulness to the ancestors for their nurture in the past as they bring closure to ancestor worship. Also tell the ancestors what kinds of respect

Christians will continue to give them, excluding the old fearful spirit ways. Then close and put the ancestors to rest.

3. Care and cleaning of ancestral graves. Family or clan gathering for festivals, such as *ching ming* or *bon*, can be unifying events, full of fun for the members. Identity and unity are keys. It is also a solemn time to remember the ancestors and to honor them with words of gratitude, written tributes for their value, and blessings of flowers or balloons. After meticulously cleaning up the gravesite and restoring its luster, hold hands around the grave while members offer prayers of thanksgiving to God and maintain a minute of special silence. Christians can excel others by doing this at least one extra time a year to honor their ancestors.

4. Family altars in the home. Suggestions made earlier for funerals are proper here. Add special meaningful items such as a list of ancestors recorded in the family Bible. David Liao even designed a model of a "corrected" Hakka ancestral tablet (1972:124). Hold family devotions near the altar and praise God for placement in that family and in his church. Thank the Lord and for His provision of protection, health, food, shelter and clothing. Consider displaying photos of the ancestors for several generations on the wall nearby. Produce a family history of the ancestors with significant details and place it on the memorial table. Read sections of it to the members for devotions. In times of crisis or need for decisions gather near the family altar to call upon God for His direction and blessing. Praise Him for His grace, mercy and will. Tell God all the troubles, confess sins and commit the future to Him.

Conclusion

This paper has attempted three things: (1) to apprehend the complex concepts driving ancestor veneration, (2) to analyze the societal context behind the cult, and (3) to apply practical suggestions in the use of functional substitutes. We conclude with eight actions that will hopefully point the way to better understanding, evaluation and experimentation.

1. Recognize the complexity of ancestral rites and practices. Understand them. Simplistic responses or polarized antagonism do more harm than good. Reinforcing the importance of this issue Charles Van Engen succinctly writes, "A careful, culturally-appropriate, biblically-faithful, and missiologically intentional theology of ancestor veneration still cries for development" (1998:66).

2. Exemplify strong models of genuine Christian filial piety. Believers are to excel in expressing true respect for their ancestors, especially while they are yet alive. Paul Hiebert's "unfinished business in mission" includes "ancestors and traditional life-cycle rites." These are "once again living issues that church leaders must confront. The debate surrounding these issues has been heated" (1993:258). Elsewhere Hiebert notes that people of different cultures "ask different questions. For example Africans and Asians ask, 'What shall we do about our ancestors?' Western theology gives little attention to ancestors, although much is said about them in the Bible" (1985:210). Creating examples and practices that honor parents and forbears may be a vital key to church growth in Asia.

3. Empathize with heartfelt understanding and compassion. Behind the disturbing elements in ancestral cults are deep feelings of desperate psychological need and spiritual pain. Differing views call Christians to sensitivity, patience, love and prayer, not contention, criticism and judging. Accepting people as they are and empathizing with their need and motives is paramount. Listen to their heart.

4. Focus on whole family evangelism. Asian family consciousness and extended relationships produce strengths for social unity and kinship continuity. "One by one" evangelism disturbs this, producing fractures in families and protective reactions. Practice the biblical approach of reaching and baptizing whole families. Change strategy by planting churches around households. Produce literature, videos and radio dramas that tell of family conversions. Evangelize with families in mind, rather than individuals.

5. Conduct sound research. Serious socio-anthropological, theological and missiological investigations provide data on the current beliefs about ancestor worship. Indigenous leaders can conduct in-depth studies and surveys at the grassroots. Cross-cultural comparative studies would enhance understanding regional variations of ancestor practices among people groups, providing a pool of possible models for new approaches and cross-fertilization of ideas. Interview unchurched folk especially.

6. Build on contact points. The capacity of ancestor worshipers through such concepts as belief in the soul, life after death, prayer, worship, relation with the invisible beyond, and spiritual communal sharing provide bridges to be explored and applied in the worship of God. Many positive points of honoring fathers relate to the heavenly Father.

7. Develop appropriate functional substitutes. Undertake experiments using the above bridges. With national believers' input create and test new approaches that give assurance and visibility to Christian respect for ancestors. Evaluate and recycle lessons learned.

8. Instruct new converts--educate church members. Teach believers (new and old) and missionaries about new approaches. Train them to be models in honoring. Instruct them how to relate to their relatives, and use functional substitutes. Learn to differentiate between worship of the Creator God and dutiful respect due to ancestors. Understand both monistic and biblical worldviews. Especially teach how to handle fear by trusting God's power and depending on believers' position in Christ.

8

Ancestor Veneration and Family Conversion Revisited

David S. Lim

Perhaps next to materialism, ancestral veneration remains the biggest hindrance in evangelizing Chinese peoples. Although this paper views this issue from its context of ministry to Chinese Filipinos, it believes that its relevance extends to ministries among other peoples whose cultures include ancestral beliefs and practices, including those in and also perhaps all other folk Buddhists (especially the Japanese and Koreans) and folk religionists in India, Africa (Kopytoff 1997) and elsewhere. Though folk or popular religion may also connote "the religion of the lower classes" in contrast to elite or official religion, this article uses it to denote the common religion that represents the underlying worldview, values, practices and institutions shared by a people across social boundaries (cf. Bell 1989; Teiser 1995). In this sense, Chinese religion is still popular even in China today (MacInnis 1989).

Christians have been called "traitors" (anti-Chinese) and considered "outcasts" (non-Chinese) by their compatriots whose ethnic and/or cultural identities are essentially defined by filial piety as the supreme virtue in their moral hierarchy of human relationships. In Taiwan, like in most overseas Chinese communities, many who are interested in Christianity but who were raised under a strong Chinese religious influence have been reluctant to commit their lives to Christ unless they are allowed to retain their ancestral tablets on the altar in the living room (Liaw 1985:188). Also, a Japanese minister confessed that he could not win his eldest brother who said, "If I became a Christian, all memory of our honored ancestors will perish" (McGavran 1985:314).

Ancestor veneration with its moral and cultural implications presents Christianity with a great conflict far beyond the churches. To non-Christians, Christians disrespect their departed family members; they have lost interest in and are disloyal to family traditions. Christians have been criticized, persecuted and even disowned by their families for, not religious, but for moral reasons. Can Christians not show that because of Christ, they remember their ancestors better and honor them more than the non-believers? Can't we revere our ancestors as simply the extension of love and respect for distant foreparents in obedience to the Fifth Commandment? If left unresolved, the eternal destiny of about fifty percent of the Buddhist world, and perhaps thirty percent of all unreached peoples, is at stake.

ANCESTOR VENERATION DEFINED

Ancestor veneration may convey a more accurate sense of what practitioners, such as the Chinese and other Buddhist-influenced and Confucian-influenced societies see themselves as doing. For people unfamiliar with how ancestor worship is actually practiced and thought of, the translation "worship" can be a cause of misunderstanding and is a misnomer in many ways. In English, the word worship usually refers to the reverent love and devotion accorded a deity or divine being. However, in these cultures, these acts of worship do not confer any belief that the departed ancestors have become some kind of deity. For these cultures, ancestor practices are not the same as the worship of the gods. The purpose of ancestor veneration is to do one's filial duty. Many of them believe that their ancestors actually need to be provided for by their descendants; and others do not believe that the ancestors are even aware of what their descendants do for them but that the expression of filial piety is what is important. Whether or not the ancestor receives what is offered is not the issue.

Rather the act is a way to respect, honor and look after ancestors in their afterlives as well as seek their continuous good relations with their living descendants. In this regard, many cultures and religions have similar practices. Some may visit the grave of their parents or other ancestors, leave flowers and pray to them in order to honor and remember them while also asking their ancestors to continue to look after them. However, they would not consider themselves as "worshipping" them.

Chinese ancestral veneration (*jìngzǔ*; and *bàizǔ*), seeks to honor the deeds and memories of the deceased. This is an extension of filial piety for the ancestors, the ultimate homage to the deceased as if they are alive. Instead of prayers, joss-sticks are offered with communications and greetings to the deceased. There are eight qualities of *De* (virtue) for a Chinese to complete his earthly duties, and filial piety is the foremost of those qualities. The importance of paying filial duties to parents and elders lies with the fact that all physical bodily aspects of one's being were created by one's parents who continue to tend to one's welfare until one is on firm footings. The respect and the homage to parents (i.e. filial piety) is to return this gracious deed to them in this life and after, the ultimate homage. Thus, Chinese ancestral veneration is a fusion of the classical teachings of Confucius and Laozi rather than a religious ritual.

Ancestral practices are modes of communication with the Chinese spirit-world. Food "sacrifices" are offered to "feed" the deceased. It also includes visiting the deceased at their graves, making offerings to the deceased in the *Qing Ming, Chong Yang* and Ghost festivals. All three are related to paying homage to the spirits. For those with deceased in the netherworld or hell, elaborate or even creative offerings such as a toothbrush, comb, towel, slippers, and water are provided so that the deceased will be able to have these items in the after-life. Often paper versions of these objects are burned for the same purpose, even paper cars and TVs. *Spirit money* (also called "*hell notes*") is burned as an offering to the dead. The living may regard the ancestors as "guardian angels" to them, perhaps in protecting them from serious accidents, or guiding their path in life.

Historical Rejection

When Christianity was propagated in such countries as China, Japan and Korea, ancestor veneration has been one of the most critical problems which it had to face. While there were times when Christian churches took a favorable attitude toward ancestor practices as a desirable socio-cultural custom, most Protestant churches took a critical attitude toward ancestor worship as idolatry.

Christianity entered China during the Tang dynasty. According to the Nestorian Monument, the Nestorians looked favorably upon Chinese "ancestor worship." They taught the importance of properly treating the dead and caring for those who had passed away. The limited record shows that their evangelistic efforts brought forth much fruit (Lin 1985:149).

The Jews entered China during the Song and Yuen dynasties. At that time the city of Kai-Feng had China's largest Jewish population. The Jewish Monument (erected in 1489) shows that worship of heaven was not complete if one did not also worship ancestors. This was done twice a year, once in the spring and once in the fall. The Jews believed that one must serve one's parents in the same manner after their death as while they were living by showing respect and offering food and other goods. Another Jewish monument dated 1663 described the word "worship" to mean, "the expression of one's uttermost respect and sincerity," or "the expression of one's deep gratitude and desire to repay kindness bestowed upon him." The food offered was intended to express gratitude.

The Jews in Kai-Feng not only worshipped Yahweh, but they also conducted "*Ji*" worship, and the "*Zai*" ceremony of self-cleansing and preparation. The purpose of these practices was to express gratitude to the ancestors. And in addition to the synagogue, the Jews in Kai-Feng erected another building to place ancestral tablets. They made tablets for such ancestors as Adam, Noah, Abraham, Isaac, Jacob and Moses. According to Jewish tradition, they offered vegetables and fruits because they believed that meat could be offered to God alone and only at the temple in Jerusalem (ibid.:149-150). It appears that Judaism as practiced in China basically accepted the Chinese traditional worship of heaven, Confucianism, and certain ancestor practices. They seem to have seen no conflict between Chinese and Jewish beliefs.

Roman Catholics

When the first Roman Catholic missionaries of the Society of Jesus (Jesuits) arrived mainly through Matteo Ricci, they also took a favorable attitude toward the deep-rooted Chinese tradition of ancestor practices for about 100 years from the beginning of the seventeenth century, and their churches increased. But when the church took a critical attitude for the following 200 years from the beginning of the eighteenth century, churches declined and almost disappeared.

The situation changed when the Dominicans and the Franciscans came to China in the mid-seventeenth century. They disagreed with the Jesuits and strongly fought against the Chinese traditional "worship" of Confucius and the ancestors. In 1704, Pope Clement XI approved a decree which totally forbade ancestor and Confucius "worship." The decree called *Ex illa die* was officially delivered to China in 1715. It was finally translated into Chinese in 1720. Emperor Kang Xi of the Ching dynasty, who previously held a favorable attitude toward Roman Catholic beliefs, and even wrote an imperial decree in 1692 stating that ancestor worship is a civic ceremony and not a religious ritual, was greatly displeased by the papal decree. In anger he signed a decree forbidding all Roman Catholic activities in China. The succeeding emperors also firmly held this position. As a result, Roman Catholic work, which had been prospering during the Ming and Ching dynasties, came to a halt (ibid.:151). This lost big opportunity may be the second in Chinese mission history, next to the church's failure to respond to the request of Kublai Khan in 1271 through Marco Polo to send 100 teachers of science and religion to reinforce the Nestorians.

In 1742, Pope Benedict XIV decreed *Ex quo* which overruled the "Eight Special Permissions" given to the Jesuits and forbade even the discussion of such matters among believers. This rejectionist

Family and Faith in Asia

stance lasted for 200 years. Then providentially, in 1939, Pope Pius XII reversed and decreed the removal of *Ex quo*. The pope accepted Chinese traditional worship of Confucius and the ancestors because he viewed these ceremonies as mere expressions of respect for the dead, and he believed that these rituals helped teach the younger generations to respect their own culture. He considered it right for the believers to bow or to practice other forms of rituals before a dead person, an image or tablet of a dead person (ibid.:151-152). This remains the official Roman Catholic position to this day.

In 1979 Cardinal Yu-Bin promoted the worship of heaven and the ancestors among Roman Catholic believers in Taiwan. He officiated at large-scale ceremonies, thus eliciting some public reaction. Unfortunately, the ceremonial rituals were not fully understood so the actual impact on Catholic mission was negligible.

PROTESTANTS

But the early Protestant missionaries took a critical attitude from the start, perhaps adopting the rejectionist view of their Roman Catholic contemporaries. Although they produced a good number of conversions, they were rejected by the Chinese, especially by the intelligentsia, for they were regarded as imperialistic enforcers of sweeping disapproval of Chinese culture. And when some missionaries took a favorable attitude, they hardly influenced the stance of Chinese believers.

Those who opposed ancestor worship consisted of the early missionaries, especially those of the China Inland Mission, the largest Protestant mission group. They had received basic theological training and brought with them not only their Christian beliefs but also Western social and cultural symbolism. They sincerely believed that only their religious system was appropriate to express the true Christian faith, and they failed to understand Chinese culture. They simply believed that ancestor worship was idolatrous (cf. ibid.:152-153).

Those who supported ancestor worship included such missionaries as William Martin, Allen Young, Joseph Edkins,

Alexander Williamson, Timothy Richard and others, most of whom belonged to Guang Xue Hui. They had received university education, and thus were more sensitive toward social and cultural realities. They knew that evangelism could not be a mere transmission of ideas and concepts; if Christianity was to be rooted in China, it must become a true part of Chinese social structure. They believed that the Christian faith must be accepted not only conceptually, but culturally and socially as well to truly transform Chinese people for God's kingdom.

Therefore, they also sought appropriate forms and symbolism for expressing Christian faith in daily living. They believed that Chinese believers must develop their own sets of meaningful forms and symbols. They saw no contradiction between Christian and Chinese beliefs, considering the Christian faith to be above Confucian teachings and filling the areas which were not covered by Confucianism. These missionaries believed that socio-cultural forms must not become obstacles for the upper class and intellectuals. Therefore, they had greater respect and appreciation for Chinese cultural traditions. These missionaries considered Chinese ancestor worship to have two major functions: (1) people expressed their reverence as well as feelings of closeness toward the deceased; and (2) as a nation, China maintained ancestor worship as a form of education: veneration of ancestors taught honor and respect for parents, and veneration of Confucius taught the importance of education (ibid.:153-154).

Ancestor worship was highlighted during the Second Conference of Protestant missionaries in China in 1890, to follow up the debate started at the First Conference in 1877. William Martin presented a paper entitled "The Worship of Ancestors—A Plea for Toleration," where he affirmed the educational and moral values in "ancestor worship;" it tied family members together and produced self-discipline and a sense of self-worth. He pointed out that the three elements of ancestor worship (posture, invocation and offering) contained hardly any idolatry: the bowing posture was not reserved for worshipping idols only, for Chinese also bowed before living people such as parents, their seniors, and the emperor to express respect. Invocations could be judged thus. If worshipers request protection and special favors from the ones they worship, it should be considered idolatry; but the Chinese people did not generally ask protection from the ancestors. And the key to viewing offering was not what was offered but to whom it was offered; if Westerners could offer flowers to the dead, the Chinese could surely offer meat, vegetables and fruits to their ancestors. Thus he recommended that foreign missionaries refrain from speaking against Chinese traditional practices: missionaries should trust the Holy Spirit and God's Word to do this work in the hearts of Chinese people. The Truth would influence them and naturally bring about the necessary changes. He also hoped that this would help advance Christianity in China.

Martin's paper ignited a big debate. Hudson Taylor (CIM) and C.W. Mateer (Presbyterian) led the opposition. They rejected Martin's viewpoint regarding the three elements of "ancestor worship." They pointed out that Martin only observed the aspects of respect and commemoration and failed to detect the element of idolatry. They claimed that if there was an element of idolatry in China, it surely could be found in the practice of "ancestor worship," and thus insisted that tolerating it would be ruining Christianity. They quoted many Scripture verses and totally rejected any possibility of toleration. Taylor was very influential at the conference; as the keynote speaker, he declared that every detail of the ancestor worship ceremony was idolatrous. He disagreed totally with Martin and said that Christians should not even discuss toleration of such.

The conference ended with the overwhelming victory for those who opposed "ancestor worship." Led by Taylor, almost all the delegates at the conference stood to their feet demonstrating their total opposition to ancestor worship (Lin 1985:157-158). It must be noted that no Chinese representative was at those two conferences. Since then, Chinese Protestantism's mainstream has been officially against "ancestor worship." After the Communist takeover of China, this issue became irrelevant with the banishing of all religions. No discussion also means that Protestants in both registered and unregistered churches there continue to hold the prevailing rejectionist view.

In Taiwan, people were receptive to early Protestant missions so that ancestor worship was not a problem. But in the 1960s the island nation enjoyed great economic progress which rekindled their national and cultural pride, causing a decline in the growth of the church. Facing the decline, church leaders became aware of the importance of the Christian faith being rooted in Chinese culture (ibid.:158). This was the beginning of a movement entitled "Searching for Roots." Those involved in this movement began to re-evaluate signs, forms, and symbolism used in Chinese folk religion (Ro 1985:184). They also evaluated the role that Christianity has played in the lives of the Chinese people (Lin 1985:160). So once again the whole problem of ancestor worship has surfaced.

In Korea, the Roman Catholic Church took a critical attitude toward the Confucian ancestor practices at the last quarter of the eighteenth century; it met strong resistance from government and society in general. When she took a favorable attitude from the beginning of World War II, this obstacle was removed, making it easier for the church to adapt itself to Korean society. When Protestant Christianity arrived in late nineteenth century, it took a critical attitude from the very beginning, which was a major barrier to conversions. But it did not necessarily hinder church growth; because making such a radical decision provided the new converts with a sense of new identity and mission (Ro 1985:5) and applying the "Nevius principles" provided for national church leadership (to win men and heads of families) early on. Yet the recent Korean official statistics of religious affiliations seem to indicate that the Catholic increase and the slight Protestant decline in the past decade may partly have to do with their differing stance toward ancestral practices.

RECENT ACCOMMODATION

Gladly there have been some attempts among Protestant theologians and church leaders to re-examine the rejectionist stance, but sadly there has been no significant breakthrough to reverse or modify it. The call for this evaluation comes from two main sources: Pastors realize in their ministry that in spite the official prohibition majority of their church members still practice ancestor veneration, albeit in different degrees and forms; and researchers have discovered that this is indeed still quite prevalent (cf. Tan 1996), even in a Japanese village that has had a relatively large number of Anglicans (38.9%) for three generations (1887-1975) (Berentsen 1985b:289-290).

Asia Theological Association (ATA) sponsored a Consultation on the Christian Response to Ancestor Practices in Taipei from December 1983, with ninety-eight participants from nine Asian countries, including those with significant overseas Chinese minorities; they issued a "Working Document" which sought to have a consensus for evangelical Protestants (ATA 1985:3-10) that still reflected the rejectionist view, though the papers were more open to contextualization. The Northern Synod of the Presbyterian Church in Taiwan co-sponsored a seminar on ancestral veneration led by scholars and clergy in November 2002, which highlighted the contrast between the Chinese and the Western worldviews in relation to ancestors (TCN 2002:1). There may have been other such conferences, but there seem to be no significant shift from the general and official rejectionist view.

The general sense is that of "natural accommodation" through a gradual process of both secularization and Christian influence, especially through education of the young in Christian schools, when the dead and the spirit-world (Hiebert's middle level) fade away from daily significance, so will ancestral veneration fade away as a Chinese tradition (Son 1985; cf. Ro 1985:5). Yet, the internet age has given birth to new forms of ancestral veneration: for Koreans, "cyber ancestral worship" is available online www.memorial-zone.or.kr where descendants can view pictures and videos of ancestors and their graveyards, listen to their voices, read their biographies and accomplishments, and submit commemorating messages.

Through its interaction with their immediate communities, Chinese Protestantism has developed a distinct morality and theology of filial piety (cf. Yip 1985:141-142). It is not difficult to notice the affinities between its moral emphasis and that of Chinese religion. Confucianism, which dominated the educational system of the imperial dynasties, has a strong concern for the morality of human relationships, especially filial piety. While it is essentially the religion of the literati, it was spread by storytellers, dramas, tracts, and proverbial sayings, Confucian morality has left an impact on popular religion, which is upheld and practiced by the populace.

Converts to Protestantism have hardly changed their Chinese worldview and value system. Attracted by the claimed superiority in terms of efficacy of Christianity, some Chinese who had been practicing traditional religion turned to Christianity in crises, such illnesses, identity crisis of teenagers, and needs of new migrants to cities. Their ready acceptance of Christianity was facilitated by some similarities between these two traditions. Deities, rituals and other manifestations of their former religion (Chinese religion) were consciously rejected, and they devoted themselves to the individual and communal practices of this new faith. Yet, their acceptance of Protestantism have been based on and informed by the ideas, categories, conceptual scheme, value system, etc., of the very religious tradition they consciously rejected. These socio-religious worldview continues to be operative in helping them to understand and appropriate the new religious tradition.

With regard to healing and exorcism, Jesus is a more powerful and promising deity, a more efficacious alternative to the traditional gods in a world constantly intruded by demons and evil spirits. With regard to morality, they interpret and appropriate Christian moral teachings in a Chinese way, upholding filial piety and family harmony in the same manner as their former religion. With regard to divine-human relationships, they relate with the Christian God in terms of the ideas of retribution and reciprocity which are essential elements in Chinese popular religion. All these are not a simple mixing of elements of Protestantism and Chinese religion, nor are these a simple acceptance of one religious tradition and rejection of another (ibid.:148-149). This natural accommodation may be viewed as the actualization of Protestantism in Chinese worldview. This actualization is not static; it will gradually develop new innovations within the slowly changing boundaries of socio-religious traditions, especially when post-modernism will be encouraging more tolerant and accommodating attitudes towards the worldviews of New Age and other new religious movements.

Yet the gap between the socio-religious traditions of Protestantism and Chinese religion remains very wide, for it is still perceived as anti-cultural and even anti-family. Hence, several suggestions of "more conscious" accommodation or contextualization by using "functional substitutes" have emerged (cf. Smith 2006:169-175). Many of these have been implemented but hardly on official or large scale, and thus with hardly any social impact.

Some have sought to transform traditional Chinese funerals into Christian Chinese funerals. For example, in Taiwan where a memorial table is traditionally established for friends and relatives to show their concern for the mourning family by burning incense sticks for the deceased, Christians have urged to set up a similar table to show respect for the deceased and love and concern for the family members (Liaw 1985:191). The Taiwan Presbyterian Church has endorsed hanging on the central wall a picture of Christ, the Ten Commandments and Bible verses on large sheets of paper and carefully framed. An enlarged and framed photo of the deceased is also hung in a prominent place in the house, but not on the spot once occupied by the ancestral tablets (Liao 1985:214; Hung 1985:202; Ro 1985:184).

Hung (1985:206) notes that Taiwanese (and Filipino Chinese, too) hire professional mourners for the funeral procession; they regard those who die without people to mourn for them with speech-wailing as being most unfortunate. Thus, they see Christians as those who "die without people mourning." He urges Christians to weep and cry at the death and funeral of a family member, but without wailing speeches. They should wail or cry aloud, possibly with such words as, "Lord, be with us and comfort us;" "Lord, sustain us in times of sadness;" "Lord, guide so-and-so to heaven safely and into your bosom," or "Rest so-and-so in heavenly peace."

In Taiwanese tradition the family holds a total of seven memorial services, one every seven days after burial. The purpose of these services is to venerate the deceased, and usually a Taoist priest or Buddhist monk leads the relatives in the rituals. These services serve the purpose of gradually relieving the bereaved of their emotional burden. Thus Christians have been encouraged to also have memorial services during which the family can sing Christian songs and share the message of the Bible, and thus serve evangelistic purposes as well (Liaw 1985:192-193; Hung 1985:202). Usually it takes once a year on the anniversaries of the day of death, and the local pastor is asked to preside over it (Liao 1985:214). This is also done in Korea, but the form and content are so "Christian" (cf. Chung 2006:140-141), so that these ceremonies hardly count as honoring their ancestor by non-Christians.

Some Christians say they continue to go to the annual meetings where people of common lineage come together to offer sacrifices to ancestors. Christians do not participate in the sacrificial offerings, but the purpose of their presence is to maintain fellowship with the relatives and to show them that they have not forsaken the ancestors and the clan people (Liao 1985:214).

Christians are encouraged to prepare their own family records similar to those possessed by clan leaders. One publisher in Taiwan has made blank forms of family records available for use by Christians. Hakka ministers are especially anxious to get Christians to prepare such records in order to show non-Christians their regard for their glorious ancestry (ibid.). In Taiwan and in the Philippines, some give donations in memory of the departed loved ones are given for Christian work or to charity institutions (cf. ibid.).

Above all, during the *Qing Ming* Festival, Christian families have been told to visit and clean their ancestors' graves, and the head of the family can lead a Christian memorial service as a substitute for offering sacrifices to the ancestors. With flowers, hymns and short devotionals, Christians can show love and respect to the deceased (Liao 1985:214; Liaw 1985:192; Hung 1985:202). The elders in my Chinese church in the Philippines used to lay flowers in the graves deceased church members every All Saints' Day, but not during *Qing Ming*.

Liao (1985:215-216) finds these to be still inadequate to build a healthy image of Christianity before the eyes of the Chinese world. So he gives six more suggestions for Taiwan context. First, a veteran Hakka pastor in Taiwan mentioned to the writer that the hardest part of removing ancestral tablets is the anguish at having to deny the beloved progenitors a place in the family; for fear that the children will forget their ancestors. He suggests that a large, beautiful frame containing the names and brief descriptions of all the main ancestors be hung at a prominent spot in the house. This is different from the photographs which portray only the most recent generations.

Second, as proposed by two church leaders from China, new Christian families should write the names of all their ancestors on the blank pages provided in a large family Bible, which can then be placed in a prominent place such as on the altar table where the ancestral tablets are usually found.

Third, churches should hold annual memorial meetings called "Ancestors' Day." In such a meeting Christians will be exhorted to give special remembrance of their past generations and to add more honor to the family's reputation by more achievements. This has been the practice of some Christians in China; some churches had this kind of meeting on the Spring Festival (presumably the fifth of April) or the Chinese (Lunar) New Year's Day to take the place of the customary sacrifices.

Fourth, annual memorial meetings may be held by Christian members of a clan or an extended family. Non-Christian members may be invited to attend. Besides a Christian service for the memory of ancestors and for the fellowship of living members, the program may include other activities such as an athletic meet or a commendation ceremony for members who have had academic or other achievements during the year.

Fifth, "some churches plant trees or flowers in the church cemetery at the ancestor worship festival." This is a useful and durable monument for the deceased. Tree planting at the graveside is a traditional Chinese practice. One tree, planted at Confucius' tomb (in Shantung province) by his disciples, is said to be living yet today.

And lastly, family records should be kept at church. Instead of keeping these at home, Christians should be able to store them in a special foyer in the church. This will strengthen the tie of the church to the families and even "force" non-Christian family members to come to church. The church might well fulfill the function of the clan hall. And in today's internet, perhaps Christians can put these records in a website, to show how they still remember and respect their ancestors.

RECOMMENDED STRATEGY

These many attempts to contextualize ancestral veneration have been individual and piece-meal, and have hardly worked. Invitations to attend memorial services hosted by Christians have been avoided by non-Christian relatives, and some have been threatened with harm (Hung 1985:204-206). The latter consider Christian funeral rites to be void of proper respect and decorum, thus the dead are buried "like rats" (K.S. Tan 1985:221-222). This poor reputation before the community is mainly because Christians have been trying to contextualize in their own terms and understanding, rather than from the viewpoint of their contemporaries. The general perception is correctly understood that there is really no change from its rejectionist stance due to church pressure and tradition.

What is required is a paradigm shift for "radical contextualization" (cf. Lim 2003) to fully identify with Chinese people and their culture, as Paul says "to become all things to all men" truly, so that we may not only be able to win some (especially heads of households, clans and communities) and thereby disciple them to win the rest, but also to be true to the essence of biblical Christianity that is multi-cultural. This approach has three theological bases, three missiological principles and three major practical implications.

THEOLOGICAL BASIS

First, There are three tenets that underpin the radical contextualization view of ancestor veneration; it is theologically not idolatrous, practically not religious, and culturally communitarian.

Filiality Not Idolatry

The Bible clearly condemns the worship of gods and the making of idols (Ex. 20:4-5). 1 Corinthians 10:4-21; 5:11, Revelation 21:8; 21:18-19, and Deuteronomy 4:2 teach that God abhors idolatry, and those who do it do not belong to God. The object of any worship, ceremony and ritual must be God alone.

Yet, I do not know of a Chinese who considers any ancestor as a god to be worshiped. Most, if not all, will find the idea of their ancestor turning into or being a god ludicrous and even abhorrent (cf. TCN 2002:1). Chinese Filipinos believe in only one universal spirit whose manifestations (*hua shen*) include all the religious figures on earth (Buddha, Mohammed, Jesus Christ, etc.). They believe this spirit is the source of existence and is benevolent and effective, which performs miracles and brings good fortune (Uayan 2005:72). So the Chinese lean towards monotheism, although for many the "supreme spirit" may not be personal as in Judeo-Christian and other theistic faiths.

Gladly, since 1982, Hiebert (1999:47) has helped us understand the primal worldview better. It has three levels of reality: the bottom level is the empirical world as experienced through human senses; the top level includes cosmic realms beyond human experience; and in between, one finds the unseen or trans-empirical realities of this world. These three levels emerge out of the intersection of this world (earth, universe) and other worlds (heaven, hell), of the seen (empirical) and unseen (trans-empirical).

In the Chinese belief system the three main worldview concerns are cosmology, the pantheon of living beings, and humans. Chinese believe the universe is permeated with the cosmic breath or life force called *Qi*, sometimes described in a bipolar manner as *Yin* and *Yang*. All of existence is the result of the interplay of these two forces. Humans are but a feeble part of this cosmos and, as such, must live in harmony with the cosmological process.

Infinite numbers of gods, deities, spirits and ancestors make up the vast pantheon of Chinese religion. Tan (1996:60-87) identifies many of the non-human beings identified by MetroManila Chinese Filipinos, showing how they also accommodate the Filipino belief system within their own. The following chart for Chinese folk belief systems appears as follows (Uayan 2005:70):

Chinese Folk Belief Systems

		Organic	Mechanical
Other Worlds		Jade emperors (*Tien*) Gods and Goddesses	*Ming Yun* *Yin* and *Yang*
This World		Earth gods Sages Mythological figures Spirits and ghosts Ancestors Animal spirits (totem)	Five elements Magic Feng Shui Divination Palmistry Luck
		People Animals	Acupuncture Matter

Hiebert et. al. (1999:50) also point out that "boundaries between the categories are often fuzzy" and the "organic and mechanical analogies form a horizontal continuum with many shades between the poles." Applying this model to the Chinese Filipino belief system, the chart looks like this:

Chinese-Filipino Folk Belief Systems

		Organic	Mechanical
Other World		God the Father, Jesus, *Tien Chu*, Gods and goddesses (Buddhist/Taoist gods, Kuan Yin/Ma-Tzu/Virgin Mary) Angels, Satan, devils	*Ming Yun*/Fate and fortune *Yin* and *Yang*
This World		Earth gods, duwendes (Buddhist/Taoist) Sages/Saints, Mythological figures (*kapre*, *agta*) Spirits and ghosts Ancestors Animal spirits (totem)	Priests/pastors/faith healers/ feng shui masters Five elements Magic Feng Shui Divination Palmistry/horoscope Good luck charms/ *anting-anting, tawas, kulam*
		People Animals and plants	Chinese medicine/doctors *Manananggal, mangkukulam* Matter

Take note that the ancestors consistently belong to the middle level and separate from the upper level. The dead ancestors exist and have to be accorded their due. They can provide help, but they can also create problems; if the living experience bad luck or worse, it may be because they have neglected to honor their ancestors. Where do they reside? In heaven or hell? In the Yellow Springs? In the earth? In the air? In the rivers? It depends on their status and on the believer. There is no single answer (Chamberlain 1987:43). They can be anywhere. But gods they are not.

It is obvious that syncretism is an important trait of Chinese religion. Of course, syncretism has been at work in all religions, but to the extent that Chinese religions are themselves "religions of harmony," they have allowed more latitude to the workings of syncretism than have the more exclusivist religions, like Christianity and Islam (Yip 1999:133-134; Ching 1993:205). Chinese religion is itself a model of syncretism, intermingling elements of ancient Chinese religious traditions (such as divination and ancestor veneration) with those of "Greater Traditions" (Confucianism, Daoism and Buddhism) into a complex whole (Yip 1999:132-133; cf. Cohen 1987:289-290; Overmyer 1986:51, 69-70).

For the gods and spirits and artifacts that are classified in the upper level, these have to be demoted and denounced as idolatrous. Any Chinese who wants to become a Christian must repent of idolatry. Yet careful study of the Chinese worldview clearly shows that ancestors are distinct from gods. Therefore ancestral veneration is to be viewed as filial piety and not idolatry. This is similar to the way that Roman Catholics understand the veneration of Mary and the saints. For those who are struggling to accept this view, referring to missiological works on how to reach "folk religions" would be most helpful (i.e, van Rheenen 1996; Hiebert et al 1999; Yip 1999).

Cultural Not Religious

Second, ancestral veneration is cultural, not religious, basically rooted in filial piety. In Chinese thought, filial piety (*xiào*) is one of the virtues to be cultivated, a love and respect for one's parents and ancestors. The Confucian classic "Book of Filial Piety" (*Xiao Jing*) written around 470 B.C.E., has historically been the authoritative source on *xiào*. The book, a conversation between Confucius and his student Zeng Shen (Zengzi), is about how to set up a good society using the principle of "filial piety," and thus for over 2,000 years has been one of the basic texts in the Chinese Imperial Civil Service Exams.

Filial piety means to be good to one's parents; to take care of one's parents; to engage in good conduct not just towards parents but also outside the home so as to bring a good name to one's parents and ancestors; to perform the duties of one's job well so as to obtain the material means to support parents as well as carry out sacrifices to the ancestors; not be rebellious; show love, respect and support; display courtesy; ensure male heirs, uphold fraternity among brothers; wisely advise one's parents, including dissuading them from moral unrighteousness; display sorrow for their sickness and death; and carry out "sacrifices" after their death.

Ancestor veneration is so important, because filial piety is considered the first virtue in Chinese culture, and it is the main concern of a large number of stories. One of the most famous collections of such stories is *The Twenty-four Filial Exemplars* (*Ershi*). These stories tell how children exercised their filial piety in the past. While China has always had a diversity of beliefs, filial piety has been common to almost all of them; respect for the family is the only element common to almost all Chinese (Baker 1979). These traditions were sometimes enforced by law; during parts of the Han dynasty, for example, those who neglected ancestor veneration were subject to corporal punishment.

For Confucius, *xiào* was not merely blind loyalty to one's parents. More important than the norms of *xiào* were the norms of *rén* (benevolence) and *yì* (righteousness). For him and Mencius *xiào* was a display of *rén* which was ideally applied in one's dealings with all elders, thus making it the norm of intergenerational relations. But in practice, *xiào* has become reserved for one's own parents and grandparents, and has been elevated above the notions of *rén* and *yì*. Hence, family-centeredness is prominent in ancestral practices.

Continuity Not Discontinuity

The third tenet for radical contextualization is to give more emphasis to continuity rather than discontinuity with the people's cultural and religious background. This is the best way to develop indigenous (Chinese) theologies and to catalyze more effective "people movements" to Christianity. In relation to ancestor veneration, this positive stance towards accommodating as much of the indigenous culture as possible would enable a better understanding of the "communion of saints."

As seen above, Chinese and oriental (and perhaps most primal) cultures (hence "folk religions") have a deep sense of interconnectedness that extends to maintaining relationships with the ancestral dead. They perceive the dead to be separated from human society merely by a curtain of invisibility. In communalistic cultures, the concepts of being surrounded by a "great crowd of witnesses" (Heb. 12:1) and "the communion of saints" (Apostles' Creed) make sense. The Christian faith is continuous with the faith of ancestral heroes, and God is as much the god of our ancestors as He was the "God of Abraham, Isaac and Jacob." To those in similar cultures, this formulaic title of God's self-disclosure and the biblical genealogies are really major texts, emphasizing the sense of continuity of God's generational presence across the divide that separates the living from the dead.

Unfortunately, much of Protestant evangelicalism has emphasized the cultural discontinuities that must be made as proof of genuine conversion. While some elements in the Christian faith will necessarily disrupt culture, most of it is continuous with the primitive revelation that we find in all religions. The "folk" sense that we are not alone, that we are part of a great community that stretches back through many generations, reflects the biblical idea of a "crowd of witnesses," its "family of God" imagery that includes the "heavenly church assembly of living spirits" (Heb. 12:23) and the creedal concept of the "communion of saints" (cf. Berentsen 1985:264-267; 1985b:289-290).

For instance, in native Filipino funerary rites, art objects and other artifacts express this deep reverence for the dead and the continuing importance of the dead for the living. The rituals connected to *Todos los Santos*, and the extended time of mourning signified by *pasiyam, padasal, babang-luksa* and other such commemorative markers, speak of a people whose relational sense is unbroken by death and who believe in the continuing claims of the dead upon the living. Many upland community festivals are meant for ancestral heroes, like Kabigat and Balitok among the Ikalahan. In these communities, the *caniao* is, at its base, not so much a religious as a social rite, a way of affirming ties with the ancestral spirits who are invited to participate in the drinking, feasting and dancing. It is also a way of identifying who belongs to the community. The *caniao* is a sign and seal of the people's sense of identity together as a community (Maggay 2005:47).

This sense of connectedness explains the anxiety Protestant converts among these tribes have that their dead should also have a burial blanket that identifies them with their clan. The practice serves as locus of identity—of who they are and what they shall be in the afterlife. Without a blanket one wanders about like an outcast, not able to belong anywhere. Their animism is not preoccupied with the worship of spiritual life forces, but with maintaining harmonious ties with ancestor *anitos* and all other spirit beings (ibid.; cf. Dunawan 2002).

Folk cultures may know more of what this means than those who have been initiated into a religion that assumes people are all atomized individuals who live entirely in the present, without any notion that humans have some connection to an invisible society of those who have gone before (Maggay 2005:48). Converts from folk cultures need to compose new songs to praise the God of Abraham, Isaac and Jacob, and record their genealogies in their art forms. To do otherwise is to repeat the "heresy" of the Judaizers who expected Gentile converts to adopt Jewish forms.

Missiological Principles

These theological tenets lead to three missiological principles in radical contextualization: cultural integration, community conversion and socio-religious transformation.

Cultural Integration

The main principle is to adopt the existent socio-religious culture as much as possible. It is to integrate the Christian faith with the ethnic and cultural identity of the people, with strong indigenous church leadership from the beginning. Missiologists have called these the four characteristics of indigenous churches: self-governing, self-propagating, self-supporting and self-theologizing (the last has been added in Hiebert 1994). Failure to do so has resulted in the transplanting of foreign churches, and not the planting of indigenous churches. Such cultural dislocations invite real syncretism, even Christo-paganism or "split-level Christianity."

Chinese religion, which diffuses and permeates Chinese society, is inseparable from Chinese culture. Except in the case of the professional religious living apart in monasteries, religion in China was so woven into the broad fabric of family and social life that there was not even a special word for it until modern times. To a great extent the basic ideas of ancestral veneration coincide with beliefs and values that pervade Chinese culture as a whole (Cohen 1987:289; Ching 1993:2). Suggesting the model of an "Asiatic mode of religion," Chan and Hunter (1994:54) stress that "religion is part of culture and the cycles of daily life." This implies that Chinese socio-religious practices and beliefs are, according to Western categories, more cultural than religious.

Can biblical Christianity become the fulfillment of Chinese religion? Can Christians use the traditional forms of ancestral veneration to enrich them with biblical meaning? And perhaps even show that Christians accept ancestral veneration as obedience to the Fifth Commandment to honor one's parents, and that they care about their ancestors more than folk Buddhists do (cf. McGavran 1985:318; Kraft 1979:309)? For this to happen, "conversion should not 'deculturize' a convert... The convert may try to adopt the evangelist's culture, instead the attempt should be firmly but gently resisted" (Willowbank Report 1978:78).

There is often no need to introduce new rites or practices in place of old ones. There are already rituals and festivals within cultures that are of themselves purely cultural and amoral (the Reformers' *adiaphora*); these should be welcomed and used by Christians, because they are familiar and give a sense of solidarity and security for the people (Davis 1993:85; cf. Kraft 1979:323). The goal is to develop local theologies and local expressions of Christianity which are culturally appropriate and wholesome; any other way would mean a perpetuation of arrogant cultural and theological imperialism (Davis 1993:86). We must seek to use the existing cultural forms and expressions except when they distinctly clash with the message of the gospel (cf. Brown 2006; Kraft 1979).

Many Protestants have no (or better, rejectionist) "theology of culture," so they do not consider indigenous ways, not realizing that most of their own socio-religious expressions have been "baptized" into Christian usage by their previously pagan ancestors. They deny and reject for others what their faith-ancestors have done. Instead they should follow Bavinck's (1960:178) view of "taking possession" of "heathen forms of life," and make them new; and in the case of ancestral veneration, retaining and enlisting its practices in the service of Jesus Christ is "perfectly proper." Tippett (1985:185) observes, "In the process of incorporating converts into their new fellowship group or congregation, indigenous forms, rites, festivals, and so forth, which can be given a new Christian value content, have greater likelihood of finding permanent acceptance than foreign forms and rituals."

Contextualization follows the logic of the divine incarnational method. Jesus (with ceremonial washing), John the Baptist (with use of baptism) and Paul (with use of the altar to the unknown god, Ac. 17) risked being misunderstood, yet they met their people where they were at in their understanding and then built a bridge of communication, taking them from the known to the unknown (Davis 1993:94). This is the principle of "becoming all things to all men" (1 Cor. 9:19-23). The alternative is either creating new forms that would most likely be easily rejected as foreign or just leaving a vacuum (which will create an "empty house" that will invite seven demons worse than the first). Of course, the content and meaning of all religious forms, rituals and festivities (and secular ones, too, like Valentine's Day, Memorial/Heroes' Days) have to constantly be explained and re-interpreted, lest they lose relevance.

Ricci successfully did this in fifteenth century China, thereby avoiding the creation of a socio-religious vacuum. He had 300,000 converts (ibid.:81-82), which could have led to a "people movement" had his approach not been stopped by the pope. Although Roman Catholicism has reverted to Ricci's position since 1939, it has experienced limited growth because its forms are still too Western.

Communal Conversion

Second, radical contextualization aims at family conversions (Smith 2006:174), and through them, also group and even people/mass conversion (cf. McGavran 1985:304-315). Unlike the prevalent "extraction evangelism" of Protestant missions, this calls for "insider movements," wherein converts are encouraged to stay in their family and community, so that they can share their faith with them (cf. Lim 2006). For this to happen missiologically, the focus must be on conversions of adults, preferably leaders of households, clans, communities and even peoples. Sadly, Protestant missions have focused on the marginalized and youth, who have been put under severe stress and persecution, especially because of the church's rejectionist stance. Rather than being major decision-makers, these converts are considered rebels and traitors when they refuse to follow family traditions. There is much wisdom in the New Testament church's practice of conversions of heads of households, responsible adults who upon conversion and immediate baptism include their whole families, thereby ensuring a solid beachhead for evangelization, and also avoiding unnecessary trauma and persecution of young converts.

Moreover, to achieve communal conversions, community involvement is necessary, perhaps even a prerequisite, for the church-planting movement (CPM) worker needs to earn his/her right to be accepted and heard by the community. In the past, successful missions have been done through works of mercy, like health care and education. At present, many forms of community development work have been used. In fact, any professional skill will do. This is the advantage of the expatriate: his or her community service can not help but be visible; hence, access to leaders is almost unavoidable! However, unless combined with a sensitivity to focus on befriending and converting the leaders, as well as urging them to take leadership to build the Christian community, there will be very minimal possibility of having communal conversions or people movements.

Because of the highly integrated character of ancestral rites in Chinese culture, changes can not be imposed from the outside. The expatriate must therefore give leadership to the culturally sensitive new believers to decide which old forms to adopt or modify and which ones to discard. These local leaders should be encouraged to use old forms and re-invest them with new meaning and value (Tippett 1987:185; and Davis 1993:83, quoting Eugene Nida). Such changes must be done as soon as possible, "When good functional substitutes have been proposed and accepted at the time of the primary religious change (conversion),...these have stood the test of time and proved effective" (Tippett 1985:185). Insider movements can happen only when from the beginning it is truly indigenous: self-governing and self-theologizing!

Socio-Religious Transformation

All this is not to say that the primal or folk worldview and its practices should not be changed. In fact, they will and must be transformed "from glory to glory." Yet in the process, the theologies, liturgies and orthopraxes that will evolve will surely contribute to the enrichment of the glorious unity-in-diversity of the Christian faith.

Historically, Christianity has been able to turn pagan and secular traditions into Christian ones, so there should be no lack of confidence that she can take on the whole Chinese religious worldview, too! The Chinese church can be spiritually formed and give relevant witness to their compatriots by developing their distinctly Chinese forms of worship, catechesis and festivals.

Fortunately, there has been one significant model of this transformation: *Tao Fong Shan* ("The Mount Where the Wind of *Tao* [or *logos*] Blows") in Hong Kong. Its buildings use Chinese temple architecture and its Christian community has sought to live out and demonstrate the most sensitive and contextual integration of the Christian faith and Chinese culture, including ancestral veneration. It was founded by the Norwegian Lutheran missionary, Karl Reichelt (1877-1952) who arrived in China in 1903 to find the poor relationship between Christians, especially Western missionaries, and the general population. He made a sustained first-hand study of the life and practices of the best of Confucianism, Buddhism and Taoism in China.

He set up a Christian monastery in Nanjing in 1922, where visiting monks and serious seekers (averaging a thousand a year) could come for meditation and discussion. He transferred to Hong Kong in 1927, which introduced "the universal, the cosmic, the all-embracing Savior Jesus Christ" to all those who visited this "monastery." Converts were baptized, but instead of letting them join the existing churches, he encouraged these "Friends of the *Tao*" to spread out and evangelize in the temples and monasteries. Reichert wrote, "Although not joining the external church, such enter the yearly increasing number of unknown and unregistered Christ-followers" (cf. Kung 1993). Although this had the potential to grow into a movement, it carried a complex structure which made it difficult to replicate. There is a recent report of a similar yet simpler movement in a Buddhist-dominated country, but this has to be confirmed.

Reichelt's approach is "from above" through the socio-religious elite, but my preferred transformation is "bottom up" through the church-planting movement (CPM) or the "house church multiplication" strategy that is growing among secularized and/or folk Buddhists in Japan, Cambodia and Myanmar today. Combined with the focus on family conversions and family-to-family evangelism, they are discipled to be less concerned about religious practices, but to grow "unto Christ" to be more generous (more caring towards and sharing with their neighbors), which is the 'agape' law of Christ" (cf. Gal.6:1-2) (Lim 2008; Brown 2007). Transformation for ancestor-worshipping cultures means freedom from fear of ancestors, nature spirits, fate and/or gods, which is the source of so much superstitions (= religious practices which have no rational or scientific basis). A transformed socio-religious culture will reflect the simple faith of the Torah, minus the blood sacrifices that have been fulfilled in Christ. It will consist only of weekly Sabbaths through house-fellowships, as in the New Testament church, and three-times-a-year community celebrations (Passover, Pentecost, Tabernacles; Deut. 16:16).

Such is the radical contextualization approach to the evangelization and transformation of peoples and nations. It is not syncretism, because it emphasizes that the content and meaning is

"Christ and his finished work on the cross" only, but that also the forms must be culture-sensitive. Those who oppose this approach can be counter-charged with "syncretism" with the secularized Enlightenment worldview of modern science and rationalism that deny the existence and powers of beings in Hiebert's "excluded middle."

PRACTICAL IMPLICATIONS

There are three practical implications so as to effect "insider movements:" effective evangelism must be personalized, contextualized and holistic.

Personalized

Evangelism must use the friendly approach: inviting people on a spiritual journey with us, not as salespeople prompting a decision to close a deal (cf. Richardson 2006). Since there is a wide variety of ancestral beliefs and practices even just among the Chinese, it is necessary that the evangelist must first find out the socio-religious background of the non-believers, and proceed with "gentleness and respect" (1 Pet. 3:15). The rule is to listen carefully, and to accept their views non-judgmentally, even if they are dead wrong. We can correct them later, if necessary, during the discipling stage.

There should be only one stumbling-block, "Christ and him crucified," the convert can learn all the rest of his teachings later and unlearn all his unbiblical worldviews later in the discipling process. Salvation is through their simple faith to follow Jesus, so they can come to him "just as they are," in their context, with no requirement for worldview change. Otherwise, who can claim to be saved, since our worldviews are not completely biblical yet (cf. 1 Cor.13:8)? Most expect too much from their converts, usually, that they not only believe in Jesus, but also follow the evangelist's religiosity of his/her brand of Christianity.

Even discipling must be personalized. Spirituality is based on our relationship with God and reflected in our relationship with fellowmen. It is not measured by adherence to religious practices which vary from culture to culture. God delights in creativity and diversity. We must allow freedom of conscience and allow each believer to find the boundaries of their religious faith in light of the Scriptures and avoid being judgmental or legalistic (Rom. 14:1-15:7).

Moreover, since Christians are known to be rejectionist towards "ancestor worship," one must avoid being categorized under or associated with mainstream Christianity. If one is suspected or accused of being part of the rejectionist community, s/he must apologize for such attitudes of the churches in the past and at the present. This is a very important act of humility that can open the opportunity for one to share the gospel.

Contextualized

Christians should show that we remember our ancestors and honor them from the bottom of our hearts, perhaps exceeding even those of non-believers (cf. 1 Tim. 5:8). We must suppress any urge to criticize the non-Christian practices (Chow 1985:144; Smith 2006:173-174).

We must allow young converts to follow their family traditions, including bowing down, offering incense (cf. Mal. 1:11), eating food offered to idols (1 Cor. 8,10) and making tablets or scrolls, just like Paul who did not object to the Corinthian practice of "baptizing the dead" (1 Cor.15:29). Out of love, they must never cause their families, clans and communities to stumble over socio-religious practices (1 Cor. 10:32-33, cf. 8:9-13).

In Korea, Yonggi Cho, the senior pastor of the famous Yoido Full Gospel Church got into big trouble with the Presbyterian churches there because he taught that a believer could bow down during "ancestral worship." He remarked, "We Koreans serve our living parents by bowing down. Why is it alright to bow down to living parents and not to dead parents? Dead parents are still their parents, thus it is not sinful to bow down to dead parents during ancestral worship" (www.goni.kimc.net/sacrifice.htm). His stance must be emulated.

Once people have received Christ (preferably baptized with their family), they must be discipled in private, and in small groups. All efforts must focus in winning their families to the same faith as soon as possible. If they (especially family-heads) regard their ancestors as gods/deities, hence worthy of their worship, they will surely realize very soon that repentance requires leaving such idolatry. If they fail to realize this, a gentle dialogic probe into the logic of their new-found faith in "Jesus is Lord" will lead them to burn their idols and paraphernalia. If they (especially family-heads, too) view their ancestors as human spirits who hover among the living, capable of providing or withholding protection, assistance and even "bad luck" unless offered food and other material needs, they can be helped to find "functional substitutes," or better, encouraged to gradually drop the practices bit by bit, without calling attention to their conversion in the community. Hiebert's "excluded middle" may be considered to be existent (perhaps in the "communion of saints"), but not relevant to earthly life.

The forms of their spirituality will most probably differ from mainstream westernized Christianity/ies. There is no divine form of Christianity which is suitable for all believers at all times. This is how indigenous theology will evolve, too. This is not a "to each his own" and uncritical theologizing. Caught in the tension of Scripture, church tradition and one's culture, each believer must choose the way to follow Christ and obey God's word in their context. We must believe that the Holy Spirit will use the word to illumine and direct each believer to be God's "priest, prophet and king" in Christ, especially in the Bible reflection or sharing time with their discipler(s) or small groups. Christians have a plurality of options rather than one single choice in ancestral veneration, as they reflect on biblical principles, cultural values and family practices. It is not the church or the pastor, but the believers themselves who will make the decisions. Some errors may occur, but the believing community around them will keep them in check (cf. Chung 2006:152-155). The major aim is to achieve family conversion and growth as well as communal conversion and socio-religious transformation.

In communal discipling, they can be taught that before Buddhism came to China with its doctrines of heaven, hell, reincarnation and transmigration of souls, there was hardly any concern for elaborate burial practices, like burning paper money, to plead for blessings and protection from ancestors (Wei 1985:130; Lin 1985:149). The classical Chinese emphasis on filial piety is much simpler and is just concerned for proper morals, "Filial piety is the root of all virtues and the stem out of which grows all moral teaching. It starts with the service of parents; it proceeds to the service of the Ruler, and culminates by the establishment of the character" (*Xiao Jing*, ch.1, in Chang 1975:838). And from one essay of Ou Yang Shieu, a noted scholar and statesman in the Sung Dynasty, "It is more important to provide respectfully and affectionately for the needs of the parents when they are alive, rather than worship them by burning paper money and spreading a feast before ancestral tablets which are more superstitious practices" (Chang 1975:839). Originally, ancestral veneration was "void of religious content" (Son 1985:244).

Holistic

Since our objective is to win entire peoples to Christ, our approach must also be holistic, so that we can be in a position to evangelize adults, even community and socio-religious leaders. When they are converted, they can lead in the education (and possible worldview change) of the rest of the populace.

Efforts must be extended to befriend Buddhist and Taoist monks and nuns. Christians should participate in the activities of the Qing Ming and Chong Yang festivals (cf. Liaw 19985:188). As we join in socio-religious and civic affairs, we show our willingness to cooperate with people of good will to establish shalom/peace and transformational communities. The best way to win people's hearts is doing sacrificial acts of love.

Moreover, the best way to honor ancestors is to love our neighbors today, through our social achievements or "good works." This is exactly what Christian spirituality is:,to glorify God as his light in the world through our good works (Matt. 5:16), which is the summary of the Torah in the Great Commandment (Matt. 22:37-39) and in the Golden Rule (7:12) to do to others what we want to be done to us, which is the positive and higher version of Confucius' dictum, "Don't do to others what you don't want to be done to you." This is perfected in Jesus' New Commandment which raises the standard to the highest level: to love one another as he loved us (John 13:34-35), which is self-sacrificially!

Christians should therefore use their time, energy, resources and skills to do community services, from their homes, offices and any public property. If needed and capable, they can build (or turn their church buildings into) community ministry centers. There is no need really to build more religious buildings for offering religious services, for any meeting turns into a church (Christian service) when it includes prayer and Bible reflection/sharing.

Conclusion

The radical contextualization approach to ancestral veneration aims for family conversions and people movements that will transform Chinese and similar cultures from within through "insider movements." With the rise of new religious movements, mostly with Buddhist and primal worldviews in our globalized world, this approach may be the most relevant and effective mission strategy in the twenty-first century, too.

Yet, it would be very hard to expect the present rejectionist denominations and churches to adopt this mission paradigm officially. Their leadership and laity have already been perceived, often accurately, by their compatriots to be isolated sub-cultural minorities that have been westernized and modernized and have completely rejected the folk Buddhist worldview and practices. Most, if not all, of them are bound to church traditions which are hardly open to questioning the macro-issue of the socio-cultural barriers between their Christianity and the wider community, which have made effective evangelism very difficult and "Christward movements" virtually impossible. They may even take pride in their rejectionist religious heritage that had invited persecution and martyrdom to their forebears. Many even have an eschatology that "only a minority ('the elect') will be saved anyway." Moreover, change of their position would require much spiritual maturity and humility, for it infers that Roman Catholics and some "Liberals" are right, and also requires some form of public apology towards their respective non-Christian communities.

What can be done most urgently and more effectively today are new church-planting movements in these ancestor-venerating contexts to break this traditional stronghold that has kept multitudes of folk Buddhists and folk religionists from eternal life in heaven and abundant life on earth. New brands of Christianity in ancestral venerating contexts have begun, but they need to multiply through insider movements and house church networks. The eternal destiny of 1.5 billion people is at stake. Without this shift, we condemn them to reject Christ through a Christianity that is perceived to be disrespectful of parents, elders and ancestors. For those who hesitate, for the sake of the gospel and by God's mercies, please support (or at least allow) others to try and make this shift for the next ten years.

9

A New Family Model for Japanese People

Mitsuo Fukuda

In 2003 approximately 270,000 couples divorced in Japan. More than one out of three marriages in Japan now ends in divorce. By the year 1998, increasing economic and emotional dissatisfaction with the family system had become evident in Japanese society. The rate of child abuse and of divorce began to climb. So-called "Freeters" or "free-arbiters" (job-hopping part-time workers), juvenile crimes and suicide rates began to increase rapidly. This decade led the way in significant societal change. In this paper, I will discuss the growth and decline of the Postwar Family Model leading up to the current breakdown of Japanese families. Secondly, I will suggest how the Japanese must begin to put their priorities back into intimacy within the family. Thirdly, I will present a new family model, called the "Intimate Family Model" and discuss how to implement this model into Japanese society.

THE BREAKDOWN OF JAPANESE FAMILIES

After World War II, Japan went through a period of high economic growth. Until the early 1970s, Japanese families had a series of common purposes. Their purposes were two-fold: to own a comfortable home, and to raise their children better. Husbands worked hard outside of the home and earned wages in order to buy electrical appliances, and to be able to make a down payment for a new home. Wives administrated the family budget and did their best to keep house and take care of the children. Children tried to meet their parents' expectations and study hard. Sometimes, they enjoyed family time through leisure activities. Happily, by working hard, almost everybody achieved these purposes.

In 1965, almost 90% of Japanese thought of themselves as belonging to the middle class. Although Japanese men worked relatively longer hours compared to other advanced countries, they could endure the hardships and trials they were going through because they looked forward to having a respectable family life. Family sociologist Masahiro Yamada coined the phrase for this type of family where husbands worked outside the home and wives kept up the house and raised the children, where both of them tried to build an affluent family, as the "Postwar Family Model." I will explain how the model had functioned and now is presently inadequate, based on Yamada's analysis in *Runaway Family: Declining of Postwar Family Model in Japan.* (Yamada 2005)

Why were the Japanese people so attached to their families? In prewar days, people derived their identity from the nation and from their village. When a person thought that he/she contributed to the prosperity of the nation and/or the village, he/she felt that he/she had won recognition as someone special. This kind of approval was "something to live for" for the Japanese.

However after the war, nationalistic tendencies began to decline and the traditional village communities were broken up. For most Japanese, family became the unique source of their identity. The family was indispensable and increasingly people began to seek fulfillment in the family setting. In 1958, 12% of Japanese answered "Family is No.1" to the question "What is most important to you in your life?" In 1998, 40% answered the same answer, and in 2003, it went up to 45%. (The Institute of Statistical Mathematics 2004) The family-centered value system had penetrated into Japanese society along with rapid economic growth. Despite recent individualistic trends, 38% of high school students answered a similar question "What do you prioritize as the most important matter in your life?" as, "to build up a happy family life." High school teacher, Toshihiro Mori, analyzes the government "High School Student White Paper 2006" and says that due to the reality of increased wage differentials, students are seeking a fulfilling family life rather than a higher social status. (Mori 2007:61)

Around 1998 various indicators began to show that Japanese families were changing. Until 1997, the annual suicide rate had been holding steadily around 24,000-25,000. However, in 1998, suddenly it shot up to 32,863 and since 1998 it has been consistently well over 30,000 annually. According to recently released statistics for 2007, 33,093 Japanese men and women took their own lives last year. This means that every day nearly 100 people take their own lives, at a rate of almost one every fifteen minutes. Since 2000, the unemployment rate has been hovering around 5% and the unemployment rate for young people has increased even more dramatically. Along with this, the number of "Freeters" (job-hopping part-time workers) has been increasing rapidly, and the number of people considered NEET (Not in Employment, Education or Training), was over 800,000 in 2004 according to the Cabinet Office. Divorce, marriages due to unplanned pregnancies, dropping out of school, school violence, withdrawal from society, stalking, and domestic violence have all been on the increase since 1998. The "Postwar Family Model" is no longer working and increasingly people are being forced out of that model.

The core assumption of the "Postwar Family Model" is that a large majority of the workers are males who will have secure employment and a steadily rising income. The economic situation has not only gotten worse, but it has also changed fundamentally. In his book, "The Future of Success," Robert B. Reich called this recent economic change "The New Economy" and he insisted that it inevitably results in employment stratification (Reich, 2000). Technology and globalization have given consumers more choices. In this new Internet-driven marketplace, companies are constantly being forced to create new products due to the ever-shifting allegiance of consumers who, with the click of a mouse, can make alternative choices.

Coping with this new, affluent society, companies need two types of workers. One category of workers is the administrators and the specialists who create new innovative products, new services and complicated systems that meet the various requests of customers. They are the core staff and professionals. They cannot expect a big salary but only long working hours. Another category of workers is the unskilled laborers who utilize the manuals produced by the professional staff of the company. They will not be hired as regular employees but only as disposable part-time workers and temporary contract workers with no opportunity of receiving a raise. The development of this new economy has caused instability within the employment market resulting in the economic foundation of the Japanese family becoming unstable.

Not only that, the stratification of the employment is negatively influencing another new family model. This new family model is based on an egoistic and narcissistic value orientation. This individualistic model began to emerge in the early 1990s. People wanted to choose desirable occupations, marry agreeable partners, enjoy exciting hobbies, and live the rich life economically as well as emotionally. They would not take a job if they didn't like it. They did not want to have to compromise anything to get married. They did not want to ever have to accept a decline in their standard of living.

That all sounded good but was too idealistic. The result was that only a few elite, over-achieving young people could actually experience this in their lives. This model ended up trapping many young people in a less than ideal situation because it made it difficult for them to compromise on anything less than the perfect marriage partner and job. Most of them just kept on waiting for the ideal "ship to come in". Over forty-five percent of the population aged from twenty to thirty-four are single and are living with their parents (Nishi and Kan, 2005:2). One trend is where a "Freeter" is forced to marry another "Freeter" because of an unwanted pregnancy and then they end up accelerating their hopelessness and poverty. Moreover, these dreamers tend to make fun of hard working people who have endured difficult situations.

Another possible family model is the "Egalitarian Dual Income Family Model" that was influenced by the Euro-American family of the 1980. This model is possible for a dual career family with high-income jobs like a teacher, a government employee, a professional or a specialist in a company. After having a child, this model only works when a wife has a full time job with flexible hours, or she has a specialized job like a doctor, a pharmacist or a researcher which makes it easier for her to come back home and work. In this time of the "New Economy," it is not easy to find such a wife in Japan.

The "Postwar Family Model" does not work in this current economic situation. The "Individualistic Model" is too idealistic to follow for many young people and the "Egalitarian Dual Income Family Model" is not realistic for most people. Despite the challenges, most young people continue to view married life as an indispensable relationship and continue to hope to find the right partner and raise children. They are still seeking their source of identity in the family. How can the Christians in Japan show a new family model for this dysfunctional society?

Put Priorities Back Into Relationships

A full-time housewife is making a cake wearing an apron in the kitchen of her own house looking out onto a large yard. Her husband is enjoying a chat with their children in the big living room. This was the ideal life presented by the media in movies, magazines and family life TV dramas. Between the postwar period and the period of high growth, this ideal family model was based upon the image of white middle-class suburban residents in the prewar days of America. In addition, commercial messages showed married couples happily drinking coffee together, causing Japanese people to dream of a perfect family that was gradually getting richer economically as well as emotionally (Sodegawa et al. 2005).

As stated above, that dream was largely reached until the 1970s. Most Japanese felt that they were approaching the dream because they could move to a better house, buy electric appliances, and educate their children to have successful academic careers. Once the recession started, however, many people lost the economic foundation of that dream. In the 1990s, most families gave up chasing that dream in the economic sphere, and only a small number of the upper class were able to reach it. However, they still held on to the dream to have quality time with their family members. Being influenced by media like family life TV dramas, a new expectation emerged that the members of a family should feel affection for one another.

Until the 1970 this new value was expressed in giving material things and in serving others in a self-sacrificing manner. A new custom spread widely after the war, that is, a husband worked long hours in a company and gave his pay envelope to his wife without breaking the seal. It showed that his sacrificial work was an expression of his love toward his family. On the other hand, the wife expression was to care for her husband and children. One symbolic ritual is called the "Aisai Bento" or a lunch box filled with his wife's affection. A husband would bring his "Aisai Bento" to his company and feel his wife's affection while he was eating. These trends related to their divided roles. If husbands played the role of working hard outside and wives played the role of keeping house and raising children, this family was recognized automatically as a loving family. Even if they did not have sufficient mutual communication, it was OK as long as they were playing their roles. Actually they were satisfied with the refrigerators afforded by the husband's salary and the special curry rice cooked by housewives.

The Postwar Family model, conditioned by continual economic growth, flourished until the end of the high-growth period. In the low-growth period, married couples needed a different set of values and practices because men employment situation became increasingly unstable and they could not expect to have an ever-increasing standard of living. Japanese people realized that their marriage relationships were dependant on the shaky foundation of their divided roles. For that reason, husbands and wives expected more than just divided roles from each other. They wanted quality communication. This higher expectation required the Japanese families to step beyond their traditional roles. They needed to travel together, go shopping and do leisure activities together, and enjoy hobbies, conversation and sex together. These new behaviors needed to engage their emotions and cause them to feel that their partner was "likable." If they could not have such an emotion, their relationships got worse and worse. In 1990 the divorce rate climbed rapidly. Now Japanese couples have a series of problems: divorce at a young age, domestic violence, child abuse and withdrawal from society.

I have a pastor friend whose name is Keishi. Keishi used to have many problems in his marriage. He often criticized his wife, Kazumi, in front of the church people, and blamed her in a loud voice. When he was a university student, he won first prize in martial arts, so his attitude toward Kazumi was like how he treated the former lower ranking members of his martial arts club. He was a typical Japanese husband. He thought that he played enough of a role as a husband by working hard outside of his family setting. He never imagined that he had to do anything more in order to have quality communication with his wife. One day, Keishi's friend, who had recently been divorced, asked Keishi if his marriage relationship was OK. The friend told him, "You are just like I was with my wife." Keishi was shocked and began to worry about his marriage. Then he visited me with his wife to ask for help. My wife and I were doing an accountability group for marriage couples, called the "Three Dailies," and had found it useful for our marriage to become a healthier couple. So, I recommended that Keishi and Kazumi start it.

Christian counselor Douglas Weiss insists that many marriages have little to no structure to encourage intimacy in their relationship (Weiss 2001). Passion in marriage is a result of making intimacy a priority for life. Passion is a dividend that comes from making consistent investments in the priorities of a marriage relationship. Many couples try to get the passion back into their relationship when what they need to do is to get their priorities back. Once you re-establish the priority of the relationship, the passion naturally follows and grows. One way to do this is by using the "three daily exercises." Each couple agrees to perform three simple daily exercises to the best of their abilities as a couple: pray together, clearly express their feelings for one another and encourage and praise one another. They should attempt to make this a top priority in their schedule.

Weiss likes to share an analogy of a broken bone and a cast. When your bone is broken, the doctor applies a structural treatment to your structural problem in the form of cast. "The cast is a structural treatment that allows the bone to heal. The cast itself is just plastic or plaster, and it has no healing properties. But when it is applied to a broken bone to hold the bone in place, surprise; healing can and does happen. The same thing happens when you place the priorities back into your marriage. No matter how sprained or broken a marriage is, healing can and does take place." (Weiss 2001:154) Attending marriage seminars might provide a clue for their future solution, but it is not enough. A structure is needed where couples can mentally focus their attention to put right insight into right practice in their daily lives.

The assumption of institutionalized training is that "knowledge is power." A teacher is a one-man show for transmitting knowledge to passive students in a classroom setting. Even if a teacher is exceptional and the educational system is perfect, our minds quickly forget the knowledge that has been instilled in us. Even if we succeed in accumulating the right knowledge, trying to change any hardwired habit requires a lot of effort. Jesus told us not only to listen to him, but also to obey him. Once we know his will, we should obey consistently by producing lasting behavioral change. It will be produced through applying "physical activities include talking, writing, reading, drawing and filing: anything that focus our attention on an insight for an amount of time" (Rock 2006). We need to intentionally focus on what pleases God in our daily lives. We should say, "focus is power" in order to see these new divine customs take root in our family life.

What happened to Keishi and Kazumi? They faithfully incorporated the three dailies into their lives. They came to understand each other better. Keishi said, "Now I can accept my own wounds and weaknesses, and realize her pains and grief. One day God told me that you were created to bear her pain together. I found my heart filled with a passion for her." Kazumi said, "I was amazed to feel so many emotions in my daily life, as well as to find many new aspects in Keishi. The more I know him, the closer I feel to him. It is like falling in love the second time." It was difficult work at first, but it became easier over time, and now it has become a core value for both of them. They experienced not only a restored relationship as a couple, but also as a family. Keishi said, "I woke up at midnight and looked at my wife and our four children sleeping in the same room. I thought that I could die for them. It was the natural flow of my thoughts. However, I could not have said such a thing before our marriage was restored." Their children also found a new sense of peace in their relationship with their parents and with each other. Blessings overflowed from the restored couple to their children.

INTIMATE FAMILY MODEL

If Japanese people really seek to have relational intimacy among family members, they need to give up on trying to be rich and prioritize building up their spouses with prayer, sharing and accepting of emotions, and affirming their love by giving and receiving praise. When the couple becomes healthier, they can become a good team in helping each other to raise up their children. When their children observe how their parents express intimacy in their daily life, they will have dignity and hope in their own lives. They could potentially form their own families after the ones in which they were raised. If family life TV dramas and commercial messages from a coffee company could imprint the ideal family image for the Japanese, how much more impact they will have when they have a real experience of intimacy in their family life. The DNA of intimacy will be planted in the families of the younger generation.

John White, a coach for house church planters, believes that the "Three Dailies" will be used not only to heal dysfunctional families, but also to bless all the families of the earth through healed families. He insisted that marriage is the basic discipleship group as well as the first and most foundational expression of the church. He encourages many Christian couples to start the "Three Dailies" and share their story with other couples to facilitate and train them to plant a church in their own home. Couples are trained and are accountable to other couples in the small church that meets in their living room. It is called an MTG, or Marriage Transformation Group (White 2003). This group meets weekly and functions as a kind of house church. The benefits are, (1) each couple gets healthier, (2) each couple comes to the larger house church gatherings with significant needs already met, which results in healthier and more positive meetings, and (3) there is potential for rapid multiplication of churches because it is easy to teach other couples about practicing the basic disciplines and about being in a church.

This kind of healed community would be highly contagious in Japan because it is what people have been consistently seeking since the time of the last world war. Healed couples will multiply by sparking other couples to do the same thing. There is no need to train teachers or to produce textbooks. When a couple experiences intimacy through doing the "Three Dailies," it is easy for them to teach a new couple because it is simple, organic and realistic. There is potential to multiply rapidly as a grass-roots movement. Now is the time to present this "Intimate Family Model" to Japanese society with testimonies by ordinary Christian couples. I believe that this model will appeal to many young couples who have little or no hope to maintain the living standard that their parents had. "Blessed are the poor in spirit, for theirs is the kingdom of heaven." (Matt. 5:3) The economic recession is a blessing for Japanese in the spiritual realm because they have an opportunity to see the kingdom of heaven expand through intimate family relationships of Christian couples.

While the Japanese young people sigh over their misfortunes at being born in an economically stagnant era, they are still super rich compared to people in other Asian countries. They should see the reality of the world around them. While 25,000 people starve to death everyday on this planet, Japanese people throw away one third of imported food. In a sense, Japan economic growth has been bought at a cost of the resources of the two-third world. They should listen to the words of the Teacher, "Better to have one handful with quietness than two handfuls with hard work and chasing the wind." (Eccl. 4:6) and moreover, they should be sent out to serve the Asian peoples.

In order to implement this new family model into Japanese

society, Christians in Japan need a huge paradigm shift. We have been trained to think that church life is made up of religious programs led by sacred clergy in a holy church building. We thought that evangelism was inviting in evangelists twice a year. However, while we were involved in the religious programs in the church buildings on Sunday as well as possibly on Wednesday night, our family life was largely neglected. The same problems in the secular world are taking place in church, too. We have been suffering with ecclesiological dualism.

Marvin R. Wilson shares many practical teachings of marriage and the family for today Christian church from a Hebrew perspective. He asserts "the dinner table of the home became, as it were, the altar of the Temple." (Wilson 1989:215) Eating is a spiritual instrument for religious service. At the table, the family sings while the father served as priest instructing his family in the words of the Scripture. The home reflecting God's glory through prayer and praise was the original form of Christian community. We have missed the most powerful evangelistic weapon, that is, "a changed family life." We rarely see couples who express their love toward their spouses in an adequate way. Roger Gehring correctly insists that houses served as bases of operations and meeting places for prayer, table fellowship and teaching in the missional outreach of Jesus' disciples (Gehring 2004:295; cf. White, 2008). We need to renounce this dualism and reunite church with family, in order for the home to function as a house of prayer, as a house of study and as a house of assembly where community needs can be served. May all the couples in Japan experience Jesus among them, and function as the 24/7 Embassy of the Kingdom of God, in order to see the promise fulfilled, that "All the families of the earth will be blessed through you" (Gen. 12:3).

10

Christianity and Buddhist Marriage in Sri Lanka

G.P.V. Somaratna

Marriage is the socially recognized and approved union between two individuals, who commit themselves to one another with the expectation of a stable and lasting intimate relationship. Marriage is commonly defined as a partnership between two members of opposite sex known as husband and wife. The wedding ceremony formally unites the marriage partners. A marital relationship usually involves some kind of contract, specified by tradition, which defines the partners' rights and obligations to each other. In addition to being a personal relationship between two people, marriage is one of society's most important and basic institutions. Marriage is the state in which men and women can live together in a sexual relationship with the approval of their social group. Every culture of the world recognizes some form of the institution of marriage. In most cultures a man or a woman is not considered complete without a spouse when they reach the age of maturity.

In Christianity and many theistic religions, marriage is considered a sacred act. In the Bible marriage is traced back to the union of Adam and Eve. As a blessing of God, the Biblical concept of marriage is not only for the purpose of perpetuating humankind, but also to enhance and complete the partners' personal growth.

Christian marriage has always been characterized by the practice of monogamy and official resistance to divorce. Traditionally, marriage was justified primarily for producing children, with partnership in the background, and avoiding fornication. The Roman Catholic Church classes marriage as a sacrament. Denunciation of marriage has usually been regarded as an error, except by extreme ascetics (Hinnells 1995:301). Catholics entering wedlock have been expected to understand it as a permanent commitment, lasting for a lifetime.

THE CHRISTIAN CHURCH IN SRI LANKA

Sri Lanka has been identified as a Sinhalese Buddhist country for over two millennia. However, the presence of Christians in the Anuradhapura Period is indicated by archaeological and literary evidence. We are, unable to ascertain the nature of their contribution to the culture of Sri Lanka. The assertion made by Senarath Paranavitana in the *Story of Sigiri* connecting the sixth century Sigiriya fortress with Christianity has not been popular amongst historians despite the fact that the Persian origin of the garden layout of the city of Sigiriya has been accepted by archaeologists. The arrival of Franciscan missionaries from Portugal in 1543 in the Kingdom of Kotte, at the invitation of Bhuvanekabahu VII (A.D. 1521-1551) marks more clearly the beginning of Christian influence on the life of Sinhalese Buddhists. Apart from those who embraced the Roman Catholic faith during this period, the Sinhalese Buddhist population generally also came under Christian influence (De Silva 1959). Thereafter, under the Dutch administration of the maritime provinces of the island the process of Christian cultural contact with Sinhalese Buddhist Society continued (De Silva 1959). The expansion of missionary activities in the nineteenth and twentieth centuries under Protestant missionary organizations resulted in further cultural influences to Sinhalese Buddhist society.

In this article we shall examine one important area in which Christianity made a lasting impact on Buddhist culture in Sri Lanka. The institution of marriage has undergone vast changes as a result of Christian impact during the last four centuries. We shall attempt to identify some of these areas in which Buddhists acquired Christian practices and made them part of their heritage.

Sinhalese Buddhism

Buddhism in Sri Lanka is referred to as Theravada, the School of the Elders. It was officially introduced to Sri Lanka in the third century B.C. Ever since that time Buddhism has played a pivotal role in forming the culture of the Sinhalese, who were regarded as the sole occupants of the island until about the thirteenth century, and have remained the dominant ethnic community of the island until today. The identification of the Sinhalese with their hereditary religion has been strengthened by the conscious efforts of the Buddhist activists of the nineteenth century. It is therefore not surprising to hear from political platforms that "Sinhalese are Buddhists," where an attempt is made to preserve national and communal identity with the hereditary religion. The Sinhalese Buddhist leaders since the second half of the nineteenth century in their struggle for national identity had to grapple with the presence of a Christian community amongst them. The Christians who formed nearly ten percent of the Sinhalese population in the nineteenth century became a stumbling block to their idea—a "nation of Sinhalese Buddhism." The "Protestant Buddhism" which raised its head in the second half of the nineteenth century has acquired Christian social and cultural aspects to modernize Buddhism in order to compete with the aggressive Christian missionary activities.

Buddhist Monks

Canonically, Buddhism is not at all involved in the changes of status that sociologically mark the individual's passage through the life cycle. Although contemporary Buddhism pays great attention to these points of transition, it has less involvement in them than is characteristic of other religions. Except for certain death ceremonies, Buddhism is only peripherally concerned with the life cycle. Birth, puberty and marriage are not marked in Sri Lanka and other Buddhist societies by rites of passage deserving religious involvement. They most certainly are life cycle ceremonies, but outside the purview of the otherworldly religion of Theravada Buddhism (Spiro 1971:232).

The *sangha*, according to its rules of discipline, was not able to get entangled in the ritualistic services of laymen (Bechert and Gombrich 1991:135). It essentially forms the Buddhist priesthood, which unlike Christianity, has no distinct secular clergy. The *sangha* need only provide the opportunity for the laity to seek their salvation, even by offering the chance to accumulate merit through pious gifts to the *sangha*. Buddhist priests conduct funerals and memorial services for the dead, which involve the transfer of merit for the benefit of the deceased. Naturally then, the monastic *sangha* plays a prominent role in the funeral proceedings.

There is an indifference to lay customs in Sri Lankan Buddhism. Buddhists monks as well as Buddhist sacred objects have not had any part in the rites of passage in traditional Sri Lanka until its encounter with Christianity in the sixteenth century. The third precept of Buddhism enjoins the abstention from illicit sexual behavior. This precept undertaken by lay Buddhists states "I undertake the course of refraining from wrongdoing in respect of sensuality (*kama*)." In the Buddhist view there is nothing uniquely wicked about sexual offenses or failings. Failure in this respect is neither more nor less serious than failure to live up to the other four precepts. The fourth precept, to refrain from all forms of wrong speech, is the most difficult one to live up to (Walshe 1986:3). Because of its ambiguity, the precept against sexual misconduct (*kamesu micchacara*) has been variously interpreted in different Buddhist societies (Obeyesekere 1991:298, Gomrich 1991:298).

Buddhist precepts are not commandments. They are regarded as rules of guidance. It is the undertaking by the person to do their best to observe a certain type of restraint. It is undertaken because the person thinks it is good. But if the person finds it unattractive he or she is free to abandon it, believing that it would have bad *karma* in the future *samsara*.

The Pali word *kama* means sensual desire. It is not exclusively confined to sex. The plural word used in this connection would be equivalent to "lust of the flesh" in the biblical vocabulary. Therefore the precepts refer to the desire for pleasure from the other four senses as well. It is *tanha* (craving) which leads to *dukkha* (sorrow). It is the root of man's desire and craving. It is the intention of the five precepts to control these desires and craving so that one would experience less and less *dukkha*. Therefore both rigid Puritanism and total permissiveness have been regarded as extremes in the Buddhist teachings. Specificity regarding lay ethics is absent in Buddhism. Some scholars have stated that this facilitated the spread of Buddhism among the peasant societies with diverse and contradictory moral codes (Obeyesekere 1971).

Buddhism and Marriage

Buddhism is not concerned with the ceremony of marriage, but non Theravada school of Buddhism, and monks of the Mahayana Buddhist orders, may be called in to recite scripture at a birth, marriage or funeral (Humphreys 1984:125). In Buddhism, priests are regarded as renouncers of lay life. Hence, they are not expected to play any role in important areas of lay life such as birth, marriage and sickness. In Buddhist doctrine, though the rules of conduct for the *sangha* are minutely regulated, there is no systematic code of lay ethics. Therefore rituals specified for these important areas of lay life have been left for popular religion to fill. The only Buddhist text dealing with lay life is the *Sigalovada Sutra*, the householder's code of discipline, as described by the Buddha to the layman Sigala. This *sutra* offers valuable advice on how householders should conduct themselves in relationships with parents, spouses, children, pupils, teachers, employers, employees, friends, and spiritual mentors.

These guidelines are not adequate to provide institutions like marriage with ceremonies that could be regarded as religiously prescribed. Such affairs of lay life do not appear to have been dealt with in canonical writings as matters of importance. The Sinhalese marriage ceremony is entirely secular. In itself it contains no Buddhist elements. When this vacuum, as compared with Christian practice was realized, Buddhists made an attempt to appropriate institutions from Christianity.

Sinhalese Buddhist Marriage before Missionaries

According to the contemporary reports it is clear that the Sinhalese Buddhists had a very lax sexual life prior to the introduction of

Christianity. In the Kandyan territories (which did not directly come under Christian influence until 1815), this situation continued well into the latter part of the nineteenth century. T. Berwick, reporting on the judicial aspects of marriage in 1870, was appalled by the Kandyan practice of marrying and dissolving marriages (1870:50). It is stated that marriage began with one glance and ended with a kick! The traditional family was a social institution. It was not regulated by law. A man could meet a woman, enquire about her consent and start a sexual relationship (Ellawala 1962). Sociologists state that sexual relations are one thing and marriage quite another. However, since there was an absence of legal demarcation, marriages became fluid affairs during this period (Harvey 2004:206). Buddhism from its inception has not defined the right kind of marriage to lay people. Therefore the prevalence of monogamy, polygamy and polyandry has been reported in many Buddhist societies (Obeyesekera and Gombrich 1990:28). All these practices have been accepted by Buddhists of Sri Lanka.

Polygamy

For economic considerations polygamy has not been popular among the lowest strata of the Sinhalese society. The laxity of sexual moral codes made it unnecessary to maintain a number of wives. For the same reason, sociologists have found no trace of the institution of professional prostitution in the Kandyan kingdom (Peiris 1956:207). Polygamy, however, is found in the historical records as an accepted fact in the upper strata of the society. For example, the Sinhalese Chronicle *Rajavaliya* records that Vira Parakramabahu (1476-1489) had two sisters as his chief wives in addition to the concubines that the kings of Sri Lanka used to have (Suravira 1976:212). The usual form of fraternal polygamy is for sisters of one family to be married to one man. This practice is common among the *binna* method of marriage, where the man goes to live in the wife's house, among the Kandyan Sinhalese (Peiris 1956:207-232).

Polyandry

The Sinhalese custom of fraternal polyandry where a wife would be shared in common by several brothers has long fascinated those interested in Sinhalese Buddhist society and culture. The practice referred to as '*eka-gei-kema*' still survives in some remote areas in spite of its condemnation by contemporary marriage laws.

The practice is also known to have existed among other Asian communities such as the people of Tibet and Sikkim, the Jats of the Punjab, the Tidying of Kerala and the Todas of the Nilgiri hills until fairly recent times. Some scholars have suggested that its existence among the Sinhalese was due to a common origin. It is likely that it is an independent development on parallel lines.

M. B. Ariyapala referring to the medieval social practices of Sri Lanka states, "polyandry and polygamy may have been rare occurrences. We get a few references to co-wives and miseries known to them. Reference is made to a man marrying a second time if the first wife proved to be barren" (Ariyapala). However, the Sinhala writings of the medieval period speak of the loose nature of Sinhalese marriage. Most Sinhalese scholars of the modern era were ashamed by the absence of a proper marriage among the Sinhalese in the past. Therefore when the issue of marriage came in their studies they glossed it over by making some sweeping statements. The eminent archaeologist, S. Paranavitana, states that the genealogy of king Parakramabahu II (1236-1270) has confused in the contemporary accounts because of the prevalence of fraternal polyandry (Ray 1959:615).

Although the practice of polyandry may have been of early origin the earliest clear record we have of polyandry among the Sinhalese is the Magul Maha Vihara inscription of the 14th century where we find the queen calling herself the chief consort of the two brother kings named Perakumba (Liyangamege 1968:84). This information is confirmed by the *Dalada Pujavaliya* of the same period (Thera 1954:35). The practice was also found in the time of the arrival of the Portuguese in the Island as Vijayabahu VI (1513-1521) and his brother Rajasingha had married one wife, and from her they had four sons and one daughter (Suravira 1976).

Family and Faith in Asia

The European writers of the colonial period, who have been fascinated by this practice, have left us vivid descriptions of the custom as it existed then. The elaborateness of the ceremony of marriage, if there was one, varied according to the social class and place in the caste system of the families of the couple.

Fernao de Queyroz whose work *The Temporal and Spiritual Conquest of Ceylon* (1645), which has been regarded as the history par excellence of the Portuguese period of the island, records (Abeyasinghe 1966:7):

> They also have taken from the Malavaras the most barbarous custom that exist among those nations; for it is a common practice for four or five brothers or more to marry one single woman, and on the contrary one single man may marry many sisters, and the youngest ever holds the first place in authority and power in the house and even in love. But in order to separate, each one's wish is sufficient, who taking what was brought to the household may go back and marry at pleasure; and if they had children the males are entrusted to the father and the female to the mother; and if all are males or females then they divide, each one taking what falls to him by lot. And Bento da Silva relates that when he was *ovidor* of Ceylon, there appeared before him a woman married to seven brothers to complain of the ill treatment she received from so many, and begged in good earnest to be relieved of some of them. And as they were still subject to their laws and customs, the *ovidor* asked her whether two would be enough for her, and she replied she would take four; and choosing those she liked, the case was settled. Such are the fruits of paganism (Kumaa 2001:24, 91).

The Portuguese historian Juao Ribeiro says in his *Fatalidado Historica da Ilha de Ceilao* (1685) that once the marriage ceremony is concluded, the first night of consummation is allotted to the husband, the second to his brother, the third to the next brother, and so on as far as the seventh night, when if there be more brothers, the remainder are not entitled to the privilege of the eldest six. He further states:

> A girl makes a contract to marry a man of her caste for they cannot marry outside it, and if the relatives are agreeable they give a banquet and unite the betrothed couple. The next day the brother of her husband takes the place, and if there are seven brothers she is the wife of all of them, distributing the nights by turns, without the first having greater right than any of the others. These first days being past, the husband has no greater claim on his wife than his brothers have; if he finds her alone, he takes her to himself, but if one of his brothers be with her, he cannot disturb them. Thus one wife is sufficient for a whole family and all their property is in common among them. They bring their earnings into one common stock, and the children call all the brothers indifferently their fathers (Pieris 1910:140).

The Dutch missionary Philip Baldaeus in his Description of Ceylon (1672) regarding the Sinhalese in Galle says:

> Incest is so common a vice among them, that when husbands have occasion to leave their wives for a long time, they recommend the conjugal duty to be performed by their own brothers. I remember a certain woman in Galle, who had confidence enough to complain of the want of duty in her husband's brother upon that account (1996:841).

On another occasion he states that "They marry as many wives as they think fit"(1996:822). Robert Percival, who stayed in the island from 1796 to 1799 reports:

> In some respect the accounts given of the matrimonial connections of the Ceylonese are incorrect. It has in particular been said that each husband has only one wife, although a women is permitted to cohabit promiscuously with several husbands. This however is not always the case;

> many of the men indeed have but one wife while others have as many as they can maintain. There is no positive regulation on the subject, and it is probable that the case with which promiscuous intercourse is carried on, and the case with which marriages are dissolved, is, together with their poverty, the true cause why polygamy is not more general among them (1803:129).

James Cordiner, who served as the chaplain of the British garrison in Colombo and the principal of all the schools in the island from 1799 to 1804 reports:

> The custom of several brothers marrying amongst them but one wife undoubtedly prevails amongst the poorer sort of people who are not Christians, and although not sanctioned by their religion, seems approved by the immemorial usage in the country (1807:96).

John Davy (1815-24) reports:

> Though concubinage and polygamy are contrary to their religion, both are indulged in by the Sinhalese, particularly the latter: and, it is remarkable, that in the Kandyan country, as in Tibet, a plurality of husbands is much more common than of wives. One woman has frequently two husbands; and I have heard of one having as many as seven. This singular species of polygamy is not confined to any caste or rank; it is more or less general among the high and low, the rich and poor. The joint husbands are always brothers (Parker 1982:10).

> The apology of the poor is, that they cannot each have a particular wife; and of the wealthy and men of rank, that such a union is politic, as it unites families, concentrates property and influence, and conduces to the interest of the children, who, having two fathers, will be better taken care of, and still have a father though they may loose one.

> These reasons were once assigned to me by a very acute old Kandyan chief, who, with his brother, had one wife only in common. The children call the elder brother, 'great papa' and the younger 'little papa." There appeared to be perfect harmony in the family (1987:215).

The last substantial account of the practice is perhaps that of Sir James Emerson Tennent in his monumental work *Ceylon* (1859), where he says that polyandry prevails throughout the interior of Ceylon, chiefly amongst the wealthier classes of whom one woman has frequently three or four husbands, and sometimes as many as seven. He notes that as a general rule, the husbands are members of the same family, and most frequently brothers. The custom was however not to remain legal for long for the British outlawed it the same year, though it is known to have survived for a considerable period thereafter.

Ponnambalam Arunachalam observed in *Twentieth Century Impressions of Ceylon* that:

> Polyandry, though illegal, continues to exist among the Kandyan peasantry, especially in the case of brothers. The law against polyandry is evaded by not registering the union at all or by registering it as with one brother only (Wright 1907).

The maximum number of husbands has been seven. If there were more than seven they had no claim over the woman. It is generally believed that a woman with five husbands was a fortunate person (Peiris 1956:205). The woman who is the wife of many husbands was similar to a royal queen (Ribeiro 1685:118).

The men who shared one wife in common did not say that they were married to one wife. Their statement was 'that they protect her in one house' (Peiris 1956:205). Similarly the woman would not say that they are her husbands. Instead she would say, "I cook food for all of them" (205). The children would refer to the men as father using the epithets indicating their chronological order.

Looseness of Marriage

From the reports available, through local and foreign informants, it is clear to us that marriage was not a serious and well-marked institution amongst the Sinhala Buddhists. We may quote the statement of de Queyroz, "among them there is no stable marriages (sic) nor union, except that which arises from personal inclination"(1645:90-91). In addition to the practices of polygamy and polyandry there was a disregard for the marriage bond both among men and women.

Robert Knox writes:

> But their marriages are but of little force or validity. For if they disagree and mislike one the other; they part without disgrace...Both women and men do commonly wed four or five times before they can settle themselves to their contention (1681:248).

Robert Percival, further states:

> It is also customary for those who intend to marry, previously to cohabit and make trial of each other's temper; and if they find they cannot agree, they break off without the interference of the priest, or any further ceremony; and no disgrace attaches on the occasion to either party. But the woman is quite as much esteemed by her next lover as if he had found her in a state of virginity. (1803:129)

There is no tendency in Buddhism to regard sexual irregularities and deviations as wicked. Adultery was regarded as something that was to be avoided. It was widely considered that premarital sex was a good thing for young men but bad thing for girls. In traditional Sinhalese Buddhist society marriage was not a sacrament and often divorce was by mutual consent (Gombrich and Obeyesekere 1990:256). Researchers report that adultery was not a very serious offence in the society before the impact of Christianity (Gombrich and Obeyeskere 1990:4,150). Robert Percival states:

The marriage ceremony, which, among nations with stricter ideas of chastity, is looked upon with a degree of mystery and veneration, is a matter of very small importance among the Ceylonese, and seems to be at all attended to only with a view to entitle the parties to share in each others goods, and to give their relations an opportunity of observing that they have married into their own caste. The marriages are often contracted by the parents while the parties are as yet in a state of childhood, merely with a view to match them according to their rank and are often dissolved by consent almost as soon as consummated. (1803:129)

Change was Necessary

Roman Catholic missionary activities since the sixteenth century terminated the historic equation of Sinhalese Buddhist identity. During British times Protestantism was the dominant religion. Protestants became the economically dominant class but the middle of the nineteenth century saw a revival of Buddhism. Buddhists made every effort to emulate the Protestant Christian model in order to give Sinhalese Buddhists a respectable status. Among those methods were imitation of organizational forms and tactics of the Protestant Christians. The rising middle class, which had their education in Christian Schools and were closely liked with the British administration, made their attempt to reinterpret Buddhism in harmony with modern concepts. Therefore "Protestant Buddhism" is a direct result in Sri Lanka of Christian experience over several centuries.

CHRISTIAN MARRIAGE

The institution of sacramentalized lifelong monogamous marriage was a Christian concept, first introduced to Sri Lanka by the Roman Catholic missionaries in the Portuguese period. Marriage in Christianity is an exclusive relationship. The total unity of persons—physically, emotionally, intellectually and spiritually—is comprehended by the concept of "one flesh" and is encapsulated in the concept of holy matrimony. This eliminates polygamy and polyandry as options. The indissolubility of marriage has been the biblical principle guiding this lifelong union.

The Introduction of Christian Marriage

The registration of marriage, which this concept necessarily entailed, was done in Sri Lanka in the *Tombo* registration books under the supervision of the Roman Catholic clergy beginning in the sixteenth century. Therefore, marriage has been referred to as *casada* in Sinhalese, this word being a derivation from the Portuguese word *casado* meaning marriage. Marriage, thus, became a sacrament to those who embraced Christianity, unlike Buddhists to whom marriage, at which nonreligious dignitary was present, was not a sacrament (Disanayake 1999:121).

The Dutch administrators continued the practice of marriage registration and connected it with the legitimacy of children for purpose of inheritance. The registration of marriages together with births and deaths was done by the school masters under the guidance of the *Predikants* (ministers) of the Dutch Reformed Church. The system of registration of marriages, births and deaths continued to be the privilege of the state church until 1860 when civil registration was introduced.

The introduction of monogamous lifelong marriage was not readily accepted. It was broken at the slightest opportunity by Sinhalese Buddhists used to a system of lax marriage. The change of colonial power from the Portuguese to the Dutch between 1642 to 1658, and later from the Dutch to the British in 1796 and the disruption caused by the period of transition from the East India Company to the British Crown, also provided an opportunity for the people to lapse into traditional practices. The presence of an independent kingdom of Kandy until 1815 also encouraged the law to be broken as the Kandyan laws did not have any rules to regulate marriages.

Sri Lankan Buddhist Reaction to Christian Marriage

Ordinance number six of 1847 introduced the formal registration of marriages, births and deaths. Severe penalties were imposed any who dared to treat lightly the social responsibilities of the marriage contract whether he or she be Tamil, Sinhalese or Western. Marriage was regarded as a very important social matter. Prior to this period Sinhalese Buddhist as well as Tamil Hindu marriages were not regulated as monogamous lifelong affairs. This ordinance became a hindrance to the current practice of polygamy and polyandry and established the system of registration of marriages (Senaratna 1999:97).

The Buddhist priests were the first to object to the formalized monogamous marriage. This may be because they did not have a role it. Bentara Attadassi Thera, writing in the early 1850s in reply to the Wesleyan missionary Daniel Gogerley's criticism of Buddhism entitled *Kristiyani Prajnapti* (1849), refers to the introduction of monogamous marriage from the point of view of the traditional Sinhala Buddhists. Attadassi further elaborated that monogamous marriage created individual families, cutting them off from other family members who could be a source of support. The law enforcing monogamous marriage was often violated in many devious ways as indicated by reports of missionaries and the police reports.

Marriage, being an extremely important social institution, was affected by the socio-economic and cultural developments in the country. The pressures which arose from the alteration of the socio-cultural milieu with the rise of a new middle class and missionary education, greatly influenced the institution of marriage.

The *Buddhist Catechism* published by Colonel Olcott in 1881 was very popular among Sinhalese Buddhists educated in Christian missionary schools. As a result the book underwent several reprints in the nineteenth century. It incorporated many Christian concepts of marriage in to the Buddhist system of values. These views were popularized among the Buddhists through the schools run by the Buddhist Theosophical Society. For example question 205 of this catechism is, "What does Buddhism teach about marriage?" The answer is:

> Absolute chastity, being a condition of full spiritual development, is most highly recommended; but a marriage to one wife and fidelity to her, is recognized as a kind of chastity. Polygamy was censured by the Buddha as involving ignorance and promoting lust.

These are not teachings of the Buddha or the instruction embodied in the Buddhist canon (Wickremesinghe 2002:31). They are the innovations of Olcott, which he derived from his own Christian upbringing. In fact the view of the Buddhist scholars is that there is no Buddhist text referring to the preference of monogamous marriage. Buddha did not teach the validity of monogamous marriage over other forms of marriages prevalent in North India in his time (Gombrich and Obeyesekere 1990:253, 273).

The *Poruwa* Ceremony

The meaning of the Sinhala word *poruwa* is a plank. *Magul poru* is the plank where the married couple is expected to stand in order to perform the wedding rituals. But Sinhala writings before the eighteenth century make no mention of *Magul Poruwa* even when they refer to royal weddings (Senaratna 1999:50). Robert Knox (1681) does not mention the *Poruwa* even in the case of the royalty and nobility neither is the *Poruwa* is mentioned by Percival in his account of Ceylon published in 1803. Cordiner also makes no mention of it in 1807. But Alexander Johnston who was the Chief Justice in the Maritime provinces of Ceylon wrote sometime between 1811-1819:

> The manner of marrying, according to the Cingalese custom, is, when a bridegroom comes, together with his relations, to the house of the brides' parents, for the purpose of marrying, there shall be spread a white cloth upon a plank called *Magoolporoewe,* and upon that white cloth there shall be scattered a small quantity of fresh rice, whereupon bridegroom and the bride shall be put or carried upon the said plank by the uncle of the bride, who shall be on her mother's side - if there is none, by any other nearest relation -

and afterwards there shall be delivered by the bridegroom to the bride a gold chain, a cloth, and a woman's jacket, besides which there shall be changed two rings between them; at the same time, the bridegroom gives a white catchy cloth to the mother of the bride, according to his capacity; after which ceremony, and while the bridegroom on the right and the bride on the left are standing upon the said plank, by the uncle of the bride, or by any of her nearest relations, as above stated, shall be tied the two thumbs, one of the bride and one of the bridegroom, by a thread, and under the knot of the said thumb there shall be holden a plate, and some milk or water poured upon the said knot, and then shall the bride be delivered to the bridegroom. In some places, the two little fingers of the bride and bridegroom are tied, and the said ceremony performed; and, in some places, a chain shall be put by the bridegroom on the bride's neck, a cloth be dressed, and then rings be changed. In some places the marriage is performed without these last mentioned ceremonies (Upham:323-324).

In this record there is no reference to a religious dignitary, auspicious times, consulting of horoscopes, *jayamangala gatha,* or various decorations done to the poruwa. It was mainly a family gathering confined to the families of the two parties.

D'Oyly also refers to a simple *poruwa* ceremony which was performed by the upper class Kandyan Sinhalese. It had no religious significance. There was no religious dignitary officiating it. There was no religious text chanted or song of blessing sung. It is also clear that the common man was not aware of such a ceremony.

The happy moment being arrived, the Bridegroom throws a gold chain over the bride's neck and then presents her with a complete set of apparel and ornaments—and the Bride being arrayed therewith steps up along with the Bridegroom on the *Mogool Poroo* or wedding plank which is covered with a white cloth. The Bride's maternal Uncle or some other near relation then takes a gold chain and therewith ties the little finger of the bride's right hand with that of the Bridegrooms left, and the couple then turn round upon the plank three times from right to left—the chain is then taken off, and the Bridegroom moves to a seat prepared for him—Magool Pata or wedding plate is then brought in from which the Director of ceremonies take rice and cakes and making balls of them give the same to the Bride and Bridegroom who make a reciprocal exchange thereof in token of conjugality (D'Oyly 1938:124-125).

The Development of Poruwa

It was later in the 1870s that the *poruwa* ceremony was introduced to commoners. In this period Buddhist leaders made a conscious attempt to imitate several Christian institutions in order to bring honor to the Buddhist marriage ceremony. The Sinhalese Buddhist leaders, lay and clergy, in the first half of the nineteenth century believed that the Christian sacrament of Holy Matrimony was one of the attractions that drew Buddhists to Christian churches. The Buddhist leaders viewed this with great alarm. On the other hand the new bourgeoisie found the sexual mores implicit in the British legal system fit well with their expectations. This new middle class was a product of the missionary educational system and the introduction of the capitalist economy by the British. In order to bring the Sinhala marriage ceremony to closer to Christian ideals and make it more respectable it had to be sacramentalized (Obeyesekere and Gombrich 1990:256).

The Buddhist newspaper, *Lakmini Pahana*, proposed the *poruwa* ceremony which was current among the Sinhalese Buddhist society, especially prevalent among the Kandyan nobility as a Buddhist counterpart to the Christian sacrament of marriage. In 1869 the *Lokarathasadhaka Samagama* (the Society for the Welfare of the World), which was the Buddhist educational society headed by Dodanduwe Piyaratna Tissa, met at Sailabimbaramaya at Dodanduwa and resolved to advise Buddhist laymen on the validity of the practice of the *poruwa* ceremony as a Buddhist invocation, in order to solemnize Buddhist weddings (Sri Lanka National Archives 1968).

Dodanduwe Piyaratna Tissa had a special reason to spearhead such a move as he lost his only brother, David Weerasooriya, on his conversion to Christianity (Darling 1991:5). David Weeasooriya was the father of Arnolis Weerasooriya Colonel of the Salvation Army. David Weerasooriya's conversion in 1862 at the height of religious controversies made Piyaratana Tissa indignant. In fact the person selected as the headmaster for the first Buddhist school organized by Dodanduwe was a Sinhalese Buddhist convert from Christianity who had had his education in a missionary school (Malalgoda 1976:234).

By 1907 the *poruwa* ceremony had acquired more fertility rites as indicated by D.J. Subasingha:

> A special dais, termed the *magul poruwa*, is prepared in the centre of the hall. On the floor is spread a mat, over which is drawn an octagonal diagram divided into eight equal parts. Over this is placed a wooden board, which is covered with a carpet, and this in its turn is covered with a cloth.
>
> Over the temporary platform described, gold and silver coins, pearls and fried paddy, and five different kinds of flowers are scattered. A canopy is suspended over the dais, at the four corners of which four pots, half filled with water and holding outspread coconut flowers placed. On each flower is an earthen lamp burning with coconut oil. At the auspicious moment announced by the astrologer, the bride and groom are conducted to the *magul poruwa*, and as they mount, a coconut is split in halves with a wood chopper. Benedictory verses are now repeated, after which the bridegroom is handed a cloth, to an end of which is tied a gold coin that goes to the dhoby is a present. Spreading out the cloth, the bridegroom wraps it around the bride's waist; she in turn presents him with a suit of clothes. This called the *Piliendavima*. The maternal uncle of the bride now mounts the dais, ties together the right thumbs of the bride and bridegroom with silver threads, whilst learned

relatives of both families chant *Ashtaka* verses containing Buddha's attributes and blessing. The uncle them pours water from an ewer over the joint thumbs, and thus gives away the bride. As the wedded couple dismount a coconut is again split into halves (Wright 1907:191-192).

In this description one can see the new addition to the simple *poruwa* ceremony. A religiosity has been added with the chanting of praises of the Buddha. However, the *poruwa* itself was still placed on the ground. There was no elaboration of the *poruwa* into the shape of a throne.

The Contemporary Poruwa

Today Buddhist weddings are influenced by Hindu culture which gives prominence to *Nekath,* auspicious times. The *Nekath* is derived from the horoscopes of the bride and the groom, which are created based on their dates and times of birth. Of the many traditional events that take place during a Buddhist wedding, the *poruwa* ceremony is the most important. Therefore it is strictly guided by *Nekath*. The *poruwa* is a beautifully decorated wooden platform on which the traditional Buddhist marriage ceremony takes place. Therefore this event is called the *poruwa siritha*. The origin of the modern *poruwa* ceremony goes back the nineteenth century when Protestant Buddhists made every endeavor to counter Christian cultural influence. Ever since its introduction, many innovations have been introduced to the *poruwa siritha*. By and large, the men and women of present day society consider it their heritage and are motivated to protect and preserve something of their past for posterity. Today's *poruwa* ceremony has been influenced by both upcountry (Kandyan) and low country (maritime) customs of Sri Lanka.

The *poruwa* is a decorated marriage platform that is used for the bride and the groom to stand on until the traditional wedding ceremony is completed. According to Sinhala rites and customs, the platform is prepared by covering it with a clean white cloth and placing rice, five kinds of medicinal herbs, a coconut and a few coins to bring prosperity to the couple. Four pots known as *pun kalas*, upon which four lamps are lit, are placed on the four corners of the *poruwa*. The lamps are lit before the ceremony to invoke the blessings of the gods in charge of the four zones (Wijetunga 1984:1668). The Master of Ceremonies, sometimes known as *Gurunnanse* or *kapuwa*, presides over the ceremony.

Kandyan or Low Country drummers would herald the ceremony as the bridesmaids watch. At an auspicious time, known as *nekat*, the bride is escorted to the hall by her father to stand before the *poruwa* till the groom joins her. At an auspicious time the couple ascends the *poruwa*. Traditionally, the groom is escorted to the right side of the *poruwa* and the bride to the left. With the reciting of the *Ashtakas* or eulogies, blessings are invoked upon the couple. After that, seven betel leaves are dropped on the dais to symbolize unity, cooperation and friendship. The little finger of the right hand of the bride and left hand of the groom are tied together with a blessed thread and water is sprinkled on the hand to denote oneness. Four virgins wearing traditional half saris sing the *jayamangala gatha* or auspicious songs, invoking health, wealth, prosperity and happiness upon the couple. This is followed by the exchange of rings and the couple is led to the *poruwa*, each of them putting the right foot forward. The beating of drums known as *magula bera* by the Low Country drummers or Kandyan drummers is an auspicious way to herald every important occasion of the wedding ceremony. These drummers accompany the couple to the dais and each important step in the ceremony is marked by the beating of drums (Herath 2004).

The newly coined words such as *Poruwa siritha* (poruwa custom) have confirmed the significance of the *poruwa* in the modern Buddhist wedding. The rites associated with it have become elaborate. *Gok* (coconut) leaves and banana bark which were associated with festive occasions in the past are being introduced to the wedding *poruwa*. Some of the wedding *poruwas* today resemble royal thrones.

Today the bride is accompanied by her father to the assembly of friends and relatives in front of the decorated *poruwa*. When the father leads to bride to the hall, the assembly rises, imitating the pattern of the church service. This practice shows how far the

Buddhist mind was attracted by the Christian sacrament of Holy matrimony and its rituals.

The Meaning of the Poruwa—Then and Now

Traditionally the wedding *poruwa* was a simple plank which was covered with a white cloth for the occasion. According to Johnston rice was sprinkled over it at the time of the ceremony. The *poruwa* being simply a plank was used for various purposes. *Porewedanda* meant a plank placed to cross the stream. The plank which was used in the paddy fields to smooth the muddy ground after ploughing is also known as *poruwa* (Leach 1982). Some anthropologists have regarded *poruwa* as a fertility symbol because of its association with rice cultivation (Gombrich and Obeyesekere 1990:262). The fact that seeds of rice are spread on the *poruwa* before the couple ascends it may be taken as further proof to this hypothesis. According to Davy's account, the couple stands on a plank of jak wood. The jak (*Artocarpus integrifolia*) being a tree which oozes milk is also treated as a fertility symbol in the Sinhalese society.

Adaptations and Innovations in Buddhist Marriage Ceremonies

Today the rituals connected with the *poruwa* ceremony are based on auspicious times calculated to the minute. This, of course has been made possible only with the introduction of clocks in the twentieth century. In the era before the use of clocks the auspicious times were not kept to the minute (D'Oyly 1938:124).

Kapurala, and *Gurunnanse* who have become the officiating priests owe their origin to the post independence era. They now dress and act like the Royal Purohita Brahmins described in the Buddhist literature. In Subasinha's account (1907) the chanting of *ashtaka* was done by the relatives. The *jayamangala gatha* was not known even at that time.

The practice of singing *jayamangala gatha* by virgins is of much later origin. These innovations were motivated by the desire to emulate various aspects of the ritual of a Christian wedding, which proved to be attractive and a status symbol to many Buddhists.

Although the term *poruwa* is used for the modern structure used in connection with Sinhalese Buddhist weddings, its original meaning is forgotten. Hardly anyone would be willing to adapt that it has origins in fertility rites. According to Obeyesekere these are royal symbols that have been attractive as a result of association with the Kandyan aristocracy (Gombrich and Obeyesekere 1990:263). The couple receives something similar to consecration of royalty. The accompaniment of drumming and music also add pomp to the occasion. The modern wedding would have hired dancers, traditional or modern, in their wedding ceremonies to add color to the occasion.

The Bride Wears White

The Christian custom is still seen in the use of a white veil by brides in many parts of the island. The color white symbolizes the union of Christ to the Church. The bride also wears a white sari. However, in the Sinhala tradition the color white is not an auspicious color. It has been used on polluting occasions such as funerals, puberty, births and weddings. The *magul poruwa* is covered with a white cloth. Alexander Johnston's report indicates that the bridegroom gives a white catchy cloth, indicating the polluting aspect of the marriage act, to the mother of the bride, according to his capacity. Traditionally widows and widowers wear white. According to Sinhalese Buddhist tradition the color white is clearly connected with sorrow. Yet following the Christian custom, Sinhalese Buddhist brides wear white in the *poruwa* ceremony disregarding the example of the colorful outfits worn by Hindu brides.

Blessings Chanted

There are two types of chants mentioned in connection with Buddhist weddings today. The *ashtaka* are sung in order ward off evil powers emanating from gods, demons, evil spirits and humans (Senaratna 1999:51). While the couple is on the *poruwa,* maids dressed in white chant the *jayamangala gatha*. Although there is no accepted order they do this usually at the end of the *poruwa* ceremony. The *Jayamangala Gatha* (meaning victorious auspicious songs) consists of nineteen four-line stanzas in the Pali text. It celebrates the Buddha's triumph over evil and passion. These songs were traditionally sung after the gathering of the paddy harvest. It is intended to expel malevolent spirits (Gombrich and Obeyesekere 1990:264-265). According to Obeyesekere, "To have these Buddhist verses sung by pre-pubertal (i.e. infertile) girls dressed in sterile white is a symbolic proceeding that from the standpoint of the traditional culture annuls the sexual and procreative aspect of marriage" (265). It is interesting to note that while in the traditional Christian wedding white is confined to the dress of the bride, in the context of the Buddhists even the other participants who sing *jayamangala gatha* are also in white.

Participation of the Clergy

According to traditional beliefs, Buddhist monks, being celibate men, are symbols of sterility. Their yellow robe is associated with impermanence and death. The mere sight of a Buddhist monk is generally regarded as inauspicious therefore the Buddhist monks have been kept apart from the marriage ceremonies. However in the recent past in Sri Lanka, as in Myanmar, Buddhist monks have been invited to chant *pirit*, an all purpose tradition to ward off any ill fortune, after the wedding ceremony is over. It is also reported that on rare occasions monks have been invited to chant *pirit* at the wedding ceremony itself. Worship of the Buddha by the couple before or after the *poruwa* ceremony is also another innovation to receive religious blessing to the couple.

THE POST-CHRISTIAN ERA

In the post independence era much of the Christian contribution to Sinhalese Buddhist social life has been taken for granted as Buddhist heritage. Most of the Christian practices acquired by the Buddhists in the colonial era have been baptized into the Buddhist system by giving them high-sounding Sinhala names. The monogamous sacramentalized institution of Christian marriage is one of them. Present-day Buddhists condemn the western culture as being sexually promiscuous and pride themselves on having higher moral standards from time immemorial. Monogamy, which is the only form of marriage advocated by the Christian church throughout history is now being thrown at Christians as a Buddhist heritage.

Modern Christian Adaptations

Some modern Christians who are not aware of the origins and the intentions of these social institutions have tried to imitate or incorporate them in the garb of indigenization and contextualization of Christianity in the Sri Lanka soil.

White or Yellow?

Among other Christian practices connected with the wedding ceremony adopted by Sinhalese Buddhists is the wearing of a white sari and face veil by the bride. The white sari was the usual wedding dress even in the case of Kandyan weddings where the veil was not often used. As a result of the research done by Gananatha Obeyesekere, Buddhist leaders during the last decade have made a deliberate attempt to shun white as the color of the *poruwa* bride even though the veil is still retained. On the other hand the Christians wear white because it symbolizes Christ's union with his bride, the church. However, there is a growing trend among the Christians who are unaware of their tradition and symbolic value of white in the sacrament of marriage to opt to go with the trends of the day. It is interesting to note that some brides now unwittingly use shades of yellow which is the color of impermanence and death according to the Buddhist tradition.

Magul Poruwa in Churches

During the 1960s in the Catholic Church some leaders who were interested in the process of accommodation with the local culture vehemently agitated for enculturation and indigenization. They questioned the validity of not permitting the *poruwa, jayamangala gatha, pun kalas, hewisi* music, the national flag and other traditions that constitute the hallowed Sinhala customs at Buddhist weddings, for church weddings as well. In 1967 on the occasion of his daughter's marriage, Santiago Fernando was very keen in observing the Sinhala customs and traditions with all of the intricacies of the *poruwa* ceremony etc. in the church. However, he failed to obtain permission from several churches. Ultimately, a French priest gave him full permission in his church in Bolawalana, to have the church wedding with all cultural regalia of Sinhala traditions. Santiago had to fight with his back to the wall to withstand the tremendous challenges in and outside the church for his radical innovation. Some Catholics, who strongly opposed Santiago, labeled him as a Marxist rebel and Satan. Ever since that time *poruwa* structures have been seen occasionally in Roman Catholic and Protestant churches at wedding ceremonies. Many of them who make these requests are unaware of its association with fertility rites.

Jayamangala Gatha

Jayamangala Gatha is a collection of Pali stanzas which eulogizes the Buddha and is sung in the hope of obtaining various victories and blessings in the Buddhist way. Today one can find Christian hymns of blessing sung according to tune of *jayamangala gatha* at the Christian marriage ceremonies by the choir. They are sung at the most sacred part of the sacrament of marriage while the vows are repeated and the rings are exchanged.

Parental Blessing

Buddhist critics have pointed out that the Christian wedding ceremony has no place for the parents of the couple. Their complaint is that the mother of the bride has no place in the Christian ceremony. It is only the father of bride who has an official role in the ceremony. The groom's parents also do not play any part in it. According to the critics the couple does not pay homage to their parents and receive their blessing on this special occasion. The fact that the roles assigned to the parents of the bride and the groom is a very recent innovation to the series of *poruwa* customs is not known to the modern onlooker. Taking this to be a valid omission in the Christian marriage ceremony some Christian churches have included hymns in Sinhala thanking the parents for nurturing and bringing up the couple.

Drums

Churches are often decorated with young coconut leaves. Flowers are kept in two large pots filled with water known as *pun kalas,* and a clay lamp lit with coconut oil is found. Those who can afford hire drummers for an auspicious *hevisi* session. Some do it inside the church before the couple enters. However, some of these practices have fallen out of use as a result of the difficulties of obtaining labor and raw material.

CONCLUSION

When Christianity was prestigious and powerful in the colonial Christian era, Buddhists tried to imitate and acquire Christian practices and values. Today being the post-Christian era, the trend has reversed. Christians, being unaware of their own heritage in Sri Lanka, have fallen into the lap of Buddhist resurgence and have acquired many of the Buddhist practices without knowing their origins. There is a tendency to follow the contemporary popular practices without knowing the non-Christian symbols attached to them. Many critics of this tendency have stated that this is a part of the syncretism that the church is undergoing. Others have indicated that it is necessary to make the Christian marriage relevant and pertinent to today's social demands as long as they do not contradict the basic Christian values.

The *poruwa* ceremony has become a very colorful and attractive event that would provide lasting memories to the couples who take part in it. Even foreigners have been attracted to the pomp and pageantry of the *poruwa* ceremonies and the rituals attached to it. The *poruwa* ceremony, being a folk innovation, can keep on adapting to suit the trends of the time and yet give a mysterious and religious touch to the event. Since the *poruwa* can be hired at a comparatively low cost and since the ceremony can be performed without its astrological and fertility symbols, some Christians would be attracted to it in this post-Christian era. It is unavoidable that some young couples would prefer to go with the trend of the day.

The intention of the institution of *poruwa siritha* as a counterpart to the Christian wedding ceremony has not only achieved its original purpose; the dreams and aspirations of its original innovators have far surpassed their intended purpose. Now they have been able even to challenge the Christians. Christians have mistakenly capitulated to the view that only Buddhists have contributed to the cultural heritage of Sri Lanka, thus undermining their own heritage as "foreign" despite its five hundred year history. The Christians are not aware of the fact that they have enriched the cultural heritage of this island. The Sri Lankan Christians have been pushed into a predicament that they feel guilty about their historical past. They wrongly think that the fathers of their faith acted destructively by demolishing the Sinhala culture. They do not know their own contribution to the enrichment of the culture of Sri Lanka. Monogamous marriage and the dignity that they introduced to the chaotic family life of the Sinhalese is one such major contribution.

11

Biblical Ideals and Buddhist Images

M.S. Vasanthakumar

The institution of marriage and the concept of family life are not human inventions or ethical achievements. Primitive or pre-scientific people who lived like animals did not evolve or improve and eventually form the advanced or civilized way of life with the matrimonial system, as many are accustomed to assume today. As the Bible clearly shows, marriage and family life for human beings were designed and instituted by none other than God himself. For it was God who created the human beings as male and female (Gen.1:27) and united them as husband and wife (Gen.2:20-25). In fact, even before the first man had any ideas or insights about marriage and family life, God saw that it was not good for man to be alone and created an appropriate person for him to have as his nuptial partner (Gen.2:18). "Marriage is bound up with the very creation of man. It is not a product of some progress or development that came about later… By (the) creative act, marriage was instituted by God" (R.C.H. Lenski, 1943:729). In fact, marital relationship was established as the first human institution by God (J. MacArthur 2005:15). "It is not a late development of an advanced civilization" (R.C. Sproul 2003:143).

BIBLICAL PRINCIPLES OF MARRIAGE AND FAMILY LIFE

Since God has designed marriage and family life for human beings, he has given several guidelines and instructions in the Bible which are necessary for a proper and meaningful marital life.

According to the Bible, the marriage bond should be monogamous and between heterosexual people only. Therefore, the Bible condemns polygamy and homosexual (including lesbian) practices vehemently. By creating only one woman to the first man, God has clearly revealed that monogamy is his intention for human marriage. God's intention is that "the two should become one flesh and not three" (R.C. Sproul 2003:145). Likewise, giving a woman to the first man, God has indicated that conjugal relationship was not designed for the same sexes. In fact, these were creation ordinances, designed for the entire human race. "Genesis 2:21-24 presents the creation of the first two human beings and their monogamous marriage as the will of God" (W.C. Kaiser 1983:182). Therefore, biblical commandments insist that the conduct of human beings should conform to what God has explicitly constituted in his creative work.

In the Old Testament polygamy is explicitly condemned in Leviticus 18:18, which states: "Do not take your wife's sister as a rival wife and have sexual relations with her while your wife is living" (NIV). Some take this verse as an example of the basic Hebrew concept that through marriage a woman's sisters become her husband's sisters. This prohibits a person from taking his wife's sister as his second wife (G.J. Wenham 1979:258; R.K. Harrison 1980:187). Others confine this to a ban on a special type of polygamy (N. Kiuchi 2007:336; R.L. Harris 1990:599), involving two sisters having one husband. But, this verse expressly prohibits all types of polygamy (W.C. Kaiser 1983:189), for the basic principle underlying monogamy is contained in it (J. Murray 1957:253-256). In fact, the term "sister" in this verse could be rendered as "another woman" (G.L. Archer 1994:259). In all other thirty four instances, the phrase "a woman to her sister" (wife's sister in NIV) is rendered idiomatically as "one woman to another" or "one wife to another" (W.C. Kaiser 1983:185). Hence, Leviticus 18:18 cannot be rendered in any other way. Further, this is confirmed by one of the Dead Sea Scroll Biblical manuscripts on this passage (A. Tosato 1984:200,203). Therefore, there is no doubt that it is a direct prohibition of polygamy.

It is true that in the Old Testament many people had several wives, including those who knew and followed God. Therefore, some have concluded that in the Old Testament polygamy was permitted or tolerated (R. Gane. 2004:324), and that the Christian church's stand against polygamy is not grounded firmly on the Bible (O.C. Fountain 1974:111). Some have gone to the extent of saying that, "we can hardly point with certainty to a single text in which polygamy is expressly forbidden and monogamy is universally decreed" (K. Barth 1957:199). But the law governing marriage had always looked to Genesis as normative (W.C. Kaiser 1983:183). Hence, an express biblical permission for polygamy never existed. In fact, those who had more than one wife in the Old Testament had deliberately gone against the divine law, which explicitly prohibits polygamy. For instance, in the Old Testament kings were specifically told not to take many wives (Deut.17:17), but generally the kings did not adhere to this divine decree. Likewise many people during that period, did not take God's prohibition of polygamy (in Lev.18:18) seriously, and had more than one wife.

In the Bible, the practices of the people cannot be considered as divine endorsements. The narrative portions of the Bible should be scrutinized in the light of the direct teachings and thus the practices of the people should be verified, whether they represent divine norms or deviations from God's ideals. In the New Testament, the teachings of Jesus Christ on marriage (Matt.5:31-32, 19:3-9, Mark.10:2-12, Luke.16:18), explicitly forbid polygamy. According to the New Testament, each man should have his own wife and each woman her own husband (1 Cor.7:1-2). "Polygamy never was God's order of things for marriage even though it is present in the society of the Old and New Testaments" (W.C. Kaiser 1983:190). Even the first mention of the polygamy in the Bible is depicted as an implicit judgment on such marriages (Gen.4;19). That God exercised forbearance with the Old Testament saints does not mean that he sanctioned their polygamy. Nowhere does God give his blessing to a plural marriage (R.C. Sproul 2003:146).

According to the Bible, the monogamous marriage bond between heterosexual people should not be broken by any means, until death of a person separates them. In other words, divorce is not allowed for Christians on any grounds. God has explicitly expressed his displeasure on divorce, for he had unequivocally stated in Malachi 2:16 that he "hates divorce." Likewise, Jesus Christ has declared, "what God has joined together, let man not separate" (Matt.19:6). Divorce is a violation of what God has created. Because it is undoing the work of God, Jesus commands us not to do it. "To break up a marriage is to usurp the function of the God by whose creative order it was set up, and who has decreed that it shall be a permanent one-flesh union" (R.T. France 2007:718).

In God's view, "a married woman is bound to her husband as long as he is alive, but if her husband dies, she is released from the law of marriage" (Rom.7:2). Therefore, Jesus has stated, that "anyone who divorces his wife and marries another woman commits adultery, and the man who marries a divorced woman commits adultery" (Luke 16:18). Reflecting on Jesus' teachings, the apostle Paul has stated, "to the married I give this command (not I, but the Lord): a wife must not separate from her husband. But if she does, she must remain unmarried or else be reconciled to her husband. And a husband must not divorce his wife. To the rest I say this (I, not the Lord): if any brother has a wife who is not a believer and she is willing to live with him, he must not divorce her. And if a woman has a husband who is not a believer and he is willing to live with her, she must not divorce him" (1 Cor.7:10-13). The mixed marriages to which Paul refers to in these verses were not Christians who had married unbelievers. In these marriages, both partners were unbelievers when they got married, but subsequently either wife or the husband has become Christian. Even in such marriages Christians are not allowed to divorce their unbelieving partner. In fact, they are admonished to live in such a way to win the unbelieving partner to the Lord (Cf.1 Pet.3:1-2). Hence it is clear that divorce is not sanctioned for Christians in the Bible.

Even though the Bible has not sanctioned divorce for Christians, some passages seem to contradict such an absolute conclusion. For instance, in the Old Testament, it appears that Moses had given permission for divorce in Deuteronomy 24:1-4. Hence, the Jews thought that Moses has not just granted permission but given a great commandment sanctioning divorce. Their question in Matthew

19:7 in response to Jesus' teaching against divorce indicates this. When Jesus said, "what God has joined together, let man not separate" (Matt.19:6), the Jews thought that he was going against the law by prohibiting divorce altogether. Therefore they asked him, "Why then did Moses command to give a certificate of divorce and send her away?" (Matt.19:7). In answering, Jesus corrects their false conceptions by saying, "Moses permitted you to divorce your wives because your hearts were hard. But it was not this way from the beginning" (Matt.19:8). According to Jesus, Moses did not command divorce, but allowed and legalized what was happening during his time. And he did this because of the hardness of human beings. In fact, "the Deuteronomy passage presupposes the practice of divorce… (Therefore) a general law of divorce can hardly be embedded here" (McConville 2002:358). Indeed, Moses did not decree divorce, but in his allowance, "a current practice is tolerated" (Stott 1978:95). Hence, this is not a command to divorce but a provision that regulates those instances when a divorce takes place… The law is concerned with what happens after a divorce…. (for) the requirement of the law comes in its final clauses in verse four" (Wright 1996:255). In fact, it does not deal with divorce in general, but merely with remarriage after divorce (J.A. Thompson 1974:243).

Prior to the Mosaic divorce regulations, it was economically difficult for women to live alone. Men often sent their wives out of their house if they disliked them. Since women were dependent on the male members of their families, those who were sent away by their husbands were forced, either to depend on other male relatives, or to remarry, or eventually to become prostitutes for their survival. In the mean time, if a woman wished to remarry, her former husband used to claim that she was still his wife and prevented her marriage.

In order to avoid such unfortunate exploitation, Moses insisted that a certificate of divorce should be given to the wives if they were sent away, which would free them from any claims by their former husbands. "When Moses took note of the ills that could be done toward women and provided for divorce, he was giving the repudiated wives a little measure of protection" (Morris 1992:483), and not giving a commandment on divorce. "The Deuteronomic legislation is a response to human failure, an attempt to bring order to an already un-ideal situation caused by human hardness of heart... The existence of divorce legislation is a pointer not to divine approval of divorce but to human sinfulness" (France 2007:719-720). It is not a divine instruction, but a concession to human weakness (Stott 1978:95). Hence, what was allowed to the sinful, hard hearted people of the Old Testament period is indeed not for the New Testament Christians, whose hearts have been changed by the Spirit of God.

While explaining what Moses did, Jesus did not fail to point out that Moses' regulation did not alter God's intention concerning the permanency of marriage. Therefore he added, "but it was not this way from the beginning," meaning, from the beginning divorce was not allowed by God. It was practiced by human beings, but not sanctioned by God. Therefore, Jesus unequivocally states, that despite the concession of Moses, remarriage after divorce is adultery. For, according to him "Anyone who divorces his wife and marries another woman commits adultery, and the man who marries a divorced woman commits adultery" (Luke 16:18). In fact, "this new and dramatic way of speaking is directly related to the absolute prohibition of divorce by Jesus" (Hagner 1993:125).

According to some, Jesus had allowed divorce on the ground of adultery. They substantiate their arguments by the so called "exceptional clause" found in Matthew's gospel. Matthew has recorded Jesus' statement in 5:32 as "I tell you that anyone who divorces his wife, except for marital unfaithfulness, causes her to become an adulteress, and anyone who marries the divorced woman commits adultery" and in 19:9 as "I tell you that anyone who divorces his wife, except for marital unfaithfulness, and marries another woman commits adultery." But Mark and Luke, when recording this statement, had purposely avoided the clause "except for marital unfaithfulness" for the obvious reason, that they were primarily writing their gospels to the gentile audiences.

Since Matthew's original readers were Jews, he has generally included some additional clauses which were directly applicable and relevant only to his Jewish readers. For instance, when Mark conveys Jesus' warning about tribulation he has stated as "Pray that this will not take place in winter" (Mark 13:18). But Matthew has an additional clause which is relevant only to the Jews. Hence his version of this warning of Jesus reads as "Pray that your flight will not take place in winter or *on the Sabbath*" (Matt.24:20). Since the Jews strictly observed Old Testament Sabbath regulations, Matthew has included this as well, whereas, the gentiles were not bothered about such laws, so Mark and Luke did not mention the Sabbath. Likewise, the exceptional clause permitting divorce is only relevant in the Jewish culture, and therefore Matthew included it in his gospel. In the meantime, it should not be forgotten that the Jews did not grant divorce for adultery, the punishment for adultery is the death penalty and not divorce procedure (Deut.22:22, John 9:1-11).

Even though there exist wide varieties of interpretation on the exceptional clause and especially on the precise meaning of the term Jesus used for "marital unfaithfulness" (in NIV but fornication in KJV cf. G.J. Wenham & W.E. Heth 1997), it seems that in the Jewish culture fornication (*porneia*) and adultery (*moicheia*) were two different types of sexual sins. Hence, whenever the Bible has used both *porneia* and *moicheia* in same context, it intends some distinction between them (Carson 1984:414 cf.Matt.15:19, Mark 7:21, Gal.5). In such contexts, *porneia* refers to the immorality of the unmarried and *moicheia* to the immorality of the married (J.R.W. Stott 1978:97). Hence *porneia* has been defined as "premarital sex" (R.C. Sproul 2003:116), and *moicheian* as "unfaithfulness to the marriage vow" (F.F. Bruce 1990:373). Even though, *porneia* could refer to any kind of illicit sexual behavior, for the Jews it is committed only by unmarried people. In Jewish societies the marriage ceremony consisted of two distinct events, one is betrothal and the other one is the wedding. Betrothed or engaged couples were considered as husband and wife (Gen.29:21, Deut.22:23-24, 2 Sam.3:14, Matt.1:18-25), and it was as binding as a wedding. Therefore, for separation legal divorce was required (Moore 1971:121; de Vaux 1965:36). Nevertheless, after a year only their marriage would be consummated and then only they would begin to live together. Therefore, until marriage, the engaged couples were expected to be faithful to one another (Neufeld, 1944:143-144) and if they fail, their sexual sin is called fornication.

Jesus gives permission for divorce on such a ground, for the marriage of the engaged couple has not been consummated and one of them has become defiled. Jesus did not advocate or allow divorce for people whose marriage has been consummated, for they have become one flesh and cannot be separated. Marriage according to Jesus, "is a divine institution by which God makes permanently one two people who decisively and publicly leave their parents in order to form a new unit of society and then become one flesh... (Therefore), the person who may have secured a divorce in the eyes of human law is still in the eyes of God married to his or her first partner" (Stott 1978:94,96). Therefore, Jesus' permission for divorce is not for married people, but it is "dissolving the betrothal agreement in an unconsummated marriage where one partner had violated the agreement by engaging in sexual relation with a third party" (Isaksson 1965:140).

As far as the explicit teaching of the Bible is concerned, divorce is not sanctioned for Christian believers on any grounds. A Christian must live with his or her spouse until his or her death. According to Jesus, divorce and remarriage is nothing else than adultery. Nevertheless, we should not apply these biblical principles to unbelievers. Hence, if a person is divorced prior to his or her conversion to Christianity, and there is absolutely no way to reconcile to his or her former spouse, there is nothing wrong for him or her to remarry. In fact, in 1 Corinthians 7:27-28 Paul allows such persons to remarry if they wish to do so. Unfortunately, these verses are not correctly rendered in the NIV, but other versions convey what Paul has written here. For instance the NASB says, "Are you bound to a wife? Do not seek to be released. Are you released from a wife? Do not seek a wife. But if you should marry, you have not sinned." Most commentators conclude that the first question in verse 27 is directed to the engaged couples and the second one to the unmarried (Elliott 1972:221-222; Fee 1987:332; Garland 2003:326). Those who follow the NIV think that these verses are addressed to the married and unmarried (Soards 1999:160). But only the first question is translated correctly in the NIV, and here the married are advised not to get divorce (MacArthur 2005:1582).

However, the second part, especially the question, "Are you released from a wife" cannot be rendered as "Are you unmarried?" as in the NIV. It could refer either to the widowed or to the divorced person (Morris 1987:113), but here it specifically refers to the divorced. For, if bound and release in the first part of verse 27 refers to marriage and divorce, then there is no reason to change the meaning in the second part. Further, the unusual term employed by Paul for release (loose in KJV) in Greek is a technical term for discharging someone from the obligation of a contract (Moulton & Milligan 1930:382). Therefore, to be released from a wife implies being released from the marriage contract. Even though Paul says not to seek a wife to such people for some specific reasons he mentioned in this chapter (i.e. the present distress 7:26), he did not prohibit them marrying. Hence, he states in verse 28, "but if you should marry, you have not sinned." There is no doubt that in these verses, Paul allows the divorced (from the broader biblical perspective divorced prior to the conversion) to remarry (J. MacArthur 2005:1582).

Paul's allowance of remarriage for those who were divorced prior to the conversion can be deduced from 1 Corinthians 7:15 as well. After stating that the believer has no authority to dissolve his or her marriage, when he or she is married to an unbeliever, Paul goes on to say that "if the unbeliever leaves, let him do so. A believing man or woman is not bound in such circumstances; God has called us to live in peace." Once again the context clearly indicates that this so-called mixed marriage is not a believers' marriage to an unbeliever, but the marriage has occurred prior to one person has been converted to Christianity. In such circumstances, Paul does not give permission to the believer to dissolve his or her marriage, but on the other hand, if the unbeliever wished to get divorce Paul did not want to prohibit it. Because in such a situation a believer has only two options, "either to denounce his or her faith in Christ and maintain the marriage or continue to hold his or her Christian faith and let the marriage be dissolved" (Barton & Taylor 2001:668). Paul's instructions clearly show that unbelievers are not expected to abide by biblical principles and norms. In a mixed marriage, if the unbeliever wants to divorce his or her spouse, Paul says the believer is not bound in such circumstances. That means, the believer is "not reduced to being a victim of circumstances. He is free from the marital vows that were broken by the unbeliever's actions" (Soards 1999:151), and fallen into "a state of what amounted to widowhood" (Bruce 1971:70). Therefore, it is apparent that the believer in such a situation is free to remarry (Morris 1987:107).

Though some insist that Paul does not speak about remarriage at all in this verse (Fee 1987:303), what he says in this verse clearly implies it. The Greco-Roman and Jewish law enshrined remarriage after divorce as a right. And the "slavery imagery (i.e. not bound) derives from the Jewish comparison of divorce deeds to emancipating deeds" (Instone-Brewer 2001:238-239), and divorce deeds of that time explicitly allow remarriage (Garland 2003:296). Hence, when Paul says that they (believers) are not bound, "any first century reader would understand him to mean that they can remarry, because they would think of the words in both Jewish and non-Jewish divorce certificates: 'you are free to remarry.' If Paul had meant something else, he would have had to state this very clearly, in order to avoid being misunderstood by everyone who read this epistle" (Instone-Brewer 2001:241). According to Paul, the Christian is not subject to any constraint because of the unbelievers' behavior. He can marry again (Conzelmann 1975:123; Ruef 1977:57; Murphy-O'Connar 1979:66). As D.E. Garland has stated:

> Paul's primary goal in this passage is to argue against a Christian dissolving his or her marriage to an unbelieving spouse for spurious religious reasons. He disallows remarriage in the case of Christians divorcing Christians in 7:11 and argues against changing one's status in 7:17-24. But in 7:17-24, he also allows for an exception in the case of the slave obtaining freedom. In the same way, the one who has been divorced would be permitted to move from being married to being set free by divorce to being married again (Garland 2003:296).

An important biblical injunction concerning the marriage is that a

Christian should not marry an unbeliever. In fact this is explicitly taught in both Testaments. In the Old Testament Moses exhorted the people saying, "when the LORD your God brings you into the land you are entering to possess and drives out before you many nations… Do not intermarry with them. Do not give your daughters to their sons or take their daughters for your sons (Deut.7:1-3). The reason for such strict commandment is that marrying people of other faiths would easily draw them away from God (Deut 7:4). The life of King Solomon demonstrates this awful fact clearly and serves as a dreadful warning to all subsequent generations (1 Ki.11:1-8). Hence such marriages were considered heinous sin among the devoted Israelites (Ezra 9:10,12; 10:1-2). In the New Testament, the injunction "Do not be yoked together with unbelievers" (2 Cor. 6:14), though could have a broader application, includes prohibition of entering into the partnership of marriage with people of other faiths as well. The concept of unequal yoke is based on two Old Testament texts, one that banned cross-breeding of animals (Lev.19:19), and the other that forbade the yoking together of an ox and an ass for plowing (Deut.22:10). "The force of the metaphor lies in the recognition that the unbelievers are of a different breed and that care must be taken as to the nature of the relationships one might enter with them" (Barnett 1977:344). Since marriage is a mutually intimate and unending relationship in this world, Christians cannot have such a correlation with unbelievers. "Those who bear Christ's yoke cannot share it with others who deny Christ" (Garland 1999:331) or who do not know Christ.

According to the Bible marriage is good and pure in God's sight. Therefore, celibacy for spiritual growth is unknown and contrary to the Bible. Unless a person is specifically called by God to a special vocation for which marriage would become a heinous hindrance, people are generally expected to get married and enjoy their earthly existence (Prov.5:18, Eccl.9:9). Hence Paul wrote, "I wish that all men were as I am. But each man has his own gift from God; one has this gift, another has that. Now to the unmarried and the widows I say, It is good for them to stay unmarried, as I am. But if they cannot control themselves, they should marry, for it is better to marry than to burn with passion" (1 Cor.7:7-9). In these verses, Paul acknowledges that not all are like him, i.e. all are not celibate. Nevertheless, he does not "mean to imply that they have somehow failed to reach his level of spiritual commitment. (For) the issue is not about how God has gifted Paul but how God has gifted them" (Garland 2003:271). Further, Paul points out that "celibacy is a spiritual gift and not a requirement" (Fee 1987:284). Like other spiritual gifts, celibacy too, is granted by God via Holy Spirit according to the divine plan and purpose (1 Cor.12:11).

Those who receive this special gift are depicted by Jesus as those who "have renounced marriage because of the kingdom of heaven" (Matt.19:12). They will have "the capacity for resistance to sensual allurements" (Barrett 1968:158), and totally dedicate their lives for an "extensive service to God" (Soards, 1999:140). Paul's contention in these verses is that "all do not have this special gift" (Vaughan & Lea 1983:72), and "those who have not received this gift should not try to remain unmarried" (Morris 1987:104). In the Old Testament, God gave this gift to prophet Jeremiah (Jer.16:2), but it was extremely unusual; and even in the New Testament celibacy is not the norm but a rare exception (Huey 1993:166). The negative circumstances can temporarily delay marital status to some (1 Cor.7:26), but they cannot permanently deprive anyone's marital life (1 Cor.7:28) unless a person is divinely called to be single for a specific ministerial assignment, and enabled by the special gift of celibacy to live without a spouse. As the seventh chapter of the first Corinthians points out "for Paul not marrying is preferable only if the capacity to remain single is given by God" (Soards, 1999:140).

Since celibacy is not the zenith of Christian spirituality, the Bible is critical about the sexual abstinence within the marriage as well. Therefore, when responding to the "pro-celibacy faction in Corinth" (Blomberg 1994:133), Paul has declared that, "the husband should fulfill his marital duty to his wife, and likewise the wife to her husband" (1 Cor.7:3). Paul acknowledges that both husband and wife have "marital duty" (NIV) or "conjugal rights" (RSV) by which he euphemistically refers coitus (Garland 2003:258). Paul's expression literally refers to debts, and implies that "married couples are indebted to one another sexually" (Fee 1987:279). Hence, within marriage sex is "a standard, natural, even necessary element" (Soards 1999:139). In fact, Paul uses the present imperative in this verse, which shows that "he regards the mutual recognition of conjugal rights as the normal condition of married life. Since husband and wife are one flesh, neither has the right to refuse intercourse with the other" (Wilson 2005:258). According to the Bible, "conjugal rights are equal and reciprocal" (Barrett 1968:156). Therefore, Paul goes to the extent of making an unorthodox assertion that in sexual act "the wife's body does not belong to her alone but also to her husband. In the same way, the husband's body does not belong to him alone but also to his wife" (1 Cor.7:4). Hence, sexual abstinence, according to the Bible is a violation of the marriage vow.

However, if both husband and wife mutually agree, short time abstinence is allowed for the specific reason of fasting and prayer. Hence, Paul says, "do not deprive each other except by mutual consent and for a time, so that you may devote yourselves to prayer. Then come together again so that Satan will not tempt you because of your lack of self-control" (1 Cor.7:5). Contrary to the Jewish devotion, Paul assumes that both partners are praying, and if one spouse refuses abstinence the other person cannot pray. (Garland 2003:261). It should not be forgotten that Paul emphasizes temporary abstinence only, for either husband or wife "cannot flee the sexual obligation by deciding on a permanent prayer meeting" (Sproul 2003:122-123). Therefore, "no separation is to be allowed which is not with mutual consent, for a limited time, for the purpose of special devotion, and with a definite intention of reunion" (Wilson 2005:258). Nevertheless, the following verse clearly shows that Paul's advice on sexual abstinence is a concession and not a commandment (1 Cor.7:7). Paul is not saying that sexual abstinence is an absolute necessity for devoted prayer or fasting. "Asceticism is a possibility in very qualified circumstances, not a norm or mode of Christian life" (Soards, 1999:140).

Even though sexual abstinence is not a part of Christian spirituality, the Bible confines sexual activities to the marriage only. Hence extramarital and premarital sex are forbidden by God. In fact, sex outside the marriage is depicted as adultery in the Bible. There are numerous explicit statements in the Bible which directly prohibits extramarital sex (Ex.20:14, Deut.5:18, Prov.6:32, Hos.4:14, Col.3:5). But many find it difficult to see any prohibitions of premarital sex in the Bible. The reason for this difficulty is mainly due to the unnecessary allegorical interpretations given to the Book of Songs of Solomon by Jewish and Christian saints. But this "corpus of love poetry" (Murphy & Huwiler 1999:221) depicts the love and marriage of Solomon and his first wife Shulamit (Olyott 1983:75) and "intends to teach lessons regarding the divine view point of courtship, marriage, and sex just as other historical books of the Bible teach us divine principles in other areas" (Fruchtenbaum 1983:2). The book describes the courtship (SS 1:2-3:5), marriage (3:6-11), wedding night (4:1-5:1) and subsequent sexual adjustments of the young couple (5:2-8:4). In the courtship section, when the lovers come physically close to one another (2:6, 3:4), literally "embracing in a lying position" (Longman 2001:115) there is a refrain which admonishes them not to "arouse or awaken love until it so desires" (2:7, 3:5), which is an explicit statement prohibiting premarital sex. For, "do not arouse or awaken love" means "to arouse sexually or more precisely becoming sexually active for the first time in one's life" (Garrett 2004:152). The refrain exhorts not to arouse sex "until it so desires." In other words, the lovers are admonished to "avoid sexual experiences until the proper time… they should avoid promiscuity and save their virginity for marriage" (Garrett 2004:153-154). In fact, the four times repeated divine plan for marriage in the Bible clearly points out the proper place for sex in human lives. In this statement "a man will leave his father and mother and be united to his wife, and they will become one flesh" (Gen.2:24, Matt.19:5, Mark 10:7, Eph.5:31), "becoming one flesh" refers to sexual union as 1 Corinthians 6:16 clearly indicates. And this comes after the couple had left their parents and united as husband and wife. According to the divine plan "only those who have left and only those who had cleaved exclusively to each other can become one flesh" (Trobisch 1971:26).

BUDDHIST PRACTICES IN PRE-CHRISTIAN SRI LANKA

Marriage and family life in Sri Lanka prior to the introduction of Christianity differed drastically from the contemporary Buddhist lifestyle. The Buddhists have absorbed many Christian concepts during the period of four centuries of western occupation of the country. Due to the Christian influence, the family life of the Buddhists has changed to a great extent. In fact, Christianity has transformed the concept of marriage and family life in Sri Lanka. Most of the changes which Christianity brought in Sri Lanka were positive and enriched contemporary Buddhist families. Some of the western norms were counterproductive, for they created negative impressions in the minds of Buddhists about Christianity, which even prevent Buddhists appreciating the positive contributions the Christian missionaries.

Prior to the introduction of Christianity, polyandry was prevalent in Sri Lanka. Polygamy too existed in the country, but it was confined to the rulers and the nobility (Geiger 1960:37). Even though some claim that polyandry was not widespread in ancient Sri Lanka (Jayawardena 1986:115), there exists ample historical evidence to counter such arguments. In the central highlands polyandry was "practiced freely" (Tambiah 1968:123). The seventeenth century western political prisoner Robert Knox had observed this in Sri Lanka. According to him, "in this country each man, even the greatest, hath but one wife; but a woman often has two husbands. For it is lawful and common with them for two brothers to keep house together with one wife, and the children to acknowledge and call both father" (Knox 1981:248-250). Not only in the central highlands, in the littoral too, polyandry persisted even after a century and a half of cultural contact with the Europeans (Tambiah 1968:123). The Catholic missionaries who endeavored to eradicate polyandry in the costal areas of the island remarked, that it was "very common among these people too, because the wife of the one brother is the wife of all the other brothers as well" (da Trindade 1972:152). Even the Portuguese courts often recognized such practices among the Buddhists (Pieris, 104-105). Though, generally it was the brothers of a family who had a common wife, sometimes non-brothers also cohabited with one woman (Sirr 1991:162-163).

Apart from polyandry, instances of group-marriage in which several brothers cohabit with their wives in common were also known in pre-Christian Sri Lanka (Pieris 1956:211). Further, it has been observed that sexual hospitality also existed in ancient Sri Lankan societies. The seventeenth century political prisoner Robert Knox has stated, that "in some cases the men will permit their wives and daughters to lie with other men. And that is, when intimate friends or great men chance to lodge at their house, they commonly will send their wives or daughters to bear them company in their chamber. Neither do they reckon their wives to be whores for lying with them that are as good or better than themselves" (Knox 1981:246-247).

Since polyandry, and in some instances polygamy, group-marriage, and sexual hospitality were prevalent in ancient Sri Lanka, the marriage bond was not so strong. According to the observation of Robert Knox, "their marriage are but of little force or validity. For if they disagree and mislike one the other, they part without disgrace… Both women and men commonly wed four or five times before they can settle" (Knox 1981:248). The sixteenth century Portuguese historian de Queyroz also makes the same observation. Thus he says, "among them there is no stable matrimony nor union except so long as they like… In order to separate, each one's wish is sufficient" (de Queyroz 1930:90-91). In fact, returning the marriage gift was the principal formality that was requisite to seek divorce (Sirr 1991:164).

The family life in ancient Buddhist societies of Sri Lanka, however, was inconsistent with the teachings of the Buddha. According to him sexual misconduct was an evil, and he insisted that the married couple should be faithful to one another (Walshe 1996:426, 467). But marital instructions did not emerge as a major concern of his doctrines, for the Buddha's teachings were addressed primarily to the monks and social reformation was not his ultimate objective. The Buddha was preoccupied with the human predicament and his struggle was to find a path to eliminate the sufferings pertaining to human existence. As Buddhism spread to various parts of the world, it absorbed and adopted the local customs and practices and accommodated itself to the new culture. The result was that Buddhism and local culture grew together. "Thus in Sri Lanka, customs and conventions relating to marriage and family life developed on their own lines. Buddhism not only made no attempt to change them, but with the eclecticism characteristic of it reconciled itself to them" (Peter 1978:281). A nineteenth century British traveler had observed:

> Though concubinage and polygamy [by this he refers to polyandry] are contrary to their religion, both are indulged in by the Singalese [sic], particularly the latter; and, it is remarkable that in the Kandyan country, as in Tibet, a plurality of husbands is much more common than of wives. One woman has frequently two husbands, and I have heard of one having as many as seven. This singular species of polygamy is not confined to any caste or rank; it is more or less general amongst the high and low, the rich and poor. The joint husbands are always brothers… it is hardly necessary to observe that chastity is not a virtue in very high estimation amongst the Singalese [sic] women, nor jealousy a very troublesome passion amongst the men. Infidelity, certainly, is not uncommon, and it is easily forgiven (J. Davy 1983:214-215).

CHRISTIAN IMPACT ON BUDDHIST FAMILY LIFE

It is not an exaggeration to say that prior to the introduction of Christianity, the moral life of people in any part of the world was not up to the standards stipulated in the Bible. It was the influence of Christian missionary activities that transformed the moral standards of the people to a great extent, and Sri Lanka is not an exception to this world wide phenomenon. The Christian missionaries, wherever they went, raised the standards of the moral life of the people via education and church discipline. Thus in Sri Lanka, all forms of immorality according to the Bible were vehemently condemned and virtually eradicated by the missionaries and the rulers of the colonial governments.

Thus with the advent of the Portuguese and of Christianity certain changes took place in the traditional attitudes and customs and practices relating to marriage, sex and family life in Sri Lanka. The main factor that effected the changes was Christianity. The Christian missionaries would not tolerate such practices as polygamy, polyandry, group marriage, cross-cousin marriage, forcing children into marriage, marital infidelity, divorce and infanticide, all of which were contrary to Christian teaching and principles. In the case of the converts they made in Sri Lanka, the missionaries made every effort to eradicate such practices (Peter 1978:290-291).

When the British captured the entire island in the nineteenth century "they attempted to change the marriage laws, basing themselves largely on a Victorian moral repugnance to polyandry; marriages should be monogamous and registration was necessary if the children were to be deemed legitimate" (Jayawardena 1986:116). Polygamy as well as polyandry was abolished in 1859 by the British governor of that time, Henry Ward (Balasingham 1968:91). Hence, today, "Buddhist sexual morality, its monogamous marriage ideals, and its divorce rules, are highly cathected derivatives from Christianity. Historically, it should be noted that these ideals were never exclusively dominant in any period of Buddhism in any part of the Theravada societies of South Asia prior to the 20th Century" (Obeyesekere 1970:61).

Not only those who became Christians adopted Victorian moral standards, those who reformed Buddhism (and Hinduism in Sri Lanka) were also influenced by the high ethical norms of the Christian missionaries. Therefore, they incorporated Christian ethical norms into their religious teachings. In fact, the nineteenth century Buddhist reformers, due to the influence of Christianity, "while rejecting Christianity as a faith... consciously or unconsciously modeled their religion on it" (H.L. Seneviratne 1999:26). Hence, many of the norms and organizational forms of resurgent Buddhism are "historical derivatives from Protestant Christianity" (Obeyesekere 1972:62). Buddhist ethics were reinterpreted in the light of Christian moral standards. Buddhist leaders eliminated much of what was contrary to Christian ethics, and incorporated many of the Christian values which they favored. Therefore, nineteenth century Buddhism has been depicted as "the mirror image of Protestant Christianity" (de Silva 1978:227), for it had "assumed salient characteristics of that Protestantism" (Gombrich & Obeyesekere 1990:7). Ironically, the very missionaries, who wished to spread Christianity throughout Sri Lanka, had provided models and methods that propelled the creation of Protestant Buddhism. On the other hand, the Buddhist leaders, who strove to overthrow Christianity, consciously or unconsciously absorbed Christian ethics and western values into their system. In fact, in the nineteenth century resurgent Buddhism, "Protestant and western norms… (were) cathected and assimilated as pure or ideal Sinhalese norms" (Obeyesekere 1972:72). As far as marriage and family life were concerned, "influenced by Victorian beliefs that the ideal unit of social organization was the monogamous British family based on a strict moral code for women, the local new rich began to condemn the liberal marriage customs and sexual mores of the Kandyans, denouncing particularly the prevalence of polyandry and divorce by mutual consent" (Jayawardena 2000:249).

CONTEMPORARY REACTIONS AGAINST CHRISTIAN INFLUENCES

Christianity has contributed much to shape Buddhist marriage and family life in Sri Lanka. Nevertheless, some of the changes Christianity has brought in Buddhist lifestyle have become counterproductive. Therefore, instead of appreciating the good influences of Christianity, contemporary Buddhists are accusing Christianity of disrupting their traditional values and distorting their treasured virtues. In fact such attitudes have often prevented Buddhists appreciating Christianity. Consequently they have become major obstacles to evangelizing them. The Buddhist leaders of the nineteenth century took Christian moral and ethical concepts to reform their religion, but they presented them as their own traditional Buddhist practices.

Therefore contemporary Buddhists think that their present high moral standard is their own traditional heritage and it did not derive from western Christianity.

One of the major Buddhist criticisms against Christianity is the Biblical concept of the marriage bond which involves the married couples "leaving their parents and cleaving to one another" (Gen.2:24, Matt.19:5, Mark 10:7, Eph.5:31). In traditional Buddhist families, married brothers with their parents lived in the same house, and continued to be under their control. Generally after the marriage the sons bring their wives to their parent's house, not only to be their helpmates, but also to look after their aging parents. Therefore, it has been often pointed out that the Christian marriage concept of leaving the parents and cleaving to the nuptial partner has prevented the married couples fulfilling their filial duties. It is true that due to western influence, many have neglected their filial responsibilities, but the blame cannot be laid on Christianity alone. According to the Bible, leaving the parents is not giving up filial duties nor deserting them. The Bible has much to say about the responsibilities of children towards their parents. In fact it warns children and pronounces severe punishments for neglecting or ill treating their parents (Ex.21:15, 21:17, Lev.19:3, 20:9; Deut.21:18-21, 27:16). Therefore, Buddhist converts, as well as Christians, need to comprehend the Biblical concept of "leaving", in Christian marriage, properly. Then they can set an example to the Buddhists, and show what is really meant by leaving the parents in marriage. In fact, proper understanding about the Biblical concept of leaving and cleaving would enable Buddhist converts to enjoy a blissful married life.

In evangelizing the Buddhist, the new converts need to be instructed about their filial duties and marital responsibilities as well. They need to honor their parents (Ex 20:12, Eph 6:1-3), and look after them when they are old (Prov.23:22). In fact, Jesus Christ has set an excellent example in this regard, for even at the moment of his agonizing death, he made the necessary arrangements for his mother's wellbeing (John 19:26-27). Christians should always follow the footsteps of Jesus in this matter as well. Yet, Jesus himself has declared on the basis of divine plan, that in marriage "a man will leave his father and mother and be united to his wife, and the two will become one flesh" (Matt.19:5, Mark 10:7). Though the Bible does not speak very often about marriage, this is the one and only statement about marriage in the Bible which is repeated four times in very decisive places and thus clearly shows the "divine plan for human marriage" (Trobisch 1971:18). Nevertheless, it should not be forgotten that "the responsibility to honor one's parents does not cease with leaving and the union of husband with wife, but does represent the inauguration of a new and primary responsibility" (MacArthur 2005:15). Leaving in Christian marriage is not deserting or ignoring the parents. "The marriage involves a new pledge to a spouse in which former familial commitments are superseded. Marriage requires a new priority by the marital partners where obligations to one's spouse supplant a person's parental loyalties" (Mathews 2001:223). Hence, leaving means "transferring one's fundamental allegiance from parents to spouse" (Blomberg 1992:290). The newly married couple should begin their own life, without their parents' direct and dictating involvements and their financial inputs.

In evangelizing the Buddhist, Christians often encounter the criticism, that it has created an attitude of disrespect towards the elders among the younger generation. Buddhist children are taught from an early age to show respect and greet the elders in their families (Wijesekera 1990:476). Therefore, they are accustomed to stand up when elderly relatives and monks approach them (Abhayawardena 1973:48). They also greet their parents and elders of the family by kneeling on the floor with clasped hands at their feet (Wijesekera 1990:477). Respect is expressed in this manner also to teachers in schools. Since Christians see such practices as a form of worship, they have completely given up this traditional way of showing respect (Wijesekera 1987:224-225). Hence, the Buddhists accuse Christianity of eradicating important traditional practices. Such accusations often prevent Buddhists considering Christianity as a worthy religion to follow. Therefore, it is necessary for Christians to reconsider the adaptation of traditional forms of showing respect. In fact there is nothing wrong in these practices, if the converts are given proper instructions concerning the intention of bowing or kneeling down before the elders. They should do this to show respect and not worship. If this is clear in their minds, adopting the traditional Buddhist forms of showing respect is a good practice for the Buddhist converts to follow. Even in the Bible, the Syrian army commander Naaman, after becoming a believer of Yahweh, was not prohibited from practicing his traditional form of showing respect to his king, by bowing down even in a pagan temple! (2 Ki..5:18-19). Even though others may have thought that he was worshipping an idol, in his mind Naaman was just showing respect to his king. Hence, it is not the outward form, but the inward intention, which is the crucial issue in adopting forms and practices of other religions. Christian mission could reach many Buddhists, if it adopts some of their traditional forms and practices. Then they will think that Christianity is not an alien intruder which disturbs and destroys their cherished customs, but an intimate companion with whom life can be continued.

Another problem often associated with Christian mission among Buddhists in relation to marriage is the prevalence of the caste system. In fact, caste plays a major role when marriages are arranged by parents for their children. Parents want their children to find nuptial partners in their own caste and class. But Christianity on the other hand proclaims that there is no class or caste division among people (Gal. 3:28), for the entire human race has descended from one single parent (Acts 17:26). Therefore, among Christian converts, mixed marriages have become a common feature. Hence, the Buddhists often accuse Christians of not taking seriously the existing caste system. For them, marrying out of one's caste is defiling and descending to a low caste. Consequently, Christians are considered to be low caste, and Christianity is deemed an inferior and insignificant religion. In fact, it is surprising; that those who follow the teachings of the Buddha in Sri Lanka are adhering to the caste system, for the Buddha was vehemently opposed to the same system in his native land. Hence, Christianity is in agreement with Buddhism at this point, and it is Christianity and not Buddhism in Sri Lanka which strives to uphold the ideal that the Buddha had sought.

CONCLUSION

Though Buddhism has high moral standards, prior to the western occupation the family life in Sri Lanka had been often went below that norm. Even though the four centuries of European rule and Christian missionary activities had almost eradicated unbiblical elements in marriage and family life in Sri Lanka, unholy practices are not uncommon in contemporary societies. They are not visible but present in various forms. It has been observed that "in isolated traditional Buddhist villages sexual morality and divorce may be far more lax than in many communities in Europe or the USA" (Obeyesekere 1972:61). Therefore, the Christians who are to be the salt and light to the world (Matt.5:13-14) should exemplify the biblical marriage principles in their lives and expound them to the Buddhists whenever they encounter appropriate occasions to do so. Christian wedding ceremonies are good opportunities for such enterprise, for generally in such functions Buddhist relatives and friends gather to greet the couples. It should be pointed out to them that the biblical marriage design, including monogamous union, prohibition of divorce and marrying unbelievers, is not to deprive people from enjoying marital life. In fact they are given as divine blessings to human beings. It has been observed that "in every marriage that ends in disaster, some stupid decisions were made with respect to God's regulations. If God's regulations were followed scrupulously, not only would there be no divorce; there would be no unhappy marriages" (Sproul 2003:149).

REFERENCES

CHAPTER 1

Beaver, R. Pierce. 1999. "The History of Mission Strategy" In *Perspectives On The World Christian Movement: A Reader.* Ralph Winter, ed. Pasadena, CA: William Carey Library.

Carus, Paul. 1997. *The Gospel of Buddha.* Nagpur, India: Kashinath Meshram, Buddha Bhoomi Prakashan.

Chamroeun, Chrann and Thomas G. Nielsen. 2008. Physical, Sexual Abuse Relegates Women to a Life in the Shadows. *The Phnom Penh Post,* September 5: 5.

Court, John. 1975. The Family in the Year 2000. Paper presented at the ANZAAS Symposium, University Of Adelaide.

Croucher, Rowland. 1994. "The Family: At Home in a Heartless World," In *GRID* Autumn, Australia: World Vision (Christian Leadership Letter).

Ekachai, Santisuda. 2008. A Fighting Chance. *Bangkok Post.* August 26.

Hume, Britt. 2008, Grandparents Under The Same Roof. Special Report, Fox News, November 17.

Latourette, Kenneth S. 1953. *A History of Christianity.* New York: Harper & Row.

Lawrence, Jill. 2007, "This Time, 'Family Values' Are Lower on the Agenda" *USA TODAY,* December 18: 1-2A.

Lenovo . 2008. "China's Spiritual Awakening" In *Business Week,* January 14, Asia Insider.

Lipski, Liz. 2008. "After 'That' Day" In *The War Cry,* Vol. 127 No. 36. The Salvation Army September 13: 13.

Liu, Melinda. 2008. "China: Playing With the Old Blood Rules." *Newsweek,* March 17: 17-20.

Marcus, Erin N. 2008. "Battered and Beaten," In *Bangkok Post*, August 26, Features Outlook.

McGavran, Donald A. 1970. *Understanding Church Growth*. Grand Rapids: William B. Eerdmans Publishing.

Meroff, Deborah. 2004. *True Grit: Women Taking on the World, For God's Sake*. Bucks, UK: Authentic, Paternoster Publishing.

Neill, Stephen. 1964. *A History of Christian Missions*. Harmondsworth, Middlesex, England: Penguin Books.

Nichols, Doug. 2008. "Advocate For Children In Crisis," E-Mail Reports And Personal Notes 11/21/08, 12/02/08.

Pickett, J. Waskom. 1933. *Christian Mass Movements in India*. Lucknow: Lucknow Publishing House.

Pierson, Paul. 1999. "A History Of Transformation" In *Perspectives On The World Christian Movement: A Reader*. Ralph Winter, ed. Pasadena, CA: William Carey Library.

Pruitt, Paul. 2008. "Reaching Chinese Internationally" In Circular Letter, November, 1-2. Colorado, USA.

Rader, Dotson. 2008. "I Have Great Hope For Love" *The Oregonian – Parade*, November 23: 4-5.

Smith, Alex G. 2003. *Multiplying Churches Through Prayer Cell Evangelism: A Manual For Church Planting Movements*. Chiang Mai: OMF.

_____.2006. The Struggle of Asian Ancestor Veneration. In *Communicating Christ In The Buddhist World*. Pasadena, CA: William Carey Library.

Suellen, Hinde. 2008. "Toddlers in Distress." In *The Sunday Mail*, October 26, Australia: The sundaymail.com.au:7.

Toffler Alvin. 1970. *Future Shock*. New York: Pan Books.

Toppo, Greg and Anthony Debarros. 2008. "More Parents Move In With Kids" *USA TODAY*, September 23.

Winter, Ralph. 1999 "The Two Structures of God's Redemptive

Mission" In *Perspectives On The World Christian Movement: A Reader.* Ralph Winter, ed. 220-230. Pasadena, CA: William Carey Library.

Writer, Larry. 2008. "Ros Packer Life After Kerry." *The Australian Women's Weekly.* October, ACP Magazines Ltd: 47-52.

Chapter 2

Berentsen, Jan Martin. 1985. "The Ancestral Rites - Barriers or Bridges," In *Christian Alternatives to Ancestor Practices.* Bon Rin Ro, ed. 287-301. Taichung: Asia Theological Association.

Bornstein, David. 2003. *How to Change the World: Social Entrepreneurs and the Power of New Ideas.* Oxford; Oxford University Press.

Bosch, David J. 1991. *Transforming Mission.* Maryknoll, NY: Orbis.

Carlton, R. Bruce. 2000. *Amazing Grace: Lessons on Church Planting Movements from Cambodia.* Chennai: Mission Education Books.

Covell, Ralph. 1993. "Buddhism and the Gospel among the Peoples of China," *Journal Of Frontier Missions* 10.3 (July): 131-140.

Davis, John R. 1993. *Poles Apart? Contextualizing the Gospel.* Bangkok: OMF Publications.

_____. 1997. *The Path to Enlightenment: Introducing Buddhism.* London: Hodder & Stoughton.

Deng, Zhaoming. 2005. "Indigenous Chinese Pentecostal Denominations," In *Asian and Pentecostal: The Charismatic Face of Christianity in Asia.* Allan Anderson and Edmond Tang, eds. Oxford: Regnum Books International.

Garrison, David. 2004. *Church Planting Movements.* Midlothian, VA: Wigtake Resources.

_____. 2005. "Church Planting Movements Versus Insider Movements: Missiological Realities Versus Mythiological (Sic) Speculations." Unpublished Monograph.

Hattaway, Paul. 2003. *Back to Jerusalem*. Carlisle: Piquant.

Hoefer, Herbert. 2001. *Churchless Christianity*. Pasadena, CA: William Carey Library.

IBMR Editorial. 2005. "Can There Be Christianity Without Church?" *International Bulletin of Missionary Research*. 29.4 (October): 169-170.

Kraft, Charles. 1979. *Christianity in Cultures*. Maryknoll, NY: Orbis.

_____. 2005. "Pursuing Faith, Not Religion: The Liberating Quest for Contextualization," *Mission Frontiers* 27.5 (September-October): 9-11.

_____ (Ed). 2005a. *Appropriate Christianity*. Pasadena, CA: William Carey Library.

Lai, Pan-Chiu. 2000. "Influence of Chinese Buddhism on the Indigenization of Christianity in Modern China," *Ching Feng* 1.2 (Fall): 13-159.

Lewis, Rebecca. 2005. "Missions in the 21st Century: Working With Social Entrepreneurs?" *Mission Frontiers* 27.5 (September-October): 20.

Lim, David. 1983. "Biblical Christianity in the Context of Buddhism," In *Sharing Jesus in the Two Thirds World*. V. Samuel & C.Sugden, eds. 175-203. Grand Rapids, MI: Eerdmans.

_____. 1987. "The Origin, Nature and Organization of the Synagogue," *Studia Biblica Et Theologia* 15/1 (April): 23-51.

_____. 2003. "Towards A Radical Contextualization Paradigm In Evangelizing Buddhists," In *Sharing Jesus In The Buddhist World*. David Lim & Steve Spaulding, eds. 71-94. Pasadena, CA: William Carey Library.

References

_____. 2004. "Church @The Frontiers: Transformation Through Church Planting Movement And Community Development." Paper presented at Sealink Conference (June). Monograph, Quezon City: CMI-Philippines.

McGavran, Donald. 1985. "Honoring Ancestors In Japan," In *Christian Alternatives To Ancestor Practices.* Bong Rin Ro, ed. 303-318. Taichung: Asia Theological Association.

_____. 2005. "A People Reborn: Foundational Insights On People Movements" ("Foreword" To Christian Keysser, *A People Reborn* (Pasadena: Wm. Carey Library, 1980), *Mission Frontiers* 27.5 (September-October): 16-17.

Parshall, Phil. 1988. "God's Communicator In The '80's," In *Perspectives on the World Christian Movement.* Ralph Winter and Steve Hawthorne, eds. 473-481. Pasadena, CA: William Carey Library.

_____. 1998. "Danger! New Directions in Contextualization," *Evangelical Missions Quarterly* 34.4: 404-406, 409-410.

Patterson, George. 1988. "The Spontaneous Multiplication of Churches." In *Perspectives on the World Christian Movement.* Ralph Winter and Steve Hawthorne, eds. 601-616. Pasadena, CA: William Carey Library.

Petersen, Jim and Mike Shamy. 2003. *The Insider: Bringing the Kingdom Of God Into Your Everyday World.* Colorado Springs, CO: Navpress.

Pierson, Paul E. 2004. *Emerging Streams of Church and Mission.* Pattaya, Thailand: 2004 Forum for World Evangelization.

Raj, P. Solomon. 2004. *A Christian Folk Religion in India.* Bangalore: Centre for Contemporary Christianity.

Richard, Herbert. 1999. *Following Jesus in the Hindu Context.* Pasadena, CA: William Carey Library.

Richardson, Don. 1981. *Eternity in Their Hearts.* Ventura, CA: Regal.

Ro, Bong Rin, ed. 1985. *Christian Alternatives to Ancestor Practices*. Taichung: Asia Theological Association.

_____ and Mark Albrecht, eds. 1986. *God in Asian Contexts*. Taichung: Asia Theological Association.

Seamands, John. 1981. *Tell It Well: Communicating The Gospel Across Cultures*. Kansas City, KS: Beacon Hill Press.

"Seeking To Nurture 'Gospel Movements'." 2005. *Mission Frontiers* 27.5 (September-October): 15.

Simson, Wolfgang. 2001. *Houses That Change the World*. Carlisle: Paternoster.

Smith, Alex. 1993. "Insights for Frontier Missions to Theravada Buddhists," *International Journal of Frontier Missions* 10.3 (July): 125-128.

Somaratna, G. P. V. 2006. *The Foreignness of the Christian Church in Sri Lanka*. Colombo: Colombo Theological Seminary.

Southerland, Dan. 1999. *Transitioning: Leading Your Church Through Change*. Grand Rapids, MI: Zondervan.

Spaulding, Steve. 2006. "Who Is Unreached In Asia." *Mission Frontiers* 28.2 (March-April): 18-19.

Tang, Edmond. 2005. "'Yellers' and Healers: Pentecostalism and the Study of Grassroots Christianity in China," In *Asian And Pentecostal: The Charismatic Face Of Christianity In Asia*. Allan Anderson and Edmond Tang, eds. Oxford: Regnum Books.

Tennent, Timothy. 2005. "The Challenge of Churchless Christianity: An Evangelical Assess-Ment." *International Bulletin of Missionary Research*. 29.4 (October): 171-177.

Travis, John. 1998. "Must All Muslims Leave Islam To Follow Jesus?" *Evangelical Missions Quarterly* 34.4: 411-415.

_____. 2000. "Messianic Muslim Followers of Isa: A Closer Look at C5 Believers And Congregations," *International Journal of Frontier Missions* 17.1: 53-59.

_____, and Anna Travis. 2005. "Contextualization Among Muslims, Hindus And Buddhists: A Focus On Insider Movements," *Mission Frontiers* 27.5 (September-October): 12-15.

_____. 2006. "Maximizing The Bible!: Glimpses From Our Context." *Mission Frontiers* 28.1(January-February): 21-22.

Tsering, Marku. n.d. *Sharing Christ in the Tibetan Buddhist World*. Upper Darby, PA: Tibet Press.

Wall, Molly. 2005. "Learning From a New Wave of Social Entrepreneurs," *Mission Frontiers* 27.5 (September-October): 18-19.

Wetchgama, Banpote. 2006. "The New Buddhists." Unpublished Paper.

Wesley, Luke. 2004. "Is The Chinese Church Predominantly Pentecostal?" *Asian Journal of Pentecostal Studies* 7.2 (July): 225-254.

Winter, Ralph. 2005. "Editorial Comment," *Mission Frontiers* 27.5 (September-October): 4-5.

Zdero, Rad. 2004. *The Global House Church Movement*. Pasadena, CA: William Carey Library.

Chapter 3

Beaver, R. Pierce. 1999. "The History of Mission Strategy" In *Perspectives on The World Christian Movement: A Reader*. Ralph Winter and Steve Hawthorne, eds. Pasadena, CA: William Carey Library, 1999.

Bruce, F.F. 1979. *Commentary on The Book Of The Acts*. Grand Rapids, MI: William B. Eerdmans Publishing.

Hesselgrave, David J. 1978. *Communicating Christ Cross-Culturally*. Grand Rapids, MI: Zondervan.

Hiebert, Paul G. 1983. *Cultural Anthropology*. Grand Rapids, MI: Baker Book House.

Latourette, Kenneth Scott. 1953. *A History of Christianity*. New York: Harper & Row.

McGavran, Donald A. 1970. *Understanding Church Growth*. Grand Rapids, MI: William B. Eerdmans Publishing.

_____. 1981. *The Bridges of God*. New York: Friendship Press.

Neill, Stephen. 1964. *A History of Christian Missions*. Harmondsworth, Middlesex, England: Penguin Books.

Nevius, John L. 1958. *The Planting and Development of Missionary Churches*. Philadelphia, PA: The Reformed and Presbyterian Publishing Company.

Pickett, J. Waskom. 1933. *Christian Mass Movements in India*. Lucknow: Lucknow Publishing House.

Pierson, Paul. 1999. "A History of Transformation." In *Perspectives on the World Christian Movement: A Reader*. Ralph Winter and Steve Hawthorne, eds. Pasadena, CA: William Carey Library.

Schramm, Wilbur, ed. 1954. *The Process and Effects of Mass Communication*. Urbana, IL: University Of Illinois Press.

Smith, Alex G. 1977. *Strategy to Multiply Rural Churches: A Central Thailand Case Study*. Bangkok: OMF Publishers.

_____. 1982. *Siamese Gold: A History of Church Growth in Thailand: An Interpretive Analysis 1816-1982*. Bangkok: Kanok Bannasarn.

_____. 2003. *Multiplying Churches Through Prayer Cell Evangelism: A Manual for Church Planting Movements*. Chiang Mai: OMF, 2003.

Smith, Donald K. 1984. *Make Haste Slowly: Developing Effective Cross-Cultural Communication*. Portland, OR: IICC.

Taylor, Mrs. Howard. 1998. *Behind The Ranges: The Life Changing Story Of J. O. Fraser*. Singapore: OMF.

Taylor, Robert B. 1973. *Introduction to Cultural Anthropology*. Boston, MA: Allyn and Bacon Inc.

Tippett, Alan R. 1987. *Introduction to Missiology*. Pasadena, CA: William Carey Library.

Unknown. N.d. *The Human Heart*. Hong Kong, Christian Communications Ltd.

Wright, G. Ernest. 1952. *God Who Acts: Biblical Theology as Recital*. London: SCM Press Ltd.

CHAPTER 4

Brewster, Dan. N.d. *Children & Childhood in The Bible: A Workbook*. Pre-Publication Draft. Compassion International.

Buddha Dharma Education Association and Buddhanet. N.d. "The Buddha Speaks About the Deep Kindness of Parents and the Difficulty in Repaying It." www.buddhanet.net/e-learning/filial-sutra.htm. Accessed 11 October 2008.

Chan, Polly. N.D. "Asian Children in MK Schools." International Children's Education www.iched.org/cms/scripts/page.php?site_id=iched&item_id=asian_children_mk_school. Accessed 12 December 2008.

Ghosh, Pi. 1996. "Evolution of Prostitution in Thailand: An Overview." Sixth International Conference on Thai Studies. Chiang Mai, Thailand.

Haas, Mary R. 1964. *Thai-English Student's Dictionary*. Stanford, CA: Stanford University Press.

Kabilsingh, Chatsumarn. 2002. "Prostitutes And Buddhism." In *A Collation of Articles on Thai Women and Buddhism*. Virada Somswasdi and Alycia Nicholas, eds. 38-47. Chiang Mai, Thailand: Women's Studies Center, Faculty of Social Sciences, Chiang Mai University and the Foundation for Women, Law and Rural Development.

Khuankaew, Ouyporn. 2002. "Thai Buddhism: Women's Ordination Or More Prostitution?" In *A Collation of Articles on Thai Women And Buddhism*. 2002.Virada Somswasdi and Alycia Nicholas, eds. 50-61. Chiang Mai, Thailand: Women's Studies Center, Faculty of Social Sciences, Chiang Mai University and The Foundation for Women, Law and Rural Development.

Knutson, Thomas J. N.D. "Tales of Thailand: Lessons from the Land of Smile." www.fulbrightthai.org/knowledge/read.asp?id=27&type=culture. Accessed 28 October 2008.

Komin, Suntaree. 1991. *Psychology of the Thai People: Values and Behavioral Patterns*. Bangkok, Thailand: National Institute of Development Administration. studyinthailand.org/study_abroad_thailand_university/suntaree/suntaree_komin_2.html. Accessed 28 October 2008.

Matzner, Andrew. 2001. "Review of *Thai Women in the Global Labor Force: Consuming Desires, Contested Selves*." by Mary Beth Mills. In *Intersections: Gender, History And Culture In The Asian Context* Issue: 5. intersections.anu.edu.au/issue5/matzner_review.html. Accessed 28 October 2008.

Montgomery, Heather. 2001. *Modern Babylon? Prostituting Children in Thailand*. New York, NY: Berghahn Books.

Mulder, Niels. 2000. *Inside Thai Society: Religion, Everyday Life, Change*. Chiang Mai, Thailand: Silkworm Books.

Nguyen, Tuong Hung. N.d. "Thailand: Cultural Background for ESL/EFL Teachers." www.hmongstudies.org/thaiculture.pdf. Accessed 24 October 2008.

Peaceful Societies. 2005. "Thai Women Cherish Motherhood." Review of "*When I Become a Mother!: Discourses of Motherhood among Thai Women in Northern Thailand*", By Pranee Liamputton, et al. www.peacefulsocieties.org/nar/050721thai.html. Accessed 28 October 2008.

Persons, Larry Scott. 2008. *Face Dynamics, Social Power and Virtue Among Thai Leaders: A Cultural Analysis.* Pasadena, CA: Fuller Graduate Schools. Unpublished dissertation.

Promphakping, Buapun. 2003. "Household, Village and Local Politics: Gender and the Politics of Common in Rural Transformation." Presented at "Politics Of The Commons: Articulating Development And Strengthening Local Practices", Chiang Mai, Thailand, July 11-14. dlc.dlib.indiana.edu/archive/00001085/00/buapan.pdf. Accessed 28 October 2008.

Pusurinkham, Sirirat. 1997. *Child Prostitution in Thailand: A Challenge To The World Christian Community.* San Francisco, CA: San Francisco Theological Seminary. Unpublished doctoral dissertation.

Rabibhadana, Akin. 1984. "Kinship, Marriage and the Thai Social System," In *Perspectives On The Thai Marriage.* Aphichat Chamratrithirong, ed. Bangkok, Thailand: Institute for Population and Social Research, Mahidol University.

Skrobanek, Siriporn, Nattaya Boonpakdi and Chutima Janthakeero. 1997. *The Traffic in Women: Human Realities of the International Sex Trade.* New York, NY: Zed Books Ltd.

Smith, Alex G. 2006. "The Struggle of Asian Ancestor Veneration." In *Communicating Christ in the Buddhist World.* Paul De Neui and David Lim, eds. 149-175. Pasadena, CA: William Carey Library.

Sudham, Pira. 1994. *People of Esarn.* Bangkok: Shire Books.

Surangkhanang, K. 1994. *The Prostitute.* Translated By David Smyth. Selangor Darul Ehsan, Malaysia: Oxford University Press.

UNICEF. 2001. "UNICEF Calls for Eradication of Commercial Sexual Exploitation of Children." Press Release 12 December, 2001. Website: http://www.unicef.org/newsline/01pr97.htm. Accessed 1 March 2009.

Young, Serenity. 2004. *Courtesans and Tantric Consorts: Sexualities in Buddhist Narrative, Iconography, and Ritual*. New York, NY: Routledge.

Zuck, Roy. 1996. *Precious in His Sight: Childhood and Children in the Bible*. Grand Rapids, MI: Baker Books.

Chapter 5

Barclay, William. 1975. *The Letter to the Romans*. Philadelphia, PA: The Westminster Press.

Boontawee, Kampoon. 1994. *A Child of the Northeast*. Bangkok: Duangkamol.

Eliade, Mircea. 1987. *The Sacred & the Profane: The Nature of Religion*. San Diego, CA: Harcourt Brace And Company.

Feig, John Paul. 1989. *A Common Core: Thais and Americans*. Intercultural Press, Inc.

Grimes, Roland L. 1994. *Beginning in Ritual Studies: Revised Edition*. Studies in Comparative Religion. Frederick M. Denny, ed. Columbia, SC: University Of South Carolina Press.

Hiebert, G. Paul. 1994. *Anthropological Reflections on Missiological Issues*. Grand Rapids, MI: Baker Books.

Komin, Suntaree. 1993. *Psychology of the Thai People Values and Behavioral Patterns*. Bangkok: NIDA.

Mejudhon, Nantachai. 1993. "Meekness: A New Approach to Christian Witness to the Thai." Wilmore, KY: Asbury Theological Seminary. Unpublished dissertation.

Ngamdee, Yinglak. 1993. *Supasit Kampangpey Lae Samnuan Thai (Proverbs, Saying and Thai Expressions)*. Bangkok: Agsarapipat Ltd.

Praya Sri Sunthorn Wohan, Noi Archanyang Kun. 1962. *Kamklong Lokaniti (The Poetry of the Laws of Life)*. Bangkok: Kurusapa Publishing House.

References

Sataanandha, Suwanna and Nuangnoy Boonyanate. 1993. *Rongroy Kwamkit Kwamchur Thai (The Belief System of the Thai)*. Bangkok, Thailand: Chulalanogkorn University Publishing House.

Schreiter, Robert J. 1994. *Reconciliation: Mission & Ministry in a Changing Social Order.* Maryknoll, NY: Orbis.

Tenney, Merill C, ed. 1962. Pictorial Bible Dictionary. Grand Rapids, MI: Zondervan.

Thai Royal Academy. 1993. *Pojananukrom (Dictionary)*. Bangkok, Thailand: Agsorncharoentasana.

The Lockman Foundation. 1962. *New American Standard Bible.* U.S.A.: The Lockman Foundation.

Tollefson, Kenneth. "Maintaining Quality Control In Christian Missions," Missiology 18/3. 1989.

Turner, Victor. 1968. *The Drums of Affliction: A Study of Religious Processes Among The Ndembu of Zambia.* Oxford: Clarendon for the International African Institute.

Turner, Victor. 1968. *The Ritual Process: Structure and Anti-Structure*. New York: Aldine De Gruyster.

Wissawate, Wit. 1967. "The Series of Lecture on Buddhist Philosophy." Bangkok, Thailand: Faculty of Arts, Chulalongkorn University.

Zahniser, A.H. Mathias. 1997. *Symbol and Ceremony: Making Disciples Across Cultures*. Monrovia, CA: MARC.

Chapter 6

Burlinghame, E.W. 1869. *Dharmapada.* Tr F. Max Müller, In *Buddhist Parables*, By E. W. Burlinghame. Reprinted In Sacred Books Of The East, Volume X, Oxford: Clarendon.

De Silva, Lyn. 1974. *Buddhism: Beliefs and Practice*s, Published by author.

Ediriweera, S.A. 2000. *Essentials of Buddhism.* Dehiwela: Buddhist Cultural Centre.

Geiger, Wilhelm. 1993. *Mahavamsa: Great Chronicle Of Ceylon,* Delhi: Asian Educational Services.

Gombrich, Richard and Gananath Obeyesekere. 1990. *Buddhism Transformed Religious Change in Sri Lanka.* Delhi; Motalal Banarsidass.

Hiebert, Paul. 1982. "Flaw of the Excluded Middle." *Missiology* 10:35-47.

_____, Dan Shaw and Tite Tienou. 1999. *Understanding Falk Religion.* Grand Rapids, MI: Baker.

Huxley, A. 1995. Buddhism and Law: The View from Mandalay. *Journal of the International Association of Buddhist Studies* 18 (1): 47–95.

Jones, K. 1989. *The Social Face of Buddhism.* London: Wisdom.

Khantipalo, Bhikkhu. 1982. *Lay Buddhist Practice,* Kandy: Wheel Publications.

Kariyawasam, A.G.S. 1995. *Buddhist Ceremonies and Rituals of Sri Lanka.* Kandy: The Wheel Publications.

Kornfield Jack. 1996. *Teachings of the Buddha.* London: Shambhala.

Malalasekera, G.P. 1999. *The Buddha and His Teaching*s. Colombo, Sri Lanka: Ministry of Cultural Affairs.

Narada Thera. 1940. *The Dharmapada: The Gift of Truth Excels All Other Gifts.* Dehiwela, Sri Lanka: Buddhist Cultural Centre.

_____. 1984. *The Discourse to Sigala the Layperson's Code of Discipline.* Kandy, Sri Lanka: Wheel Publications.

_____. 2000. *Buddhism in a Nutshell.* Dehiwela, Sri Lanka: Buddhist Cultural Centre

_____. 2007. *A Manual of Buddhism.* Dehiwela, Sri Lanka: Buddhist Cultural Centre.

Obeyesekere, Gananath. 1984. *The Cult of the Goddess Pattini*. Chicago: University Of Chicago Press.

Perera, G.A. N.d. *Buddhist Paritta Chanting Ritual*. Dehiwela, Sri Lanka: Buddhist Cultural Centre.

Perera, H.R. 1988. *Buddhism in Sri Lanka: A Short History*. Kandy, Sri Lanka: Buddhist Publication Society.

Rahula, Walpola. 1994. *What The Buddha Taught*. Colombo, Sri Lanka: Department of Cultural Affairs.

Richardson, Rick. 2000. *Evangelism Outside the Box: New Ways to Help People Experience the Good News*. New York, NY: IVP.

Report of the Presidential Commission on the Buddha Sasana. 2002. Colombo, Sri Lanka: Ministry Of Buddha Sasana.

Soma Thera. 1967. *The Way of Mindfulness, Tr. Of Sutra and Commentary*. Kandy, Sri Lanka: Buddhist Publication Society.

Thanissaro, Bhikkhu. 1997. *Dharmapada, A Translation*. Valley Center, CA.: Buddha Dharma Educational Association.

Weeraratne, W.G. ed. 1990. *Encyclopedia of Buddhism,* Vol. V. Colombo, Sri Lanka: Department Of Buddhist Affairs.

Wickremeratne, Swarna. 2006. *Buddha in Sri Lanka*. New York, NY: State University of New York Press

CHAPTER 7

Berentsen, Jan-Martin. 1985. "Ancestor Worship in Missiological Perspective," In *Christian Alternatives to Ancestor Practices*. Bong Rin Ro, ed. Taichung, Taiwan: Asia Theological Association.

Bowers, Russell H. 2003. *Folk Buddhism in Southeast Asia*. Cambodia: Training Of Timothys.

Grunlan, Stephen A. and Marvin K. Mayers. 1979. *Cultural Anthropology: A Christian Perspective*. Grand Rapids, MI: Zondervan.

Henry, Rodney L. 1986. *Filipino Spirit World*. Manila, Philippines: OMF Literature Inc.

Hung, Daniel. 1983. "M Blockage: Ancestor Worship," EMQ. 19(1).

Hwang, Bernard. 1977. "Ancestor Cult Today," *Missiology* V(3).

Hickey, Gerald. 1964. *Village in Viet Nam*. New Haven, CT: Yale University Press.

Hiebert, Paul G. 1985. *Anthropological Insights for Missionaries*. Grand Rapids MI: Baker Book House.

_____. 1993. "Popular Religions," *Toward the Twenty-First Century in Christian Mission*, Grand Rapids MI: Eerdmans.

Kraft, Charles H. 1991. *Christianity in Culture*. Maryknoll, NY: Orbis.

Liao, David C. E. 1972. *The Unresponsive: Resistant or Neglected?* Chicago, IL: Moody Press.

Liaw, Stephen. 1983. "Ancestor Worship in Taiwan and Evangelism of the Chinese." In *Christian Alternatives to Ancestor Practices*. Bong Rin Ro, ed. Taichung, Taiwan: ATA.

Lowe, Chuck. 2001. *Honoring God and Family: A Christian Response to Idol Food in Chinese Popular Religion*. Wheaton, IL: EMIS.

Maguire, Jack. 2001. *Essential Buddhism: A Complete Guide to Beliefs and Practices*. New York, NY: Pocket Books.

Nyanasamvara, Somdet Phra. N.d. *Forty-Five Years of the Buddha (Book One)*. Thailand: The Buddhist University.

Peiris, Ralph. 1956. *Sinhalese Social Organization*. Colombo: Ceylon University Press.

Reimer, Reginald E. 1975. "The Religious Dimension of the Vietnamese Cult of the Ancestors." *Missiology*. III (2).

Ro, Bong Rin, ed. 1985. *Christian Alternatives to Ancestor Practices*. Taichung, Taiwan: Asia Theological Association.

Samagalski, Alan. 1984. *China – A Travel Survival Kit*. Hong Kong: Lonely Planet Publications.

Shibata, Chizuo. 1985. "Some Problematic Aspects of Japanese Ancestor Worship," In *Christian Alternatives to Ancestor Practices*. Bong Rin Ro, Ed. Taichung, Taiwan: ATA.

Tan, Kim-Sai. 1985. "Christian Alternatives to Ancestor Worship In Malaysia." In *Christian Alternatives to Ancestor Practices*. Bong Rin Ro, Ed. Taichung, Taiwan: ATA.

Taylor, John V. 1963. *The Primal Vision*. London: SCM Press.

Taylor, Robert B. 1973. *Introduction to Cultural Anthropology* .Boston: Allyn and Bacon Inc.

Tylor, Edward B. 1889. *Primitive Cultures*. New York: Henry Holt and Company.

Van Engen, Charles E. 1998. "Reflecting Theologically About the Resistant." In *Reaching the Resistant: Barriers and Bridges for Mission*. Pasadena, CA: William Carey Library.

Weerasingha, Tissa. 1989. *The Cross and the Bo Tree*. Taichung, Taiwan: Asia Theological Association.

Wei, Yuan-Kwei. 1985. "Historical Analysis of Ancestor Worship in Ancient China." In *Christian Alternatives to Ancestor Practices*. Bong Rin Ro, Ed. Taichung, Taiwan: ATA.

CHAPTER 8

Asia Theological Association. 1985. "A Working Document Towards a Christian Approach to Ancestor Practices," ed. Bong Rin Ro. *Christian Alternatives to Ancestor Practices*. Taichung: Asia Theological Association..3-10.

Baker, Hugh. 1979. *Chinese Family and Kinship*. New York: Columbia University Press.

Bavinck, J. H. 1960. *An Introduction to the Science of Missions*. Philadelphia: Presbyterian & Reformed Publishing Co.

Bell, C. 1989. "Religion and Chinese Culture: Toward an Assessment of 'Popular Religion'," *History of Religions* 29.1: 35-57.

Berentsen, Jan-Martin. 1985. "Ancestral Worship in Missiological Perspective," Ed. Bong Rin Ro. *Christian Alternatives to Ancestor Practices.* Taichung: Asia Theological Association. 261-285.

_____. 1985a. "Individual and Collective in the Family Context: The Fourth Commandment in Japanese Perspective," ed. Bong Rin Ro. *Christian Alternatives To Ancestor Practices.* Taichung: Asia Theological Association. 61-76.

_____. 1985b. "The Ancestral Rites - Barriers or Bridges," Ed. Bong Rin Ro. *Christian Alternatives to Ancestor Practices.* Taichung: Asia Theological Association. 287-301.

Brown, Rick. 2006. "Contextualization Without Syncretism," *International Journal of Frontier Mission* 23.3: 127-133.

_____. 2007. "Insider Movements: The Conversation Continues: Biblical Muslims," *International Journal of Frontier Mission* 24.2 (Summer): 65-74.

Chamberlain, Jonathan. 1987. *Chinese Gods.* Subang Jaya, Malaysia: Pelanduk Publications.

Chan, Kim Kwong & A. Hunter. 1994. "Religion And Society In Mainland China In The 1990s," *Issues And Studies* 30.8: 54-75.

Chang, Lit-Sen. 1975. "Evangelization Among Buddhists and Confucianists," *Let the Earth Hear His Voice.* Minneapolis: World Wide Publication.

Ching, Julia. 1993. *Chinese Religions.* Maryknoll, NY: Orbis.

Chow, Lien-Hwa. 1985. "Christian Response to Filial Piety in Chinese Classical Literature," Ed. Bong Rin Ro. *Christian Alternatives to Ancestor Practices.* Taichung: Asia Theological Association. 135-146.

References

Chung, Kyung-Wha. 2006. "Ancestral Worship by Korean Christians in the Light of Christian Faith," ed. E. Acoba et al. *Naming the Unknown God*. Mandaluyong: OMF Literature.

Cohen, Alvin P. 1987. "Chinese Popular Religion," ed. Mircea Eliade. *Encyclopedia of Religion, 16 Vols*. New York: Macmillan. 3: 289.

Davis, John R. 1993. *Poles Apart? Contextualizing the Gospel*. Bangkok: OMF Publications.

Dulawan, Lourdes. 2002. "Inculturation: Ifugao Culture and Tradition." http://interactive.ifugao.org//modules.php?name=news&file=article&sid=9.

Elder, Gove. 1985. "Responses of Thai-Chinese Churches to the Ancestral Problem," ed. Bong Rin Ro. *Christian Alternatives to Ancestor Practices*. Taichung: Asia Theological Association. 225-233.

Hiebert, Paul. 1994. *Anthropological Reflections on Missiological Issues*. Grand Rapids: Baker.

_____. R. D. Shaw & Tite Tienou. 1999. *Understanding Folk Religion*. Grand Rapids: Baker.

Hung, Daniel. 1985. "Mission Blockade: Ancestor Worship," ed. Bong Rin Ro. *Christian Alternatives to Ancestor Practices*. Taichung: Asia Theological Association. 199-208.

Kopytoff, Igor. 1997. "Ancestors as Elders in Africa," ed. R. R. Grinker & C. B. Steiner. *Perspectives on Africa: A Reader in Culture, History, and Representation*. 412-421. Oxford: Blackwell.

Kraft, Charles. 1979. *Christianity in Cultures*. Maryknoll: Orbis.

_____(ed). 2005. *Appropriate Christianity*. Pasadena: Wm. Carey Library.

Kung, Timothy. 1993. "Evangelizing Budddhists," *International Journal of Frontier Mission* 10.3 (July): 118-123.

Liao, David. 1985. "Christian Alternatives to Ancestor Worship in Taiwan," ed. Bong Rin Ro. *Christian Alternatives to Ancestor Practices.* Taichung: Asia Theological Association. 209-218.

Liaw, Stephen. 1985. "Ancestor Worship in Taiwan and Evangelism of the Chinese," ed. Bong Rin Ro. *Christian Alternatives to Ancestor Practices.* Taichung: Asia Theological Association. 181-197.

Lim, David. 1983. "Biblical Christianity in the Context of Buddhism," ed. V. Samuel & C. Sugden. *Sharing Jesus in the Two Thirds World.* Grand Rapids: Eerdmans. pp.175-203.

_____. 2003. "Towards A Radical Contextualization Paradigm in Evangelizing Buddhists," *Sharing Jesus in the Buddhist World*, ed. David Lim & Steve Spaulding. 71-94. Pasadena: William Carey Library.

_____. 2006. "Catalyzing 'Insider Movements' in Buddhist Contexts." Paper Presented at SEANET Missiological Forum V, Chiangmai, Thailand (January).

_____. 2008. "Biblical Worship Rediscovered: A Theology for Communicating Basic Christianity." *Communicating Christ Through Story and Song: Orality in Buddhist Contexts,* ed. Paul H. De Neui. 27-59. Pasadena: Wm. Carey Library.

Lin, Chi-Ping. 1985. "Ancestor Worship: The Reactions of Chinese Churches," ed. Bong Rin Ro. *Christian Alternatives to Ancestor Practices.* Taichung: Asia Theological Association. 147-161.

Macinnis, D. E. (ed.). 1989. *Religion in China Today: Policy and Practice.* Maryknoll, NY: Orbis.

Mcgavran, Donald. 1985. "Honoring Ancestors in Japan," ed. Bong Rin Ro. *Christian Alternatives to Ancestor Practices.* Taichung: Asia Theological Association. 303-318.

_____. 2005. "A People Reborn: Foundational Insights on People Movements" ("Foreword" to Christian Keysser, *A People Reborn* (Pasadena: Wm. Carey Library, 1980), *Mission Frontiers* 27.5 (September-October): 16-17.

Maggay, Melba. 2005. "Toward Contextualization From Within," ed. E. Acoba et al. *Doing Theology in the Philippines.* 37-50. Mandaluyong City: OMF Literature.

Overmyer, D. L. 1986. *Religions of China.* San Francisco: Harper & Row.

Richardson, Rick. 2006. *Re-Imagining Evangelism: Inviting Friends on a Spiritual Journey.* Downers Grove: Inter-Varsity Press.

Ro, Bong Rin (ed.). 1985. *Christian Alternatives to Ancestor Practices.* Taichung: Asia Theological Association.

_____. 1988. "Chinese Concept of God and the God of the Bible," ed. Bong Rin Ro & Mark Albrecht. *God in Asian Contexts.* Taichung: Asia Theological Association. 165-191.

Schwab, Philip. 1985. "Biblical Understanding of Ancestor Practices," ed. Bong Rin Ro. *Christian Alternatives to Ancestor Practices.* Taichung: Asia Theological Association. 93-116.

Shibata, Chizuo. 1985. "Some Problematic Aspects of Japanese Ancestor Worship," ed. Bong Rin Ro. *Christian Alternatives to Ancestor Practices.* Taichung: Asia Theological Association. 247-260.

Smith, Alex. 2006. "The Struggle of Asian Ancestor Veneration," ed. Paul De Neui & David Lim. *Communicating Christ in the Buddhist World.* Pasadena: William Carey Library. 149-175.

Son, Bong Ho. 1985. "Socio-Philosophical Background for Change of Attitudes Toward Ancestor Worship," ed. Bong Rin Ro. *Christian Alternatives to Ancestor Practices.* Taichung: Asia Theological Association. 235-246.

Taiwan Church News. 2002. "Taiwan Christians Discuss the Ancestor Question." http://www.wfn.org/2002/11/msg00193.html.

Tan, Chiu Eng. 1996. "The Cosmos, Humans and Gods: A Comparison of Nonchristians and Christians on Chinese Beliefs In Metromanila. Ph.D. Thesis: Trinity International University.

Tan, Kim-Sai. 1985. "Christian Alternatives to Ancestor Worship in Malaysia," ed. Bong Rin Ro. *Christian Alternatives to Ancestor Practices.* Taichung: Asia Theological Association. 219-224.

Tan, Lucy. 1985. "Ancestor Worship Judged by Scripture," ed. Bong Rin Ro. *Christian Alternatives to Ancestor Practices.* Taichung: Asia Theological Association. 77-91.

Teizer, S. F. 1995. "Popular Religion," *The Journal of Asian Studies* 54.2: 378-395.

Tippett, Alan. 1987. *Introduction to Missiology.* Pasadena: Wm. Carey Library.

Uayan, Jean. 2005. "Chap Chay Lo Mi: Disentangling the Chinese-Filipino Worldview," ed. E. Acoba. *Naming the Unknown God.* Mandaluyong: OMF Literature. 65-77.

Van Rheenen, Gailyn. 1996. *Communicating Christ in Animistic Contexts.* Pasadena: Wm. Carey Library.

_____ (Ed.). 2006. *Contextualization and Syncretism: Navigating Cultural Currents.* Pasadena: Wm. Carey Library.

Wei, Yuan-Kwei. 1985. "Historical Analysis of Ancestor Worship in Ancient China," Ed. Bong Rin Ro. *Christian Alternatives to Ancestor Practices.* Taichung: Asia Theological Association. 119-133.

Yang, Chi-Shou. 1985. ed. Bong Rin Ro. *Christian Alternatives to Ancestor Practices.* Taichung: Asia Theological Association. 192-206.

Yip, Ching-Wah Francis. 1999. "Protestant Christianity and Popular Religion in China," *Ching Feng* 42.3-4 (July-December): 130-156.

CHAPTER 9

Gehring, W. Roger. 2004. *House Church and Mission: The Importance of Household Structures in Early Christianity.* Peabody, MA: Hendrickson.

Nishi, Fumihiko and Mari Kan. 2005. "Oya To Doukyo No Jyakunen Mikon-Sha No Saikin No Jyokyo Sono-1 (The Recent State of the Young Unmarried Persons Living with Their Parents, No.1)." *Tokei (Statistics) August, 2005* ed. Nihon Tokei Kyokai (Japan Statistical Association: Tokyo, Japan, http://www.stat.go.jp/training/2kenkyu/zuhyou/parasit1.pdf

The Institute of Statistical Mathematics *Kokumin-Sei No Kenkyu: Dai 11-Ji Zenkoku Chosa (The Research Of National Character, 11th National Investigation)*, Tokyo, Japan, 2004.

Toshihiro, Mori. 2007. "Kakusa-Shakai To Koukousei No Genjyo (The Gap-Widening Society and the State of High School Students)." *Kakusa-Shakai To Wakamono-No Mirai (The Gap-Widening Society and the Future of the Young Generation).* Zenkoku, Minshushugi, Kyoiku, Kenkyukai, eds. Tokyo, Japan: Doji-Sha.

Reich, Robert B. 2000. *The Future of Success: Working and Living in the New Economy.* New York: Alfred A Knopf.

Sodegawa, Yoshiyuki, Yukari Hanashima, and Masahiro Morizumi. 2005. *Dankai To Dankai Junior No Kazokugaku: Heisei Kakudai Kazoku (Family Sociology for the Baby Boomers and Baby Boom Echo: The Extended Family in Heisei Era).* Tokyo: Dentsu.

Weiss, Douglas. 2001. *Intimacy: A 100-Day Guide to Better Relationships.* Lake Mary, FL: Siloam Press.

White, John. 2003. "A New Kind of LTG." An E-Mail Letter In A Personal E-List, Named "House Church Coach." April 30.

White, John. 2008. "Gehring: Church Centered in the Home." LK10.Com, http://lk10.com/practices-and-patterns/simple-church/gehring--church-centered-in-the-home.html

Wilson, Marvin R. 1989. *Our Father Abraham: Jewish Roots of the Christian Faith.* Grand Rapids, MI: Wm. B. Eerdmans.

Yamada, Masahiro. 2005. *Meiso-Suru Kazoku: Sengo Kazoku Model No Keisei To Kaitai (Runaway Family : Declining Of Postwar Family Model In Japan).*, Tokyo: Yuhikaku.

Chapter 10

Abeyasinghe, Tikiri. 1966. *Portuguese Rule in Ceylon*. Colombo: Lake House.

Ariyapala, M.B. 1968. *Society in Medieval Ceylon*. Colombo: Dept. of Cultural Affairs.

Baldaeus, Philip. 1996. *Description of the Great Island and Most Famous Isle of Ceylon*. New Delhi: Asian Educational Services.

Bechert, Heinz And Richard Gombrich. 1991. *The World of Buddhism*. London: Thames and Hudson.

Berwick, T. 1870. *Judicial Report: Kandy Administration Report*. Colombo: Government Press.

Cordiner, James. 1807. *A Description of Ceylon*. London: Longman, Hurst, Rees, and Orme.

Darling, Evangeline. 1991. *Story of a Christian Mission*. Dehiwela: Sri Devi Printers.

Davy, John. 1987. *An Account of the Interior of Ceylon and of its Inhabitants with Travels in That Island*, First Printed 1821, Dehiwela: Tisara.

De Silva, K.M. 1959. *University of Ceylon: History of Ceylon*, Vol. 3. Colombo: Ceylon University Press.

D'Oyly, John. 1938. *Letters to Ceylon 1814-1824*. London: Heffer and Sons Limited.

De Queyroz, Fernao. 1982. *The Temporal and Spiritual Conquest of Ceylon*. India: Asian Educational Services.

Disanayake, J.B. 1999. *Gamaka Suvanda Siv Siya Gav Aseya*. Colombo: Lakehouse.

Ellawala, H. 1962. *Purana Lanakave Samaja Itihasaya*. Colombo: Cultural Department.

Gombrich, Richard, Ed. 1991. *The World of Buddhism*. Delhi: Motilal Banarsidas.

Gombrich, Richard and Gananatha Obeyesekere. 1990. *Buddhism Transformed*. Delhi: Motalal Banarsidass.

Harvey, Peter. 2004. *An Introduction to Buddhism*. Cambridge: University Press.

Kumaa, Hemantha. 2001. *Pavula Ha Vivahaya*. Mulleriyava, Wiejesooriya: Book Centrem.

Herath, H.M.D.R. December 24, 2004. "The Practicality of Kandyan Wedding Rituals" (Sinhala) *Lakbima*.

Hinnells, John R., Ed. 1995. *A New Dictionary of Religions*. Oxford: Blackwell.

Humphreys, Christmas. 1984. *A Popular Dictionary of Buddhism*. London: Buddhist Society.

Knox, Robert. 1681. *Historical Relation of the Island of Ceylon*. London: R. Chiswell.

Leach, Edmund. 1982. *Social Anthropology*. London: Fontana Books.

Liyangamege, Amaradasa. 1968. *The Decline of Polonnaruwa and the Rise of Dambadeniay*. Colombo: Government Press.

Malalgoda, Kitsiri. 1976. *Buddhism in Sinhalese Society, 1750-1900*. Berkeley, CA: University of California Press.

Obeyesekere, Gananath. 1963. "The Great Tradition and the Little in the Perspective of Sinhalese Buddhism." *Journal of Royal Asiatic Society*. XXII(2).

Olcott, Henry Steel. 1942. *Buddhist Catechism*. Reprinted. Kessinger Pub.

Parker, H. 1982. *Village Falk Tales of Ceylon*. Dehiwela: Tisara Press.

Peiris, Ralph. 1956. *Sinhalaese Social Organization: The Kandyan Period*. Colombo: University Of Ceylon Press.

Pieris, P.E., Ed. 1910. *History of Ceylon with a Summary of De Barros and De Couto, Antinio Bacarro and the Documentos Remittidos with Paranagi Hatana and Kustantinu Hatana.* Colombo: Government Press.

Percival, Robert. 1803. *An Account of the Island of Ceylon.* India: Asian Educational Services.

Ray, H.C., Ed. 1959. *University of Ceylon, History of Ceylon,* Vol. 1, Part 1. Colombo: University Press.

Ribeiro, Juao. 1685. *Fatalidado Historica Da Ilha De Ceilao.* Asian Educational Services (English).

Senaratna, P.M. 1999. *Srilankakave Vivaha Caritra*, Colombo: Gunasena.

Spiro, Milford E. 1971. *Buddhism and Society: A Great Tradition and its Burmese Vicissitudes*, London: George Allen And Unwin Ltd.

Sri Lanka National Archives. 1968. Document No. 5/63/1/45/68.

Suravira, A.V., Ed. 1976. *Rajavaliya.* Colombo: Lake House.

Wickremesinghe, K.D.P. 2002. *The Biography of The Buddha,* Colombo: PLW Company.

Wijetunga, Harischandra. 1984. *Practical Sinhalese Dictionary*, Colombo: Cultural Department.

Walshe, M.O.C. 1986. *Buddhism and Sex.* Buddhist Publication Society.

Wright, Arnold. 1907. Twentieth Century Impressions of Ceylon.

CHAPTER 11

A. BOOKS ON BUDDHISM AND SRI LANKA

Abhayawardena, ed., 1973. *Sinhalese Customs and Manners.* Colombo: Cultural Department.

References

Balasingham, S.V. 1968. *The Administration of Sir Henry Ward: Governor of Ceylon 1855-1860*. Dehiwela: Tisara Prakasakayo.

Davy, John. 1983. *An Account of the Interior of Ceylon and of its Inhabitants with Travels in That Island*. Dehiwela: Tisara Prakasakayo (Reprint Of 1821 Edition).

De Silva K.M. 1978. "Christian Missions in Sri Lanka and Their Response to Nationalism 1910-1948" In *Studies in South Asian Culture: Senarat Paranavitana Commemoration Volume VII*. L.Prematilleke, K.Indirapala & J.E.Van Lohuizen-De Leeuw. ed., Leiden: Brill.

Geiger, H.W. 1960. *Culture of Ceylon in Mediaeval Times*. Wiesbaden: Otto Harrasowitz.

Gombrich, Richard F. & Obeyesekere, Gananath. 1990. *Buddhism Transformed: Religious Change in Sri Lanka*. Delhi: Motilal Banarsidass Publishers.

Jayawardena, K. 1986. *Feminism and Nationalism in the Third World*, Colombo: Sanjiva Books.

_____. 2000. *Nobodies to Somebodies: The Role of the Colonial Bourgeoisie in Sri Lanka*. Colombo: Social Scientists' Association/Sanjiva Books.

Knox, Robert. 1981. *An Historical Relation of Ceylon*. Dehiwala: Tisara Prakasakayo [Reprint Of 1681 Edition].

Obeyesekere, Gananath. 1972. "Religious Symbolism and Political Change in Ceylon" *Two Wheels of Dhamma: Essays on the Theravada Tradition in India and Ceylon*. Bordwell L.Smith, ed., Chambersburg: American Academy of Religion.

Peter, W.L.A.Don. 1978. *Education in Sri Lanka Under the Portuguese*. Colombo: Catholic Press.

P.E. Pieris, *Ceylon and the Portuguese, 1505-1658*. Colombo, Sri Satguru Publishers, 1986.

Pieris, Ralph. 1956. *Sinhalese Social Organization: The Kandyan Period*. Colombo: Ceylon University Press Board,

Sirr, Henry Charless. 1991. *Ceylon and Cingalese: Their History, Government, and Religion Volume 11*. New Delhi: Asian Educational Service.

Seneviratne, H.L. 1999. *The Work of Kings: The New Buddhism in Sri Lanka*, Chicago/London: University Of Chicago Press.

Tambiah, H.W. 1968. *Sinhala Laws and Customs*. Colombo: Lake House Investment Ltd.

Trindade, P. Da. 1972. *Chapters on the Introduction of Christianity to Ceylon*. Colombo: Catholic Press.

Walshe, Maurice, Tr. 1996. *The Long Discourses of the Buddha: A Translation of the Digha Nikaya*. Kandy: Buddhist Publication Society.

Wijesekera, Nandadeva. 1987. *The People of Ceylon*. Colombo: M.D.Gunesana Company.

_____. 1990. *The Sinhalese*. Colombo: M.D.Gunesana Company.

B. BIBLICAL COMMENTARIES AND THEOLOGICAL WORKS

Archer, Gleason L. 1994. *A Survey of Old Testament Introduction*. Chicago: Moody Press.

Barnett, Paul. 1977. *2 Corinthians: The New International Commentary on the New Testament*. Grand Rapids: Eerdmans Publishing Company.

Barrett, C.K. 2000. *1 Corinthians: Black's New Testament Commentary*. Peabody: Hendrickson Publishers.

Barton, Bruce & Taylor, Linda K. Ed., 2001. *Life Application New Testament Commentary*. Wheaton: Tyndale House Publishers.

Blomberg, Craig L1992.. *Matthew: The New American Commentary*. Nashville: Broadman Press.

_____. 1994. *1 Corinthians: The NIV Application Commentary*. Grand Rapids: Zondervan Publishing House.

References

Bruce, F.F. 1990. *Hebrews: The New International Commentary on the New Testament*. Grand Rapids: Eerdmans Publishing Company.

Carson, D.A. 1984. *Matthew: The Expositor's Bible Commentary Volume 8*. Grand Rapids: Zondervan Publishing House.

Conzelmann, H. 1975. *1 Corinthians*. Tr. J.W. Leitch. Philadelphia: Fortress Press.

Fee, Gordon D. 1987. *1 Corinthians: The New International Commentary on the New Testament*. Grand Rapids: Eerdmans Publishing Company.

France, R.T. 2007. *Matthew: The New International Commentary on the New Testament*. Grand Rapids: Eerdmans Publishing Company.

Fruthtenbaum, Arnold G. 1983.*Biblical Lovemaking: A Study of the Songs of Solomon*. Tustin: Ariel Ministries Press.

Gane, Roy. 2004. *Leviticus, Numbers: The NIV Application Commentary*. Grand Rapids: Zondervan Publishing House.

Garland, David E. 1999. *2 Corinthians: The New American Commentary*. Nashville: Broadman & Holman Publishers.

_____. 2003. *1 Corinthians: Baker Exegetical Commentary on the New Testament*. Grand Rapids: Baker Book House.

Garrett, Duane. 2004. *Song of Songs: Word Biblical Commentary*. Nashville: Thomas Nelson Publishers.

Hamilton, Victor P. 1990. *Genesis 1-17: The New International Commentary on the Old Testament*. Grand Rapids: Eerdmans Publishing Company.

Harris, R. Laird. 1990. *Leviticus: The Expositor's Bible Commentary Volume 2*. Grand Rapids: Zondervan Publishing House.

Harrison, R.K. 1980. *Leviticus: Tyndale Old Testament Commentary*. Downers Grove: InterVarsity Press.

Huey, F.B. Jr. 2001. *Jeremiah Lamentation: The New American Commentary*. Nashville: Broadman & Holman Publishers.

Instone-Brewer, D. 2001. "1 Corinthians 7 in the Light of the Jewish Greek and Aramaic Marriage and Divorce Papyri" *Tyndale Bulletin*. 52, 225-243.

Kaiser, Walter C. 1983. *Toward Old Testament Ethics*. Grand Rapids: Zondervan Publishing House.

Kiuchi, Nobuyoshi. 2007. *Leviticus: Apollos Old Testament Commentary*. Nottingham/Downers Grove: Apollos/Inter Varsity Press.

Lenski, R.C.H. 1943. *The Interpretation o St. Matthew's Gospel*. Minneapolis: Augsburg Publishing House.

Longman, Tremper. 2001. *Song of Songs: The New International Commentary on the Old Testament*. Grand Rapids: Eeardmans Publishing Company.

Macarthur, John. 2005. *The Macarthur Bible Commentary*. Nashville: Thomas Nelson Publishers.

Mathews, Kenneth A. 2001. *Genesis 1-11:26: The New American Commentary*. Nashville: Broadman & Holman Publishers.

Mcconville, J.G. 2002. *Deuteronomy: Apollos Old Testament Commentary*. Leicester/Downers Grove: Apollos/Inter Varsity Press.

Moore, G.F. 1971.*Judaism in the First Century of the Christian Era Volume 2*. New York: Schocken.

Morris, Leon. 1987. *1 Corinthians: Tyndale New Testament Commentary*. Leicester: InterVarsity Press.

Moulton, J.H. & Milligan, G. 1930. *The Vocabulary of the Greek Testament*. London: Hodder & Stoughton.

Murphy-O'Connor, J. 1979. *1 Corinthians: New Testament Message*. Wilmington: Glazier.

Murphy, R. & Huwiler. 1999. *Proverbs, Ecclesiastes, Song of Songs: New International Biblical Commentary*. Peabody: Hendrickson Publishers.

References

Murray, John. 1957. *Principles of Conduct*. Grand Rapids: Eerdmans Publishing Company.

Neeufeld, Ephraim. 1944. *Ancient Hebrew Marriage Laws*. London: Longman's Green & Co..

Olyott, Stuart. 1983. *A Life Worth Living and a Lord Worth Loving: Ecclesiastes & Song of Solomon*. Welwyn: Evangelical Press.

Ruef, J. 1977. *1Corinthians: Westminster Pelican Commentary*. Philadelphia: Westminster Press.

Soards, Marion L. 1999. *1 Corinthians: New International Biblical Commentary*. Peabody: Hendrickson Publishers.

Sproul, R.C. 2003. *The Intimate Marriage: A Practical Guide to Building a Great Marriage*. Phillipsburg: P&R Publishing Company.

Stott, John R.W. 1978. *The Message of the Sermon on the Mount*. Leicester/Downers Grove: Inter Varsity Press.

Thompson, J.A. 1974. *Deuteronomy: Tyndale Old Testament Commentary*. Leicester/Downers Grove: Inter Varsity Press.

Tosato, A. 1984. "The Law of Leviticus 18:18: A Re-Examination in *Catholic Biblical Quarterly*. 46, 199-214.

Trobisch, Walter. 1971. *I Married You*. Leicester: Inter Varsity Press.

Vaughan, Curtis & Lea, Thomas D. 1983. *1 Corinthians: Bible Study Commentary*. Grand Rapids: Zondervan Publishing House.

Vaux, R. De. 1965. *Ancient Israel Volume 1*. New York: Mcgraw Hill.

Wenham, Gordon J. 1979. *Leviticus: The New International Commentary on the Old Testament*. Grand Rapids: Eerdmans Publishing Company.

Wenham, Gordon J. & Heth, William E. 1997. *Jesus and Divorce*. Carlisle: Paternoster Press.

Wilson, Geoffrey B. 2005. *New Testament Commentaries: Romans to Ephesians*. Edinburgh: The Banner of Truth Trust.

Wright, Christopher J.H. 1996. *Deuteronomy: New International Biblical Commentary*. Peabody: Hendrickson Publishers.

INDEX

A
Aachan, 56
Aaron, High Priest, 55
Abraham, family networks, 55
Accommodation as functional substitute, 193–194
Adam
  animal sacrifices, 54
  Bible marriage, 229, 257, 258
  need for Eve, 50
Adultery, 240, 262–264
Africa
  AIDS orphans, 21
  extension of the church, 15
  Kaguru tribe fertility issues, 171–172
Agriculture. *See* Farming
Ahosikarma
  Christian ritual of reconciliation, 122
  contextualized practice, 122
  defined, 118–119
  effectiveness of, 129–130
  liminality, 122–123, 125–128
  reincorporation, 122
  separation, 122–125
AIDS causing African orphans, 21
Aisai Bento, 222
Alters. *See also* Shrines
  ancestral veneration substitutes, 180
  worship at family alters for filial piety, 166–167

America
  divorce statistics, 7
  domestic violence statistics, 8
  family disintegration, 6–7
  family values, 7
  farming as profession, 12
  multi-generational domiciles, 12–13
  Native Americans, mission strategy, 17
  out-of-wedlock births, 7
  presidential attributes, 6–7
  senior-housing, 95
  traditional family statistics, 7
Ancestor veneration
  ancestor worship, 162, 163, 165–166
  ancestral cults in Buddhism, 176–177
  biblical principles, 173–174
  biblical vs. culture worldviews, 168–171
  in China, 184–185
    festivals, 185
    food sacrifices, 185
    as obstacle to conversion, 183–184
    Protestants, 188–191, 192–193
    Roman Catholics, 187–188
  consulting ancestors, 171–172
  fertility and fruitfulness of the land, 172
  human fertility, 171–172

313

relationship between the living and the dead, 172
sickness and disease, 172
contextualization
  continuity, less discontinuity, 202–204
  cultural, not religious, 201–202
  filiality, not idolatry, 197–201
  practical implications, 211–213
  radical contextualization, 197, 214
conversion hindrance, 183–184
cyber ancestral worship, 192
death and the afterlife, 162–163
defined, 184–185
deification, 163
functional substitutes, 177–180
  accommodation, 193–194
  contextualization, 212
  family alters in the home, 180
  funerals and body disposal, 178–179
  grave care and cleaning, 180
  memorials to the deceased, 179–180
  understanding of ancestor worship, 182
Genghis Khan, 161–162
guardian spirits, 164, 185
living dead, 163–164, 165, 170, 171
missiological challenges, 174–176
missiological principles, 201–210
  communal conversion, 207–208, 213
  cultural integration, 204–206
  socio-religious transformation, 208–210
  motivations for ancestor worship, 166–168
    Christian filial piety, 181
    family bonding, 168
    fear of ghosts, 167
    funerals, 166
    social customs, 168
    visiting graves, 167
    worship at family alters, 166–167
  powers to the living, 165–166
  practical implications, 210–214
    contextualized, 211–213
    holistic, 213–214
    personalized, 210–211
  Protestants, 188–191
  recent accommodation, 191–196
  rejection of Christianity, 186–187
  respect for ancestors, 163
  Roman Catholics in China, 187–188
  understanding of, steps to, 180–182
Ancestors' Day, 196
Ancestral tablet, 173, 186
Ancestral worship, 19. *See also* Ancestor veneration
Andrew, family networks, 58–59
Animals
  to describe human emotions, 66
  for food, 142
  sacrifices, 54–55, 175
Animism
  ancestor worship, 176
  in Sri Lanka, 131–132
Anthropological Reflections on Missiological Issues, 111
Antioch

Index

extension of the church, 15
missionary sending church, 52
Apostles. See Disciples
Aquila, 54
Aristobulus, 54
Ariyapala, M. B., 235
Armenia, extension of the church, 15
Arunachalam, Ponnambalam, 239
Ashtaka, 248, 249, 250
Asia Theological Association (ATA), 192
Astrology, for Sinhala Buddhists, 145–146
ATA (Asia Theological Association), 192
Augustine, 16
Auspicious
blessings chanted, 252
date for naming a child, 164
drums, 255
good days, 145
punctuality, 157
times, 145–146
times for poruwa, 250
weddings, 247, 248, 249
white color, 251
Australia
children's mental illnesses, 7–8
suicide statistics, 10

B

Babylonian captivity of the church, 34–35
Baldaeus, Philip, 237
Bangladesh, atrocities against women, 20
Baptism
baptizing the dead, 211
infant baptism, 54
ritual of reconciliation, 128
Barclay, William, 119, 120
Barrett, David, 43
Bass, Clarence B., 119, 120
Beaver, R. Pierce, 17
Benedict XIV, Pope, 187–188
Berentsen, Jan-Martin, 171
Berwick, T., 234
Beyond the Ranges, 74
Bhikkhuni, Dhammananda, 89
Bhuvanekabahu VII, 230
Bible. See Scripture
Bimbisara, 5, 176
Birth, out-of-wedlock births in America, 7
Bodhi trees
in household shrines, 137, 138
respect for, 155
reverence for, 142
Bonding, liminality
baptism, 128
confession and forgiveness, 126–127
period of probation, 127–128
steps, 126
Boniface, 16
Book of Filial Piety, 201
Brahmanism, ancestral cults, 176
Breytenbach, Cilliers, 119
Brothels. *See* Prostitution
Bruce, F. F., 52
Buddha puja, 143, 157
Buddha statue
in household shrines, 138
respect for, 155
reverence for, 142
Buddhism
ancestral cults, 176–177
in China, 19

China's Spiritual Awakening, 21–22
communicating the gospel to, 63–68
dharma, 3, 4
expressionless faces, 10
filial piety, 80–82
The Great Renunciation, 2
incense for worship, 5
karma, 3, 133
nirvana
  defined, 3
  self-salvation, 4
Sinhalese Buddhism, 133
women not allowed to achieve, 5–6
premises in a Buddhist context, 33–34
Protestant Buddhism, 231
respect for religious things, 154–157, 158
Sangha brotherhood
  history of, 3
  ordaining of family members, 4
  as substitute for family, 5
scriptural instruction on family issues, 2–6
  The Great Renunciation, 2
  respect for parents and ancestors, 5
Sinhala Buddhists. *See* Sinhalese Buddhism
Sri Lanka. *See* Sri Lanka
Theravada Buddhism
  household shrine, 137
  monks, 231–233
  in Sri Lanka, 131, 137, 231
women as lower valued, 5–6
world growth of, 47
worldview differences, 64
Buddhist Catechism, 243–244
Bunkhun
  defined, 82
  distortions of genuine filial obligation, 90–91
  gendered difference of filial obligation, 87, 99
  Grateful Relationship Orientation, 83, 90
  mother and child relationship, 83–84
  obligations of children, 84–85
  obligations of parents, 84–85
  parent and child indebted goodness, 79
  relationship cycle, 83
Business Week, China's spiritual awakening, 21–22
Byambasuren, Dashiin, 161

C

C-1 to C-6
  contextualization continuum, 33–34
  Jesus' Insider Movement, 39
  premises in Buddhist context, 33–34
Calvin Institutes, 17–18
Cambodia
  ancestral worship, 175
  church planting movements, 31
  domestic violence statistics, 8–9
  socio-religious transformation, 209
Capitalism and Communism, 11
Carey, William, 17
Caste system, 278
Catholics. *See* Roman Catholic

Index

Celibacy
  biblical principles, 267–268
  for monks, nuns and novices, 5
Cell church, 41–42
Ceylon
  Ceylon, 239
  marriage, 241
  polyandry, 236–237, 239
  poruwa, 244–245
  Twentieth Century Impressions of Ceylon, 239
Chan, Kim Kwong, 205
Child Prostitution in Thailand: A Challenge to the World Christian Community, 93
"A Child of the Northeast", 112–118
Children
  biblical responsibilities to parents, 92–96, 276
  bunkhun obligations, 84–85
  Child Prostitution in Thailand: A Challenge to the World Christian Community, 93
  domestic violence against, 8–9
  mental health issues, 7–8
  prostitution, 21, 77–79
  prostitution and filial obligation, 21, 85–91
    causes for, 79
    distortions of genuine obligation, 90–91
    gendered difference, 87–90, 99
  Thai filial obligations to parents, 79–85
    Buddhist teachings, 80–82
    bunkhun, 82–85
China
  ancestor functions after death, 163
  ancestor veneration, 184–185
    festivals, 185
    food sacrifices, 185
    as obstacle to conversion, 183–184
    Protestants, 188–191, 192–193
    Roman Catholics, 187–188
  ancestor worship, 165, 174–175
  ancestral cults, 177
  ancestral tablet, 173
  angry youth, 9–10
  Back to Jerusalem, 45
  Buddhism, 19
  care of the aged, 14
  China Inland Mission, 188
  ching ming festival, 167
  Chong Yang festival, 185
  church planting movements, 31
  Confucianism, 19
  culture and religion, 205
  family worldview, 19, 59
  filial piety, 19, 166, 201–202
  folk belief systems, 198–199
  Ghost festival, 185
  Judaism, 186–187
  offerings to ancestors, 164
  one-child policy, 13–14
  Qing Ming festival, 185, 195
  socio-religious traditions, 193–194
  Spiritual Awakening of Buddhism, 21–22
  Taoism, 19
  worldviews, 198
Ching ming festival, 167
Chong Yang festival, 185
Christ. *See* Jesus
Christians, honorific title for Christ, 155

317

Christ-ward movements, 32
Chrysostom, John, 15
Church
   call to paradigm shift, 34–39
   cell church, 41–42
   community church, 42–43, 45
   extension of. *See* Extension of the church
   growth
      by adding members, 51–52
      households and family net works, 52–53, 57–58
      by multiplying churches, 52
   house churches
      biblical basis for, 39, 40
      family households, 53
      family plus others from the community, 53
      house church network, 41, 42
   local church
      defined, 35
      long-term growth hindrance, 37–39
      maintenance, 35, 36
      quality growth hindrance, 35–36
      quantity growth hindrance, 36–37
   mega-churches, 41
Church Growth phenomena, mega-churches, 31
Church planting movements (CPMs)
   among Muslims and Hindus, 31
   communal conversion, 207
   Insider Movements vs., 32
   Jesus' mission, 39
   socio-religious transformation, 209
Clement XI, Pope, 187

Cloth, as ritual object, 118
Clovis, King of the Franks, 16
Comblin, Jose, 119
Communal conversion, 207–208, 213
Communication
   accuracy, 65–66
   to Buddhist families, 63–68
   to family networks. *See* Family network
   feedback, 65
   indigenous communication, 68–70
   local methods of, 66–68
   media, 67–68
   modern technology, 48
   social context, 65
   transfer of meaning, 64
Communism, 11
Community church, 42–43, 45
Confucianism
   ancestor worship, 191
   Book of Filial Piety, 201
   in China, 19
   Chinese ancestral veneration, 185
   Chinese Christians, 189
   filial piety, 192, 201–202
   Roman Catholics in China, 187–188
Consolidation stage of transition, 22–23
Constantine, 36
Contextualization
   ancestor veneration
      continuity, less discontinuity, 202–204
      cultural, not religious, 201–202
      filiality, not idolatry, 197–201
      practical implications, 211–213

Index

radical contextualization, 197, 214
recommended strategy, 197
C-1 to C-6, 33
critical contextualization, 111–119
divine incarnational method, 206
as functional substitute, 212
Insider Movements, 32
premises in a Muslim context, 33–34
radical contextualization, 197, 214
Continuity, less discontinuity, 202–204
Conversions, mass, 45
Cordiner, James, 238, 244
Cornelius, 53
Court, John, 13
Covenants, family networks, 54–55
CPMs. *See* Church planting movements (CPMs)
Crawford, Christa Foster, 77–99
Crispus, 53–54
Critical contextualization, 111–119
  checks against syncretism, 111
  critical response, 111, 121–122
  exegesis of culture, 111
  exegesis of Scripture and the hermeneutical bridge, 111
  new contextualized practices, 111
Critical response, 111, 121–122
Croucher, Rowland, 13
Culture
  ancestral veneration, 201–202
  biblical vs. culture worldview of ancestor veneration, 168–171
  exegesis of culture, 111
  missiological principles in radical contextualization, 204–206
Cyber ancestral worship, 195

D

da Silva, Bento, 236
Daham pasal, 134
Daham pasala, 135
Dalits (Daliths) conversion to Buddhism, 18
Dark Ages, 16
Davy, John, 238–239, 250
Day of Pentecost, call to repent, 55
de Queyroz, Fernao, 236, 240, 272
Death. *See also* Funerals; Gravesites
  abode of the dead, 169
  ancestor worship, 162–163
  ghosts. *See* Ghosts
  guardian spirits, 164, 185
  living dead, 163–164, 165, 170, 171
  memorials to the deceased, 179–180
DeBarros, Anthony, 12
Dee from Thailand, 77–79, 96–98
Deification of ancestors, 163
Devil dancing, 147
Dharma, 3, 4, 133
Dharmapada, 141, 142
Disciples
  choice of brothers as, 58–59
  family units, 18, 27–28
  financial support, 43–44
  friendship evangelism, 36
  Great Commission, 27–28, 31–32
  Insider Movements, 32
  new Thai converts, 101–102
  nominalism, 35
  training in the community, 57

319

Discussion techniques, 67
Disease, as cause for consulting ancestors, 172
Disintegration of the family, 6–11, 26
   in America, 6–7
   angry youth in China, 9–10
   children's mental illnesses, 7–8
   domestic violence, 8–9
   suicides, 10
Divine incarnational method, 206
Divorce
   American statistics, 7
   biblical principles, 259–264
   exceptional clause, 262, 263
   in Japan, 217, 223
   release from marriage contract, 265
Domestic violence
   of Asian men, 8–9
   in Cambodia, 8–9
   family values trends and, 8
   in Thailand, 9
Dowry, marriage through fornication, 115, 118
D'Oyly, John, 245–246
Drama troupe, 68–70
Dreams of Buddhists, 146–147
Drums, 255

E

Economics
   economic flow to rural areas, 60
   economically independent families, 11
   Japan
      administrators and specialists, 220
      Egalitarian Dual Income Family Model, 221
      employment stratification, 219, 220
      Freeters or free-arbiters, 217, 219, 220
      Individualistic Model, 220, 221
      Intimate Family Model and, 226
      The New Economy, 219, 220
      new family model values, 220
      unskilled laborers, 220
      wastefulness, 226
Edict of Milan, 36
Education of Sinhaha Buddhists, 151–154
Egalitarian Dual Income Family Model, 221
Eight Special Permissions, 187
Eightfold Path, 4
Eliade, Mircea, 128
End-of-day rituals, 146
Ershi, 202
Ethelbert of Kent, 16
Ethics
   Christian impact on Buddhist family life, 274–275
   Five Precepts, 133, 151–152. *See also* Five Precepts
Eunice, 54
Evangelicalism, 34
Eve
   animal sacrifices, 54
   Bible marriage, 229, 257, 258
Evil eye, 144
Exceptional clause, 262, 263
Excluded middle, 150
Extended family model, 12–13
Extension of the church
   Antioch, 15
   Armenia, 15
   family, group and people movements, 14–15

Ireland, 15–16
North Africa, 15
the Reformation, 16–18

F

Face-saving
  shame, 20–21
  in sports defeats, 20
Family
  biblical principles, 257–270
  bonding by ancestral practices, 168
  Christian impact on Buddhist family life, 273–275
  defined, 48
  evangelism. *See* Family group approach to evangelism
  Intimate Family Model, 225–227
  network. *See* Family network
  purpose of, 18–19
  Sinhalese Buddhism, 133–134
Family group approach to evangelism
  Five Finger Family Evangelism, 29–30
  historical changes after the Reformation, 14–18
  modern socio-cultural issues, 18–23
  myths and objections, 23–26
    cultural factors, 25
    individual believer separation from unsaved families, 24–25
    individual vs. family evangelism, 24
    individual vs. group salvation, 26
    long-term stability, 25
    nominalism, 25
    one on one salvation, 26
    post-conversion nurture, 25, 30
    salvation as individual choice, 23–24

    student choices, 24
    work distribution, 25–26
    youth and family ministry, 24
Family network
  biblical validity, 50–54
  blended family, 50
  bridges of transmission, 58–60
  for church growth, 52–53
  church growth, 57–58
  communicating the gospel, 63–68
  communication issues, 47–48, 50, 58–60
  covenants, 54–55
  defined, 48–49
  early history of families, 11–12
  indigenous communication, 68–70
  in-laws, 60
  missiological strategy suggestions, 70–76
  single parent family, 50
  social category, 49
  social group, 49
  social science help, 49–50
  spectrum of familial kinds, 49–50
  in Thailand, 60–63
  theological insights, 54–57
  trinity, 50
Farming
  American livelihood, 12
  fertility and fruitfulness of the land, as reason for consulting ancestors, 172
Fatalidado Historica da Ilha de Ceilao, 236–237
The feast, 128–129
Feig, John Paul, 103
Feminist movement, 6
Fertility issues, consulting ancestors, 171–172

Fertility rites, 247–248
Fertility symbol of *poruwa*, 250
Filial obligation, 96–98
   as cause of prostitution, 79
   power of Christ in transformation, 91–98
      biblical honor and obedience, 93–94
      biblical responsibilities of children, 92–93
      family and societal transformation, 96–98
      protection of biblical care, 94–96
   prostitution, 85–91
      distortions of genuine obligation, 90–91
      gendered difference, 87–90, 99
   Thai children to parents, 79–85
      Buddhist teachings, 80–82
      bunkhun, 82–85
Filial piety
   Book of Filial Piety, 201
   breakdown, in China, 14
   Buddhist teachings, 80–82
   in China, 19, 166, 201–202
   Confucianism, 192
   contextualization, 197–201
   expression of, 166
   marriage bonds, 276
   motivation for ancestor worship, 166–168
      Christian filial piety, 181
      family bonding, 168
      fear of ghosts, 167
      funerals, 166
      social customs, 168
      visiting graves, 167
      worship at family alters, 166–167

Sutra, 80–82
Filipino. *See* Philippines
Five Finger Family Evangelism, 29–30
Five Precepts
   chanting at the household shrine, 139
   compared to Ten Commandments, 151–152
   defined, 133
   end-of-day rituals, 146
   instruction of, 151, 152
   purpose of, 133
   rules of guidance, 232
   sexual offenses, 232
   Sri Lankan Buddhism, 232–233
   wrong speech, 232
Flowers
   for Buddhist worship, 139, 142
   representing friendship, 118
Food
   Preta, 143
   sacrifices, 185
   Sinhala Buddhist beliefs and practices, 142
Fornication, 263–264, 269–270
Four Noble Truths, 4
The Franks, 16
Fraser, J. O., 74
Freeters or free-arbiters, 217, 219, 220
Friendship evangelism, 41, 45
Froth and bubble, 150
Fukuda, Mitsuo, 217–227
Functional substitutes, ancestor veneration, 177–180
   accommodation, 193–194
   contextualization, 212
   family alters in the home, 180
   funerals and body disposal, 178–179

Index

grave care and cleaning, 180
memorials to the deceased, 179–180
understanding of ancestor worship, 182
Funerals. *See also* Death; Gravesites
ancestor worship, 162–163
ancestral veneration substitutes, 178–179
Christian Chinese funerals, 194
fear of ghosts, 167
filial piety, 166
Filipino, 203
memorials to the deceased, 179–180
sati or *suttee*, 19–20
Taiwanese, 194–195
Future Shock, 2
The Future of Success, 219

G

Gamaliel, 39
Garland, D. E., 266
Gautama, Siddharta, 2–4
Gecko as omen, 144
Gehring, Roger, 227
Gendered difference of filial obligation, 87–90, 99
Ghosts
ancestral veneration, 164, 167
Cambodian beliefs, 175
Chinese Ghost festival, 185
guardian spirits, 164, 185
Global Christianity, 34–35
God
as Creator, 50–51
spiritual connection, accountability and continuity, 51
"The God of Abraham, Isaac and Jacob", 174, 202, 203, 204
as a unified trinity, 50
Gogerley, Daniel, 243
Golden Rule, 214
Gospel movements, 32
Grateful Relationship Orientation, 83, 90
Gravesites. *See also* Death; Funerals
ancestor worship, 165, 167
care and cleaning of, 180, 195
Great Commandment, 214
Great Commission
church planting movements, 31–32
family movements, 27–28
The Great Renunciation, 2
Gregory the evangelist, 15
Gregory the Great, 16
Group commitment stage of transition, 22–23

H

Haiti, child prostitution, 21
The Heart of Pak, 66
Hell notes, 185
Hero worship, 37
Hiebert, Paul G.
ancestor veneration, 181, 198, 212
Chinese folk belief systems, 199
critical contextualization, 111–112
excluded middle, 150
people as social beings, 48
theory of critical contextualization, 105–106
Hinduism
church planting movements, 31
in Sri Lanka, 131–132
Holistic approach to Insider Movements, 213–214

Homosexuality, 6, 258
Hong Kong, *Tao Fong Shan*, 208–209
Honor killing for family shame, 20–21
Honorific titles, 155
Horoscopes, 145
House churches
   biblical basis for, 39, 40
   family households, 53
   family plus others from the community, 53
   house church network, 41, 42
Household shrine, 136–139
Housing
   independent living, 95
   multi-generational, 12–13
The Human Heart, 66
Hume, Britt, 12
Hung, Daniel, 167, 174, 194
Hunter, A., 205
Hwang, 162

I
Idioms, 67
Idolatry
   biblical principles, 173–174
   filiality, not idolatry, 197–201
IM. *See* Insider Movements (IM)
Inauspicious
   Buddhist monks, 252
   Monday as inauspicious day, 145
   persons as bad omens, 144
   times, 146
Incorporation stage of transition, 22–23
Independent living housing, 95
India
   atrocities against women, 20
   child prostitution, 21
   Dalits (Daliths) conversion to Buddhism, 18
   honor killings, 20–21
   sati or *suttee*, 19–20
Indians (Native Americans), mission strategy, 17
Individualistic Model, 220, 221
Indonesia, ancestor worship, 164
Industrial Age, family networks, 11–12
Infant baptism, 54
Inheritance of lands by families, 11
Initiation stage of transition, 22–23
Insider Movements (IM)
   biblical basis for, 39–40
   church planting movements vs., 32
   churches in Buddhist lands, 41–44
   cell churches, 41–42
   community church, 42–43
   counting church membership, 43
   financial support, 43–44
   frontiers of Insider Movements, 44–46
   communal conversion, 207–208, 213
   contextualization, 33–34
   frontiers, 44–46
   gatherings for celebrations at church, 40, 42
   paradigm shift of church, 34–39
   practical implications, 210–214
      contextualized, 211–213
      holistic, 213–214
      personalized, 210–211
   understanding of, 32–34
International Society for Frontier Missiology, 32
Internet, cyber ancestral worship, 192
Intimate Family Model, 225–227
Ireland, extension of the church, 15–16
Israel, ancestral worship, 174
Itipiso Gatha, 146, 147

Index

J
Jacob, family networks, 51, 55
James, family networks, 58
Japan
   Aisai Bento, 222
   ancestor veneration
      as obstacle to conversion, 184
      Protestants and, 191–193
   ancestor worship, 174–175
   ancestral cults, 177
   ancestral deification, 163
   ancestral tablet, 173
   bon festivals, 167
   divorce
      marriage problems, 223
      Postwar Family Model, 223
      statistics, 217
   economics
      administrators and specialists, 220
      Egalitarian Dual Income Family Model, 221
      employment stratification, 219, 220
      Freeters or free-arbiters, 217, 219, 220
      Individualistic Model, 220, 221
      Intimate Family Model and, 226
      The New Economy, 219, 220
      new family model values, 220
      unskilled laborers, 220
      wastefulness, 226
   expressionless faces, 10
   family alters, 166
   family breakdown, 217–221
   family importance, 218–219
   filial piety, 166
   ideal life dream, 221–222
   Intimate Family Model, 225–227
   juvenile crime rates, 217
   marriage
      "knowledge is power", 224
      Marriage Transformation Group (MTG), 226
      priorities, 223–224
      "Three Dailies", 223–224, 225, 226
   NEET, 219
   postwar economic growth, 217–218
   Postwar Family Model
      changing values, 222–223
      core assumption, 219
      current trends, 219
      defined, 218
      relationship priorities, 221–225
   Runaway Family: Declining of Postwar Family Model in Japan, 218
   socio-religious transformation, 209
   suicide rates, 217, 219
   unemployment rate, 219
Jataka tales, 4
Jayamangala Gatha, 254
Jerusalem
   church concentrations in, 52
   church expansion, 52–53
Jesuits in China, 187–188
Jesus
   divine incarnational method, 206
   family networks, 58–59
   financial support, 43
   Insider Movements, 39, 45
   marriage and divorce, 260–261, 264, 276–277
   miracles, 56
   power in transformation, 91–98

biblical honor and obedience, 93–94
biblical responsibilities of children, 92–93
family and societal transformation, 96–98
protection of biblical care, 94–96
power of Christ to transform family obligation, 91–98
reconciliation to Peter, 121
simplicity of Insider Movements, 44–45
spiritual transformation, 46
told healed persons to return to families, 56
virgin birth, 56
Jewish Monument, 186
John the Baptist
   Christian ritual of reconciliation, 124–125
   divine incarnational method, 206
   family networks, 58
Johnston, Alexander, 244–245, 250
Joseph, 55, 121
Joseph of Arimathea, 39
Joshua, 54
Judaism in China, 186–187

K

Kabilsingh, Chatsumarn, 89
Kaguru tribe of East Africa, 171–172
Kama
   Christian ritual of reconciliation, 122
   contextualized practice, 122
   defined, 118–119, 232
   effectiveness of, 129–130
   liminality, 122–123, 125–128
   reincorporation, 122
   separation, 122–125
Kamgong, Pi, 112–118
Kandy
   marriage and divorce, 234, 242
   polyandry, 238, 239
   polygamy, 234, 238
   poruwa, 245, 246, 249
Kang Xi, Emperor, 187
Karma, 3, 133
Kataragama, 137
Kazumi, 223–225
Keishi, 223–225
Khan, Genghis, 161–162
Kharma, never ending cycle of life, 170–171
Khuankaew, Ouyporn, 9, 89
Knox, Robert, 240, 244, 272
Komin, Suntaree
   bunkhun, defined, 82
   distortions of genuine filial obligation, 90
   filial piety, 83
   value clusters, 102, 106
Korea
   ancestor worship, 174–175, 211
   ancestral cults, 177
   ancestral tablet, 173
   cyber ancestral worship, 192
   filial piety, 166
   funerals, 195
Kristiyani Prajnapti, 243
Kuan Yin, 5

L

Laos, ancestral worship, 175
Laozi, 185
LaTourette, Kenneth Scott, 14–15, 57–58
Lawrence, Jill, 6–7

Lay leaders, 37
Lenovo, 21–22
Liao, David, 180, 195–196
Li-kae, 68–70
Lim, David S., 31–46, 183–215
Liminality
  bonding
    baptism, 128
    confession and forgiveness, 126–127
    period of probation, 127–128
    steps, 126
  Christian *kama* and *Ahosikarma*, 125–128
  marriage through fornication, 117, 118
  rites of passage, 109–110
Lipski, Liz, 10
Liu, Melinda, 13–14
Local church
  defined, 35
  long-term growth hindrance, 37–39
  maintenance, 35, 36
  quality growth hindrance, 35–36
  quantity growth hindrance, 36–37
Lois, 54
Lord's Prayer, 56, 151
Low Country drummers, 249
Luke, marriage and divorce, 262, 263

M

Magbanwa, Fred, 61
Magul Poruwa, 244, 247, 254
Maha-mangala Sutra, 134
Malinowski, Bronislaw, 162
Mao, 13
Marcus, Erin, 8
Mark, marriage and divorce, 262–263

Marriage
  biblical principles, 257–270, 279
  divorce, 259–264
  monogamy, 258
  New Testament, 259
  Old Testament, 258–259, 262
  unbelieving partner, 260
  Buddhist, 233, 250–252
  blessings chanted, 251–252
  bride wears white, 251
  clergy participation, 252
  white or yellow sari and veil, 253
  caste system, 278
  characteristics, 229–230
  Christian marriage, 241–244
  defined, 229
  family networks and, 49, 60
  through fornication, 112–117, 115, 118
  group-marriage, 272
  marital duty, 268–269
  Marriage Transformation Group (MTG), 226
  mixed marriage, 260, 265–266, 278
  monogamous, 243–244, 253, 258
  parental blessings, 254–255
  plank for weddings, 250
  polyandry, 235–239, 271–272
  polygamy, 50, 234, 258–259
  poruwa, 244–250, 256
    contemporary *poruwa*, 248–250
    defined, 244
    development of, 246–248
    Magul Poruwa, 244, 247, 254
    meaning of, 250
    reactions against Christian influences, 276–277
    registration, 242, 243

remarriage, 261, 264–266
Roman Catholic beliefs, 230
same-sex, 6
Sinhalese Buddhism, 233–241
   looseness of marriage, 240–241
   necessary change, 241
   polyandry, 235–239, 271–272
   polygamy, 234
   in Sri Lanka
      Buddhist, 233, 250–253
      Christian, 241–244
      before missionaries, 233–241
   unequal yoke, 267
Martin, William, 189–190
Marx, Karl, 11
Mateer, C. W., 190
Matthew, marriage and divorce, 262–263
Mayhew, Thomas, 17
McGavran, Donald
   church extension and outreach, 14–15
   contextualization, 33
   family networks, 70–71
   web movements, 48–49
McGilvary, Daniel, 61
Media for communication, 67–68
Mega-churches, 31, 41
Mejudhon, Nantachai, 103–105
Mejudhon, Ubolwan, 101–130
Memorials to the deceased, 179–180
Memorization of Sinhala Buddhists, 154, 159
Men, domestic violence against women, 9
Mencius, 202
Mental health, Australian issues, 7–8
Merits
   ancestral cults, 176

Buddhist daily devotions, 149
Buddhist dreams, 146–147
of sons for parents, 87–88
transfer to ancestors, 176
Mission Frontiers, 32, 45
Missionaries
   ancestor veneration, 204–210
   communal conversion, 207–208, 213
   cultural integration, 204–206
   socio-religious transformation, 208–210
   challenges of ancestor veneration, 174–176
   mass conversions, 45
   strategy to reach family networks, 70–76
   tentmakers, 45
Moggallana, 137
Monasteries for missionary training, 16–17
Mongolia, Genghis Khan, 161–162
Monks
   celibacy, 5
   ordination of sons, 87–89
   Sinhalese Buddhism, 132
   in Sri Lanka, 231–233
   veneration of, 157
Montgomery, Heather, 90–91
Moravia
   Herrnhut small group structure, 38
   mission movement, 17
Mori, Toshihiro, 219
Moses
   family networks, 51, 55
   intermarriage, 267
   marriage and divorce, 260–262
MTG (Marriage Transformation Group), 226

Index

Mulder, Niels, 82
Multiplying Churches Through Prayer Cell Evangelism: A Manual for Church Planting Movements, 29, 74
Music for communication, 67–68
Muslims
   church planting movements, 31
   premises in a Muslim context, 33–34
Myanmar, socio-religious transformation, 209
Myths and objections to family group approach to evangelism, 23–26
   cultural factors, 25
   individual believer separation from unsaved families, 24–25
   individual vs. family evangelism, 24
   individual vs. group salvation, 26
   long-term stability, 25
   nominalism, 25
   one on one salvation, 26
   post-conversion nurture, 25, 30
   salvation as individual choice, 23–24
   student choices, 24
   work distribution, 25–26
   youth and family ministry, 24

N

Naaman, 278
Narcissus, 54
Nathaniel, family networks, 58–59
National Geographic, Buddhism growth, 47
National heritage, lack of respect for, 157–158
Native Americans, mission strategy, 17
Neill, Stephen, 14–15
Nestorian Monument, 186
Networks. *See* Family network
Nevius, John L., 71–72
New Testament
   biblical concept of reconciliation, 119–120
   biblical honor and obedience, 94, 95
   celibacy, 268
   head of household conversions, 207
   Insider Movements, 40
   mixed marriage, 267
   polygamy, 259
Ngamdee, 127
Nicene Creed, 151
Nicodemus, 39
Nirvana
   defined, 3
   self-salvation, 4
   Sinhalese Buddhism, 133
   women not allowed to achieve, 5–6
Noah, family networks, 54
Nominalism
   individuals vs. families, 25
   of local churches, 35–36
Novices, celibacy, 5
Nuns, celibacy, 5

O

Obeyesekere, Gananatha, 253
Offerings. *See* Tithes and offerings
Olcott, Colonel, 243–244
Old Testament
   biblical honor and obedience, 94–95
   celibacy, 268
   Insider Movements, 40
   mixed marriage, 267
   polygamy, 258–259
   principles of marriage, 258–261, 262

329

Omens
  evil eye, 144
  gecko, 144
  good and bad omens, 143–144
Onesiphorus, 54
Ongkulimand, 118
Ou Yang Shieu, 213

P

Packer, Ros, 1
Paradigm shift of church, 34–39
Parakramabahu, Vira, 234
Parakramabahu II, 235
Paranavitana, Senarath, 230, 235
Parents
  biblical commandment to honor, 93, 174
  biblical responsibilities of children, 92–96, 276
  blessings at weddings, 254–255
  bunkhun obligations, 84–85
  honoring, 156
  parents' discourse, 128–129
  Sinhala Buddhist worship of, 140–141
  Thai filial obligations from children, 79–85
  Buddhist teachings, 80–82
  bunkhun, 82–85
Passover
  lamb sacrifice, 55
  meetings of Christians, 40
  salvation of families, 55–56
Patriarchy, recruitment into prostitution, 9
Patrick from Ireland, 15–16
Paul
  baptizing the dead, 211
  celibacy, 267–269

child obedience, 93
church as household of God, 57
divine incarnational method, 206
family networks, 52–54, 58
house churches, 39
marriage and divorce, 260, 264–266
Pentecost
  Day of Pentecost, 55
  meetings of Christians, 40
  Pentecost Day, 51
People movements
  church growth, 57–58
  history after the Reformation, 14–18
  Insider Movements, 32
Perakumba, 235
Percival, Robert, 237–238, 240–241, 244
Permeation stage of transition, 22–23
Persecution of Christians
  Saul the persecutor, 52, 53
  Stephen, martyrdom of, 52
Personalized evangelism, 210–211
Persons, Larry Scott, 83, 90
Peter
  family networks, 53, 55, 58
  reconciliation to Jesus, 121
Pharaoh, 55
Philippian jailor, 53
Philippines
  ancestor veneration, 198
  ancestral worship, 175
  child prostitution, 21
  family records, 195
  folk belief systems, 199–200
  funerals, 203
  grave care on All Saints' Day, 195
  missionary movements, 45
Phongpaichit, Pasuk, 86
Pickett, Waskom, 14–15

Index

Pius XII, Pope, 188
Pliny, Younger, 15
Polyandry, 235–239, 271–272
Polygamy
    among Sinhalese Buddhists, 234
    biblical principles, 258
    family networks, 50
    New Testament principles, 259
    Old Testament principles, 258–259
Portugal
    marriage, 272
    polyandry, 271
Poruwa, 244–250, 256
    contemporary *poruwa*, 248–250
    defined, 244
    development of, 246–248
    Magul Poruwa, 244, 247, 254
    meaning of, 250
Postwar Family Model
    changing values, 222–223
    core assumption, 219
    current trends, 219
    defined, 218
Prayer
    Lord's Prayer, 56, 151
    for outreach to family networks, 72, 75
    temporary abstinence during, 269
Precepts of Buddhism. *See* Five Precepts
Precious in His Sight: Childhood and Children in the Bible, 92–93
Premarital sex, 263–264, 269–270
Premises to contextualization, 33–34
Preta, 143
Priestley, Mark, 10
Prisca, 54
Probation period, 127–128

Promphakping, Buapun, 84, 87–88, 90
Prostitution
    Child Prostitution in Thailand: A Challenge to the World Christian Community, 93
    of children, 21, 85–91
    filial obligation, 85–91
        causes for, 79
        distortions of genuine obligation, 90–91
        gendered difference, 87–90, 99
    patriarchy and recruitment of young girls, 9
Protestants
    ancestral veneration and, 188–191
    Protestant Buddhism, 231
    Protestant's Modern Mission Era, 17
    Sinhalese Buddhism and, 241
Proverbs, 67
Psalms, God's creations, 51
Punctuality of Buddhists, 157
Pusurinkham, Sirirat
    biblical honor and obedience, 94
    prostitution in Thailand, 91, 93
    women's position in Thai families, 96

Q

Qi, 198
Qing Ming festival, 185, 195
Question and answer techniques, 67

R

Rabibhadana, Akin, 88–89
Rahab, 54
Rahu Kaalam, 145–146
Rahula, 2–4
Rajasingha, 235
Rama V, King, 102
Ratana Sutra, 147

Reconciliation
  biblical concept, 119–121
  defined, 106–107
  ritual of, 107–110
Redemptive lift, 37
The Reformation, extension of the church, 16–18
Reich, Robert B., 219
Reichelt, Karl, 208–209
Reimer, Reginald, 173
Reincorporation rites, 128–129
Respect for others, 277–278
Reverence as Buddhist teaching, 141–142
Revolution of 1917, 11
Ribeiro, Juao, 236–237
Ricci, Matteo, 187, 206
Rice-name ceremony, 164
Rite of Passage, 22–23, 108–110, 112
Rite of reincorporation, 128–129
Rite of separation, 122–125
Rituals
  Aisai Bento, 222
  Christian *kama* and *Ahosikarma*, 122–130
    contextualized practice, 122
    defined, 118–119
    effectiveness of, 129–130
    liminality, 122–123, 125–128
    reincorporation, 122
    ritual of reconciliation, 122
    separation, 122–125
  daily Buddhist rituals, 148
  devil dancing, 147
  end-of-day rituals, 146
  Itipiso Gatha, 146, 147
  molecules of ritual, 108
  omens, 144
  Ratana Sutra, 147
  of reconciliation, Christian
    critical response, 121–122
    liminal stage, 123, 125–127
    reincorporation, 128–129
    rites of separation, 128–129
  of reconciliation, critical contextualization
    "A Child of the Northeast" novel, 112–118
    ahosikarma, 118–119, 122–130
    kama, 118–119, 122–130
  of reconciliation, Zahniser's theory, 107–110
  rice-name ceremony, 164
  Rite of Passage, 22–23, 108–110, 112
  rite of reincorporation, 128–129
  rite of separation, 122–125
  ritual, defined, 108
  Sinhalese Buddhism, 134
  symbols, 108
  worship at the household shrine, 138–139
Roman Catholic
  accommodation of local culture, 254
  in China, 187–188
  marriage beliefs, 230
  marriage registration in Sri Lanka, 242
  Roman Catholic Counter Reformation, 16
  Sinhalese Buddhism and, 241
  in Sri Lanka, 149
Rome, manes worship, 163
Romney, Mitt, 6
Runaway Family: Declining of Postwar Family Model in Japan, 218

S
Sacred and profane, 148–149,

154–155
Sacrifices
  animal sacrifices, 54–55, 175
  food sacrifices, 185
Same-sex marriage, 6
Sangha brotherhood
  history of, 3
  ordaining of family members, 4
  as substitute for family, 5
Sariputta, 137
Sati or *Suttee*, 19–20
Saul the persecutor, 52, 53
Schramm, Wilbur, 65
Schreiter, Robert S.
  biblical concept of reconciliation, 119–121
  reconciliation definition, 105, 106–107
  schematic representation of reconciliation definition, 107
Scott, James, 7–8
Scripture. *See also* New Testament; Old Testament
  ancestor veneration, 168–171
  ancestor worship, 173–174
  celibacy, 267–268
  children's responsibilities to parents, 92–96, 276
  exegesis of Scripture and the hermeneutical bridge, 111
  family biblical principles, 257–270
  family networks, validity of, 50–54
  Insider Movements, 39–40
  marriage biblical principles, 257–270, 279
  Precious in His Sight: Childhood and Children in the Bible, 92–93
  reconciliation concept, 119–121
  Ten Commandments. *See* Ten Commandments
"Searching for Roots", 191
Senior-housing, 95
Sexual practices
  adultery, 240, 262–264
  Five Precepts, 232
  fornication, 263–264, 269–270
  homosexuality, 6, 258
  marital duty, 268–269
  polyandry, 235–239, 271–272
  polygamy
    among Sinhalese Buddhists, 234
    biblical principles, 258
    family networks, 50
    New Testament principles, 259
    Old Testament principles, 258–259
  premarital sex, 263–264, 269–270
  same-sex marriage, 6
  sexual hospitality, 272
Sexual revolution, 6
Shamanism in Vietnam, 164
Shame
  honor killings, 20–21
  in sports defeats, 20
Shaw, R. D., 199
Shrines
  alters, 166–167, 180
  Buddhist, 136–139
  household shrine, 136–139
  worship at family alters, 166–167
Sickness, as cause for consulting ancestors, 172
Sigalovada Sutra, 133–134, 233
Silas, family networks, 53
Sinhalese Buddhism
  astrology, 145–146
  Christian influence, 230
  Christianity in Sri Lanka, 149–150

333

daham pasal, 134
Daham pasala, 135
daily rituals, 148
dreams, 146–147
education and instruction, 151–154
end-of-day rituals, 146
family, 133–134
fear, 147
Five Precepts. *See* Five Precepts
food issues, 142
froth and bubble, 150
good and bad omens, 143–144
guardian deities, 137
honoring of parents, 156
household shrine, 136–139
Itipiso Gatha, 146, 147
learning of religion, 134–136
local gods, 137–138
Maha-mangala Sutra, 134
marriage before missionaries,
  233–241
    looseness of marriage, 240–241
    necessary change, 241
    polyandry, 235–239
    polygamy, 234
memorization, 154, 159
monks, 132
national heritage, lack of respect
  for, 157–158
popular beliefs and rituals, 132
poruwa, 246
practice aids, 132
Preta, 143
Protestant Buddhism, 231
punctuality, 157
Rahu Kaalam, 145–146
Ratana Sutra, 147
respect for religious things,
  154–157, 158
reverence, 141–142
sacred and profane, 148–149,
  154–155
Sigalovada Sutra, 133–134
Theravada Buddhism
    household shrine, 137
    monks, 231–233
    in Sri Lanka, 131, 231
    worship of parents, 140–141
Sivaraksa, Sulak, 89
Skrobanek, Siriporn, 91
Smith, Alex G.
    ancestor veneration, 161–182
    evangelism of Buddhists, 97
    family evangelism, 1–30
    family networks, 47–76
Social category, defined, 49
Social customs, ancestor worship, 168
Social entrepreneurs, 45
Social group, defined, 49
Social science definition of family
  networks, 49–50
Social solidarity, 22
Societal and family transformation,
  96–98
Socio-religious transformation, 208–210
Solomon, 267, 270
Somaratna, G. P. V., 131–159, 229–256
Spencer, Herbert, 162
Spirit money, 185
Spirits. *See* Ghosts
Spiritual showmanship, 38
Sri Lanka
    Buddhist monks, 231–233
    caste system, 278
    Christian church, 230
    Christian impact on Buddhist
      family life, 273–275
    Christianity in Sri Lanka, 149–150

Index

Five Precepts, 232–233
kama, 232
Kandy
  marriage and divorce, 234, 242
  polyandry, 238, 239
  polygamy, 234, 238
  poruwa, 245, 246, 249
marriage, Buddhist, 233, 250–252
  blessings chanted, 251–252
  bride wears white, 251
  clergy participation, 252
  white or yellow sari and veil, 253
marriage, Christian, 241–244
  Buddhist reaction to, 243–244
  introduction of, 242
marriage before missionaries, 233–241
  group-marriage, 272
  looseness of marriage, 240–241
  necessary change, 241
  polyandry, 235–239, 271–272
  polygamy, 234
modern Christian adaptations, 253–255
  drums, 255
  Jayamangala Gatha, 254
  Magul Poruwa, 254
  parental blessing, 254–255
  white or yellow sari and veil, 253
poruwa, 244–250, 256
  contemporary *poruwa*, 248–250
  defined, 244
  development of, 246–248
  Magul Poruwa, 244, 247, 254
  meaning of, 250
post-Christian era, 252–253
pre-Christian Buddhism, 271–273
priests or clergy, 232, 233, 252
reactions against Christian influences, 275–278
religions of, 131–132
rice-name ceremony, 164
sexual hospitality, 272
Sigalovada Sutra, 233
Sinhala Buddhists. *See* Sinhalese Buddhism
Theravada Buddhism, 131, 137, 231
Stalin, Joseph, 11
Statue. *See* Buddha statue
Stephanus, 54
Stephen, martyrdom of, 52
Story of Sigiri, 230
Storytelling, 66, 72
Student ministries, 72–73
Subasingha, D. J., 247–248
Subasinha, 250
Substitutes. *See* Functional substitutes
Suddhodhana, 3–4
Suicide
  in Australia, 10
  family disintegration and, 10
  in Japan, 217, 219
Sunday school, Sinhalese Buddhism, 152, 153
Superstar complex, 37
Surangkhanang, 77
Symbols
  Chinese Christians, 189
  defined, 108
  ritual objects, 118
  symbolic serving, 128–129
Syncretism
  checking against, 111
  in Chinese religion, 200–201

T

Tabernacles, 40

335

Tablet, ancestral, 173, 186
Taiwan
   accommodation suggestions, 195–196
   ancestor worship, 190–191
   ancestral cults, 177
   child prostitution, 21
   Christian response to ancestor practices, 192
   family records, 195
   funerals, 194–195
Tao Fong Shan, 208–209
Taoism in China, 19
Taylor, Hudson, 190
Taylor, John V., 163–164
Taylor, Robert B., 48, 49
The Temporal and Spiritual Conquest of Ceylon, 236
Ten Commandments
   compared to Five Precepts, 151–152
   honoring parents, 93, 174, 205
   idolatry, 173–174
Tennent, James Emerson, 239
Tentmakers, 45
Thailand
   ancestral cults, 176
   change as slow process, 102–103
   child prostitution, 21, 77–79
   church planting movements, 31
   domestic violence, 9
   economic flow to rural areas, 60
   filial obligations and prostitution, 85–91
      causes for, 79
      distortions of genuine filial obligation, 90–91
      gendered differences, 87–90, 99
   filial obligations of children to parents, 79–85
      Buddhist teachings, 80–82
      bunkhun, 82–85
   Five Finger Family Evangelism, 29–30
   interdependency, 126–127
   new convert witness to family, 101–103
   power of Christ to transform family obligation, 91–98
      biblical honor and obedience, 93–94
      biblical responsibilities of children, 92–93
      family and societal transformation, 96–98
      protection of biblical care, 94–96
   prostitution and filial obligation, 85–91
      distortions of genuine obligation, 90–91
      gendered difference, 87–90, 99
   religious acceptance, 102
   rites of passage, 112
   rituals of reconciliation
      ahosikarma, 118–119, 122
      "A Child of the Northeast" novel, 112–118
      Christian *ahosikarma*, 122–130
      Christian *kama*, 122–130
      critical response, 121–122
      kama, 118–119, 122
      liminal stage, 123, 125–127
      reincorporation, 128–129
      rites of separation, 123–125
   value clusters, 102, 129–130
Thammakaya, Wat, 1–2
Thera, Bentara Attadassi, 243

Index

Theravada Buddhism
  household shrine, 137
  monks, 231–233
  in Sri Lanka, 131, 137, 231
Therng, Thor, 61
"Three Dailies", 223–224, 225, 226
Tid-Joon, 112–118
Tienou, Tite, 199
Tillich, Paul, 108
Timothy, 54
Tippett, Alan, 50–51, 206
Tiridates, King, 15
Tissa, Dodanduwe, Piyaratna, 246–247
Tithes and offerings
  for full-time ministers, 43–44
  house church network, 42
  local churches, 36–37
Toffler, Alvin, 2
Tollefson, Kenneth, 110
Toppo, Greg, 12
Totemism, 176
Toynbee, Arnold, 177
Travis, John, 33–34
Trees. *See Bodhi* trees
Tribes, networks, 48
Trinity as family unit, 50, 56
Tripitaka, 4
Turner, Victor, 108–109, 110
Twentieth Century Impressions of Ceylon, 239
The Twenty-four Filial Exemplars, 202
Tylor, E. B., 163

U

United Nations 1959 Universal Declaration of Human Rights, 2
United States. *See* America
U.S. Center for World Mission, *Mission Frontiers*, 32, 45

USA TODAY, family emphasis trends, 6, 7, 12

V

Value clusters, 102, 129–130
Value of family in the 21st century
  Buddhist scriptures, 2–6
  changes following the Reformation, 14–18
  family disintegration, 6–11, 26
    in America, 6–7
    angry youth in China, 9–10
    children's mental illnesses, 7–8
    domestic violence, 8–9
    suicides, 10
  family group approach, myths and objections, 23–26
  Five Finger Family Evangelism, 29–30
  importance of family, 1–2
  modern socio-cultural issues, 18–23, 27
  practical applications and suggestions, 26–30
  principles for reaching whole families, 23, 28–29
  renewed emphasis on family, 11–14, 27
Van Gennep, Arnold, 22, 108–109, 110
Vasanthakumar, M. S., 257–279
Vietnam
  ancestor worship, 164, 165, 168, 174–175
  ancestral cults, 177
  ancestral tablet, 173
  beliefs concerning the soul, 173
  church planting movements, 31
  filial piety, 166
  offerings to ancestors, 164
  rebuilding of alters, 176

337

shamanism, 164
Vijayabahu VI, 235
Violence. *See* Domestic violence

W
Ward, Henry, 274
Web movements, 48–49
Webs of families, 48–49
Weddings. *See* Marriage
Weerasooriya, David, 247
Wei, Yuan-Kwei, 176–177
Weiss, Douglas, 223–224
Wesleyan Awakening, 38
Western shape, 35
Westminster Catechism, 18
White, John, 225–226
Widows, atrocities against, 20
Wilson, Marvin R., 227
Winter, Ralph, 16
Wisdom, sayings of, 67
Wissawate, Wit, 128
Witherspoon, Reese, 1
Woharn, Praya Sri Sunthorn, 127
Women
    atrocities against, 20
    domestic violence against, 9
    as inferior to men, 5–6, 9
    sati or *suttee*, 19–20
    Woman of Samaria, 56
Word pictures, 67
Worldviews
    ancestor veneration, 168–171
    of Buddhists, 64
    Chinese beliefs, 198
    Chinese families, 19, 59
    levels of reality, 198

X
Xiao Jing, 201

Y
Yamada, Masahiro, 218
Yasodhara, 2–4
Yin and *Yang*, 198
Yu-Bin, Cardinal, 188

Z
Zachaeus, 56
Zahniser, A. H. Mathias
    reconciliation theory, 105, 107–110
    rite of passage structure, 109
    ritual of reconciliation schematic, 110
Zeng Shen, 201
Zuck, Roy, 92–93